The Study of Judaism

Bibliographical Essays

The Study of Judaism

Bibliographical Essays

Contributors: Richard Bavier, Henry Friedlander, Lloyd Gartner, Jacob Neusner, Fritz A. Rothschild, Seymour Siegel, Frank Talmage, John T. Townsend.

ANTI-DEFAMATION LEAGUE OF B'NAI B'RITH

SBN 87068-180- X

Library of Congress Catalog Card Number: 72-79129
Manufactured in the United States of America

Publication of this book was made possible through a grant from
the Rose and Jay Phillips Foundation.

TABLE OF CONTENTS

INTRODUCTION

by JACOB NEUSNER

Jacob Neusner is Professor of Religious Studies, Brown University, and a past president of the American Academy of Religion. Professor Neusner is the author of the multi-volumed *History of the Jews in Babylonia* as well as numerous other studies.

INTRODUCTION

Would that for every complex subject we might find one good book as an ideal introduction to its intricacies—definitive, competent, lucid, simple. Above all, it would be a book which all agree is sound and reliable. In the whole history of the intellect no such book has ever appeared, with one exception. Judaism and Christianity agree that the Hebrew Scriptures—*Tanakh* to the Jews, *Old Testament* to the Christians—constitute a complete, clear, and reliable account of the relationship between God and man. Yet here too, the verdict of history was, "Insufficient." The Christians went on to produce the New Testament, the Jews, the Oral Torah contained in the Talmud and related literature. So even the biblical authors cannot claim to have produced that "one good book."

We have, and should want, no single, adequate introduction to the complex religious tradition of Judaism. Appropriately, every generation has given its account of that tradition, each beginning with the repudiation of at least part of the antecedent heritage of learning, and ending pathetically certain of the permanence of its own creation. The best one can hope for is a reliable guide to the state of learning of one's own time. Until now, even that has been difficult to come by. Scholarly books include bibliographies, but these often are mere lists of books to which the author has referred. We do not even discover what the author has learned from many of them. Introductions to the "state of the question" of important problems in the history and theology of Judaism are virtually non-existent. Whereas for specialists in the study of Judaism the absence of sophisticated perspective and self-awareness proves an obstacle to clear thinking, for non-specialists—scholars in other fields of religious studies who wish to make use of Judaic data,

1

students in undergraduate and graduate programs, ministers, priests, and divinity students—it is simply a disaster. Judaism is among the least known of the religious traditions of the West, and is also among the most difficult to seek out and study. Since accurate information is so hard to acquire, lack of study produces a superfluity of experts. Every Jew who has read a book or two—and some who have not—considers himself not merely a primary datum in the history of Judaism, but also a significant authority. Everyone's opinion carries preponderant weight, it seems, and, in particular, every rabbi knows it all. Men of good will turn to one such "master" after another for accurate and clear information on the study of Judaism, because the field is in a primitive, scarcely cultivated state.

The bibliographical essays before us do much to improve matters. They are not simply lists of books, but thoughtful essays on important problems in the study of Judaism. They address serious students in the field of religion who are not experts in the study of Judaism. They recount what comes first and what comes afterward, what may be important in one way, what in another. Their collective testimony is not that the study of Judaism is too complex for the non-specialist, but that it is a very serious and engaging undertaking. No one should be intimidated by the achievements of scholars, but encouraged by them. All should take note of what it takes to reach a sound understanding. The bibliographies ought to make clear that Judaism, in its own right and not merely as a precursor of Christianity or as the "religion of the Old Testament," constitutes a challenging and rich religious heritage, one that will reward careful research with unexpected insight.

Librarians will find suggestions as to titles needed for a Judaica collection on problems of interest to university scholarship. Students now have a measure of guidance on the range of questions to which Judaic studies supply answers. In the construction of courses on Judaism, the several papers before us provide suggestions on major themes and how they may be explored. In all, by taking the initiative in commissioning and publishing these bibliographical papers, the Anti-Defamation League of B'nai B'rith has made an important contribution to the understanding of the

Judaic tradition and of the Jewish people and to the development of Judaic studies in colleges, universities, and seminaries.

Richard Bavier introduces the topic of most immediate concern to Christians, "Judaism in New Testament Times." His selections and perspective are of special interest, for he is neither a scholar of Judaism in late antiquity, nor a Jew. A graduate of Gettysburg College, he brings to the subject no academic bias and exhibits no apologetic motive. What he does contribute is exceptional intelligence and a fine critical mind. Now well-advanced in his graduate studies in the field of Religious Thought in the Brown University Department of Religious Studies, Bavier spent a year reading the scholarly literature about ancient Judaism and its sources, in English translation. The educational result is so gratifying that others, who are neither scholars nor masters of ancient languages and literatures, should find encouragement. Bavier has read widely and here presents a lucid and thorough introduction to the field. He serves as a wise guide for other beginners, perhaps better than the scholar who is so impressed by details that he is unable to see the subject as a whole. Above all, Bavier demonstrates that Judaism in late antiquity may be studied with profit by students of varying interests, but with no preliminary preparation.

The thorough "Bibliography of Rabbinic Sources" by Professor John T. Townsend, Professor of Biblical Languages and New Testament at the Philadelphia Divinity School, is an important complement to Bavier's essay. Townsend has assembled a full list of important compilations of rabbinic traditions, both traditional and critical editions, as well as some fundamental secondary works. His introduction places these bodies of works in historical and scholarly perspective. Townsend's patience and care have reaped a valuable reward for us all. I know of no equivalent work.

Frank Talmage, of the University of Toronto, treats a more painful, and more pertinent topic. The Jewish-Christian relationship was rarely characterized by charity of understanding on either side. Only in quite recent times, and primarily in America, have the two great religious traditions sought a constructive and mutually respectful way of living together. Talmage, a scholar of medieval Judaism both in its own terms and in relationship to

Christianity, here adds to the valuable contributions he has already made. His account of the Jewish side of the relation is new and important, as suggestive, in its own way, as Moore's "Christian Writers on Judaism," which stood at the beginning of the self-conscious study of the other side of the question. The scholarly consideration of the Christian writing on Judaism is more advanced, and one may gain a satisfactory view by consulting a few modern works. In treating the more recent writings, the relationship since World War II and similar matters, upon which, to date, we have little perspective, Talmage again proves original and breaks new ground. In all, he has done more than introduce a few books; by his manner of doing so, he has also advanced the understanding of the Christian-Jewish relationship.

Professors Fritz A. Rothschild and Seymour Siegel, of the Jewish Theological Seminary of America, introduce the complex and difficult subject of modern Judaism with a listing of important items, and by judicious discussion of important problems in the field. "Modern Judaism" is primarily the creation of philosophers; it represents the philosophical experience of "being Jewish." Some of the formative figures in modern Judaism were also well-informed in, and even sophisticated masters of, the several movements of modern philosophy; all of them focused their best efforts upon the issues posed by those movements to religions in general and to Judaism in particular. Consequently Professor Rothschild and Professor Siegel treat modern Judaism as, fundamentally, an intellectual enterprise. At the same time, they have indicated the existence of works on other formative influences in the development of the modern Judaic experience. Their account is catholic and comprehensive. They prove to be reliable guides to a subject which they not only know thoroughly, but also appreciate deeply, a most valuable combination.

Lloyd Gartner, of the City University of New York and at present at the Institute for Contemporary Jewry of the Hebrew University, brings us up to the present. What has happened to the Jews in contemporary times? The apocalyptic events of our own day are difficult to sort out, document, interpret. Gartner, an important scholar of American and European Jewry in modern times, proves to be a reliable guide. His annotated bibliography is thorough and meticulous. Gartner's approach is not limited by parochialism. Characteristic of the attitude of the Institute for Contemporary Jewry, the comparative viewpoint, which sees world Jewry as a single entity of several parts, produces new insights into the whole. Since so much has been written on the State of Israel, librarians will be especially grateful for Gartner's assistance in sorting out the lasting from the ephemeral and merely sentimental.

Professor Henry Friedlander, of the City University of New York, provides a responsible and careful introduction to literature on the "Holocaust," that is, the destruction of European Jewry between 1933 and 1945. For Jews, the extermination of six million people merely because they were Jews has proved a traumatic event, affecting both the religious outlook, and political, social, and historical perceptions. One cannot understand contemporary Jewry and Judaism without both accurate knowledge of what happened and a comprehensive account of how Jews and Judaic thought have responded to what happened. Friedlander introduces both, guiding the reader through vast, but inchoate writings, including both books and journals centering on this subject. I know no better account of the more important literature on the "Holocaust," particularly in the English language.

Judaism in New Testament times, Jewish-Christian relations, contemporary Judaic theology, modern Jewry—these are four central themes in the study of the history of Judaism. They are also of the greatest interest to Christians and to students of the history of Christianity and of Western civilization. From the beginnings to the present, Jews have known too little about Christians, and Christians about Jews. Consequently, suspicion took the place of trust, dislike supplanted respect, and violence drove out social harmony. The remedy does not lie only in accurate information, meticulous scholarship, and dispassionate inquiry; but surely these stand at the beginning of a better way. While many sorts of dialogue between Christians and Jews may go forward, it is in scholarly discourse, characterized by rationality, respect for the opinions of others, and mutual respect, that the way ahead is smoothest. The bibliographies before us serve as guideposts at the crossroads.

*   *   *

The reader may wonder at the omission of a bibliography on Judaic biblical studies, for the Judaic tradition of the study of the Hebrew Scriptures began before the final formation of the Scriptures, more than twenty centuries ago. No field in Judaic studies contains scholarship of greater interest than the biblical one. Our view, however, is that the complicated questions of what is "Jewish" about Judaic biblical scholarship, how to justify and define the particularly Judaic viewpoint in that field—these require more detailed attention than seemed possible within the limits of the present volume. In this regard, we follow the view of Professor Nahum N. Sarna (in *The Teaching of Judaica in American Universities. The Proceedings of a Colloquium* [New York: 1970, Ktav Publishing House Inc.], pp. 35ff.):

> The Bible is a Jewish point of view if only by virtue of its being the product of the Jewish people and of its having been regarded as the most faithful witness to the national past, the primary source for the knowledge and use of the national language, the font of truth, wisdom, law, and morality for the people of Israel. . . . The history of Jewish exegesis is replete with critical observations ranging from textual to historical problems. In fact, there is hardly an issue, in what is today known as "lower" and "higher" criticism, to which the rabbinic and medieval exegetes did not respond in the light of their own presuppositions and with the limited tools available to them. . . .

What requires description is not only the history of Judaic biblical studies, but also the modern extension of that history: the development of a scholarly, and yet markedly Judaic, approach to biblical studies in Western universities and seminaries. For that considerable task another set of bibliographical studies is required and, in time, will doubtless be worked out.

The reader should note that each contributor has adhered to his own bibliographical style.

JACOB NEUSNER
*Professor of Religious Studies
and Head of the Graduate Program
in History of Religions: Judaism
Brown University*

Providence, Rhode Island

JUDAISM IN
NEW TESTAMENT
TIMES

by RICHARD BAVIER

Richard Bavier is a doctoral candidate in Religious Thought in the Brown University Department of Religious Studies.

I have chosen the following books as examples of various kinds of scholarship. Some are theological expositions, others devotional works, political and economic analyses, and some utilize the history-of-religions approach. A student beginning the study of Judaism in New Testament times should remember that here, no less than in the study of Christian beginnings, opinions differ as to what principles of interpretation should be applied, and to what end investigations should be directed.

A treatment longer than a book list and shorter than a series of reviews seems best. Critical remarks appear where I thought them helpful. I have concentrated upon works in the English language, except where untranslated books are particularly significant. In most cases, classics on individual topics have appeared in translation. All the books included are important in one way or another, although other important works have not been considered. I have aimed for a balanced selection which would not be overly technical, and yet would take a student beyond the stage of popularized histories of Judaism. I strongly urge readers to see Judah Goldin's fine bibliographical essay in C. A. Adams' (ed.) *A Reader's Guide to the Great Religions* (New York: The Free Press, 1965), and Jacob Neusner's "Jews and Judaism Under Iranian Rule: Bibliographical Reflections," in *History of Religions* (Vol. 8, No. 2, November, 1968).

ANTHOLOGIES

References to translations of primary sources appear in a book list at the end. A student can profit from the many volumes of selections from rabbinic writings. *A Rabbinic Anthology* edited by Claude G. Montefiore and Herbert Martin James Loewe (New York: Meridian Books, 1960) contains samples on a wide variety of topics. Montefiore has chosen and arranged the materials and, while he claims that he was governed by the emphasis of the rabbis themselves, at times his liberal Jewish background shows through. For a reader aware of this, the anthology is all the more illuminating. Since the book is ordered on thematic rather than on chronological principles, a student interested primarily in first-century rabbinism might be inconvenienced by this arrangement.

Two shorter but excellent translations of rabbinic writings are *The Living Talmud* of Judah Goldin (Chicago: University of Chicago Press, 1957), and *Judaism,* edited by Salo W. Baron and Joseph L. Blau (New York: The Liberal Arts Press, 1954). The former contains the *Pirke Abot,* a collection of quotations attributed to Pharisees and rabbis who lived between the fifth century B.C.E. and the third century C.E. Bold-face type sets off the original sayings, which are followed by a series of classical commentaries by later rabbis. The reader immediately sees certain patterns and dominant attitudes towards, for example, the secular powers and the scholarly way of life. Problems of historicity are always present, yet *Pirke Abot* yields remarkable parallels with New Testament material. An interested student may look also at Judah Goldin's translation, *The Fathers According to Rabbi Nathan* (New Haven: Yale University Press, 1955). The book presents Talmudic commentary on *Pirke Abot,* and serves as an interesting tool for the study of the development of rabbinic tradition.

Judaism was published in The Library of Religions, ". . . to make available to American students the most essential texts in the religious literature of the world." Among the selections are extracts from the apocryphal writings, from Philo and Josephus, from and about the sectarians, from different stages of the rabbinic period, and from the liturgical tradition. A reader is exposed to a wide range of literature, all of which is roughly contemporaneous with New Testament times.

THEOLOGIES

As general introductions to the theological dimension of rabbinic thought, I recommend Solomon Schechter's *Some Aspects of Rabbinic Theology* (New York: Macmillan, 1923), and George Foot Moore's *Judaism* (Cambridge: Harvard University Press, Vols. I–II, 1927; Vol. III, 1930). Schechter's volume takes a thematic approach to rabbinic material, covering some facets not emphasized in the anthologies mentioned above. In the four decades since first publication, Schechter's scholarship has proven itself comprehensive and accurate. An excellent apologete, he shows strong sympathy with the ancient rabbis as well as a keen understanding of questions asked by modern men. Like many of the books in this bibliography, *Some Aspects of Rabbinic Theology* does not limit itself to the sources from the New Testament period.

George Foot Moore's massive *Judaism in the First Centuries of the Christian Era: The Age of the Tannaim* remains the classic systematic treatment of important theological elements in rabbinic literature. The first volume contains a summary of the historical background and a statement of the author's methodology. In addition, the shorter Volume III includes extensive notes and discussions of problems raised in the text. *Judaism* serves two good purposes. On the one hand, the work represents an eminently competent survey of rabbinic theology; on the other hand, it stands as an example of an important stage in the history of scholarship in the field. In this vein I mention an issue which gets increasing attention. A student should remember that both Schechter and Moore dealt with rabbinic *theology*, as that term was understood in the early part of this century. They date themselves when they undertake to describe "normative Judaism." What place rabbinic theology had in rabbinism and what place rabbinism maintained in the lives of all Jews of that era, are questions still under hot debate.

HISTORIES

In 1921, George Foot Moore claimed that Emil Schürer's *A History of the Jewish People in the Time of Jesus* (Edinburgh: T & T Clark, 1885) was ". . . destined more than any other in its time to influence Christian notions of Judaism. . . ." I cannot improve upon Moore's fine essay, "Christian Writers of Judaism," which appeared in *The Harvard Theological Review* (Vol. 14, 1921, pp. 197–254). Moore's scathing critique of Schürer is accompanied by pointed criticism of the work of other Christian scholars. Moore in no way takes away from the completeness of Schürer's coverage of historical people and events. However, when Schürer turns to interpretation, he demonstrates astonishingly little sympathy toward his subject. His chapter, "Life Under the Law," criticizes the stagnant legalism of Pharisaic and rabbinic Judaism. This chapter, Moore felt, ". . . was written to prove by the highest Jewish authority that the strictures on Judaism in the Gospels and the Pauline Epistles are fully justified." Schocken Books has published (1961) an abridgement of Schürer. It remains an exhaustive manual on the period and a factor to be dealt with in understanding modern Christian attitudes towards Judaism.

A beginning student will be greatly helped by Morton Smith's "Palestinian Judaism in the First Century," found in Moshe Davis (ed.), *Israel: Its Role in Civilization* (New York: Harper & Row, 1956). Smith attacks the myth of "normative Judaism" and its counterpart, creeping Hellenism. Referring his readers to fuller treatments of the issues, he sketches the great diversity of shades of Judaism which coexisted in first-century Palestine.

Equally helpful, Smith's analysis of Josephus as historian arms a student with a sophisticated perspective on this central source. He exposes ways in which *Jewish Antiquities* reflects political changes in the Roman Empire. This, in turn, leads to a better understanding of the picture Josephus draws of the sects. The supposed popularity of the Pharisees, as reported in *Jewish Antiquities,* looks suspicious in light of their minor role in *The Jewish War* (here they are put at six thousand out of a population of about one million, only half again as numerous as the Essenes).

A bibliography for Judaism in New Testament times would be

incomplete without reference to Salo Wittmayer Baron's *A Social and Religious History of the Jews,* Volume Two, (New York: Columbia University Press, 1952). Baron's mastery of political, economic, and liturgical developments make his second volume one of the most helpful single works for a broad understanding of Palestine from the Maccabean revolt to the formation of the Talmud. Religious factors are considered, but economic and political currents receive equal emphasis. A student investigating the cultural base common to both Christianity and Talmudic Judaism will be grateful for Baron's integrated approach. For expansions of the discussion of particular events and trends, see the hundred-plus pages of notes and fine bibliographical notations which the author provides.

Two essays in *The Jews: Their History, Culture and Religion,* edited by Louis Finkelstein (New York. Harper & Row, 1960) are especially relevant to our topic. Elias J. Bickerman's "The Historical Foundations of Postbiblical Judaism," covers the time from Ezra-Nehemiah to the Maccabees. This is not a historical narrative but an exposition of the social, economic, and literary environment out of which Jewish adaptations and reactions arose. The author criticizes clichés commonly held about the period; for example, that the Law was a burdensome legalism which fostered an ironclad exclusivism within the Jewish community. Nor, he claims, were the Jews under continuous persecution. In fact, from the Persians on the secular powers did more to aid than to hinder Judaism.

Bickerman points to some interesting quotations from Greek philosophers, who took the Jews to be a "philosophic race," on the order of noble savages, embodying the best of Greek speculative thought. Most important, however, is the author's treatment of Oriental historiography and its shaping influence upon the Chronicler. Bickerman also investigates the literary antecedents of Ben Sirah, and finally comes to a thought-provoking conclusion about the connection between the Jews' willingness to translate their holy writings and their survival as a religious community.

Judah Goldin's essay, "The Period of the Talmud," is hard to match as a short introduction to a critical millenium in the history

of Judaism. The essay begins as a historical narrative wherein
the author brings together insights from many historians, ancient
and modern. Goldin adds his own helpful comments on the milieu
which characterized the Jews in Palestine before the fall of Jerusalem to Titus. Gradually, discussion of outstanding rabbinic
figures and scholarly methods replaces the narrative of events.
Clearly, Goldin feels that after 70 C.E. scholarship became central
in Judaism and functioned as a cohesive agent. He cannot deal
exhaustively with the many great figures and accomplishments of
such a long time span, but he does produce to-the-point biographical sketches and lucid analyses of scholarly theory.

One of the ablest and fullest treatments of Palestine in Late
Antiquity is Solomon Zeitlin's *The Rise and Fall of the Judean
State* (Philadelphia: The Jewish Publication Society of America,
Vol. I, 1962; Vol. II, 1967). Through two volumes, Zeitlin ex-
plores the Second Commonwealth from many perspectives. He
deals at length with political and religious institutions, contemporaneous literature, liturgy, economics, and the cultural milieu.
Part Three of his Volume II is a concise and illuminating presentation of what is known about Palestinian daily life. If our aim
is to understand the minds of rank-and-file Jews, not just the élite,
then more work like Zeitlin's in this area is desirable.

The author has drawn sharp criticism for his handling of Jesus,
his followers, and their place in Judaism in that period. He treats
Christian beginnings superficially, often glossing over problems
around which New Testament scholars have debated for years.
A reader will have to decide for himself whether Zeitlin's Jesus
fits consistently into the picture of first-century Palestine which the
author has drawn in *The Rise and Fall of the Judean State*. In
any event, because of its fine analysis of all aspects of the Second
Commonwealth, and because of the challenges which it issues to
New Testament scholarship, the book will remain an important
contribution for years to come.

Histories of the Jews in Late Antiquity have usually been histories of the Palestinian Jews. Insofar as the Babylonian Jews are
considered at all, they play a peripheral role. There is obviously
some justification for this practice. The Temple still stood in Palestine; the sects were there; the rabbinic academies began in Pales-

tine. On the other hand, as Palestine was slowly emptied of Jews following the Bar Kochba rebellion, the importance of Babylonian Jewry grew steadily. In order to shed light upon the development of this Babylonian community, Jacob Neusner brings the tools of a historian of religion to his, *A History of the Jews in Babylonia,* Volume I (Leiden: E. J. Brill, 1965). He examines religious, political, and all forms of social issues, adding helpful appendices on particular problems. Professor Neusner's, *There We Sat Down: Talmudic Judaism in the Making* (New York: Abingdon Press, 1972) can also be of great help in understanding the relationship of the Babylonian and Palestinian communities.

Traffic of all kinds linked Jerusalem to the Exile community, which by this time had been established for centuries. Hillel came from Babylonia to Jerusalem where he founded his school. Because large numbers of Jews lived in both the Roman and Parthian Empires, all Jews benefited from special dispensations granted them to woo their support. Hope of reinforcements from the Diaspora settlements inspired the rebels in 66 C.E. These facts, among others, make Babylonia Jewry a significant part of Judaism in the New Testament period.

INSTITUTIONS AND SECTS

Hugo Mantel's *Studies in the History of the Sanhedrin* (Cambridge: Harvard University Press, 1961) is generally held to be the finest recent work on this subject. Mantel carefully sorts out and examines the references from Josephus, the New Testament, and the Talmud in an effort to define the power and jurisdiction of the Sanhedrin. As interpreter of the Law, the Sanhedrin, like the Law itself, seems to have been viewed as a governmental arm by outsiders, and as a religious institution by the Jews themselves. In the course of his investigation, Mantel deals with the Sanhedrin officers and the authority attributed to them. He also provides a reconstruction and analysis of the migration of the Sanhedrin after the destruction of the Second Temple. Finally, the author views the New Testament accounts of Jesus and Paul before the Sanhedrin in light of what the earlier chapters of his book have shown.

Louis Finkelstein's *The Pharisees: The Sociological Background of Their Faith* (Philadelphia: The Jewish Publication Society of America, 1962), deals with the social functions of this sect, as well as with theological topics. Often apologetic, the author presents the Pharisees as champions of the plebeian class. Realizing that many of our sources from that period were written by Pharisees, he might have been more skeptical about their reports of their own popularity and their criticisms of opponents. The author goes into Pharisaic antecedents and the sect's influence upon rabbinism, thus placing the sect in its historical context. In the first volume a survey of the history of scholarship on the subject makes clear Finkelstein's own method and goals. *The Pharisees* is an able presentation of Pharisaism as a Golden Age in Judaism.

A more specialized study of this topic can be found in Jacob Neusner's textbook, *From Politics to Piety: Pharisaic Judaism in New Testament Times,* (Englewood Cliffs: Prentice Hall, 1972). This book integrates primary and secondary material of the rabbinic tradition with historical data and issues concerning the Pharisaic sect.

W.R. Farmer's *Maccabees, Zealots and Josephus* (New York: Columbia University Press, 1956) takes a look at two periods of political unrest in ancient Palestine. The author argues that the attitudes, symbolisms, and behavior of the Maccabean patriots were revived in the first century C.E. by the Zealots, whom Josephus labeled "brigands." I include the book for two reasons. First, it is an example of recent research around a largely original thesis; second, it gives a highly readable account of political extremism in the years before the war with Rome.

Farmer's argument raises an interesting question. Did the Zealots *consciously* pattern themselves and their activities upon their own understanding of the Maccabees? An answer to this question could tell us much about religious behavior in the period. The author, however, faces an obstacle here which bothers him throughout—the Zealots left no literature. Still, Farmer calls upon a good deal of circumstantial evidence to show that the political environment, the desire for revenge, and the mythological rationalizations of the two groups were similar.

When Jesus was taken and tried in Jerusalem, was he convicted as a subversive against Rome, or as a threat to Jewish authority? S. G. F. Brandon's *Jesus and the Zealots* (Manchester: University of Manchester Press, 1967) finds that both factors were involved. After bringing together all the references to the Zealots, the author tries to get behind the bias of Josephus and the New Testament. The Zealots emerge as patriots and religious purists, in the tradition of the Yahwist prophets and the Maccabees. Like Jesus, these extremists looked forward to the establishment of a theocracy over Israel. Besides these and other ideals which Jesus and the Zealots held in common, Brandon points to certain New Testament passages which suggest a historical link of some kind. He decides that while the author of Mark tended to suppress the political nature of the early tradition, some traces remain. Coming as it does directly after the murder of the Baptist, Brandon sees the Markan report of the feeding of the five thousand as an abortive rebellion. The other Synoptics list a Simon the Zealot among the disciples, an indication that Jesus' thoughts and plans were not incompatible with this particular Zealot's. On these and other grounds, Brandon finds it entirely unlikely that Jesus was as unaware of powerful political forces as the Gospels present him. If he concentrated his zeal upon the downfall of the contemporaneous Jewish leadership rather than upon Rome, it was because he saw these leaders standing in the way of the theocracy desired by many factions in Judaism.

Gershom Scholem's *Major Trends in Jewish Mysticism* (Jerusalem: Schocken Books, 1941) and *Jewish Gnosticism, Merkabah Mysticism and Talmudic Tradition* (New York: Jewish Theological Seminary of America, 1960) are definitive works in this area. He includes an important critique of the aversion of earlier scholars, notably Graetz, toward mysticism. For his own treatment, Scholem adopts a theory of religious symbolism very close to Paul Tillich's. He states that he will differentiate mystics as those who experience, "direct contact between the individual and God."

The author furnishes descriptions of the Merkabah throne-world and the ecstatic voyage. He covers initiatory and preparatory rites, attitudes towards the magical power of knowledge, and the myth-

ologies of the sects. Scholem is especially helpful when he comments on the sectarian's views of Torah and the central symbols—
Creation, Revelation, and Redemption. By linking the mystics to
these elements common to all phenomena in Judaism, he makes
possible the sort of integration and comparison of material which
is highly desirable.

A reader may have difficulty with Scholem's tools of interpretation. His definition of mysticism, that is, "direct contact between
the individual and God," can lead to confusion. This principle
works well for Evelyn Underhill in her analyses of Christian
mysticism, and equally well for Scholem when he considers later
Jewish mystics. The Merkabah mystics, however, emphasized the
aloof Kingship of God. Also, the author's appropriation of R.
Otto's term "numinous" as a description of Merkabah hymns can
be distracting. The vacuous content of this unnecessarily technical
term adds little which Scholem has not already ably stated in more
familiar language.

BIOGRAPHIES

I urge a student to read all of *Heroes and Gods,* by Moses Hadas
and Morton Smith (New York: Harper & Row, 1965), but Part
Two is especially important for this bibliography. Part One deals
with the hero and the development of his tradition. Chapters One
and Two are helpful methodological statements, in which some
generalizations about the hero type are made. Part Two contains
selections from "lives" of Pythagoras (Porphyry), Moses (Philo),
Jesus (Luke), and Apollonius of Tyana (Philostratus). In addition, a short discussion of these "lives" as examples of a literary
genre brings into relief the common Graeco-Roman cultural milieu
from which they all arose.

The four selections aid in understanding marks of distinction
as well as similarities. The introduction to and abridgement of
Luke's Gospel present the life of Jesus from the perspective of an
aretologist. Comparison of this section with the other "lives," those
in *Heroes and Gods* and in works devoted to individual Jewish
figures, can lead to a broader understanding of Jewish and Christian holy types.

You may read Nahum Glatzer's *Hillel the Elder: The Emergence of Classical Judaism* (New York: Schocken Books, 1956) profitably in conjunction with *Heroes and Gods*. On the one hand, it supplies examples of the way the Talmudists preserved traditions about their holy men; and on the other hand, the book represents a modern aretology. Thus Glatzer does not consider problems of historicity, and often extrapolates beyond the unavoidable shortcomings of his sources. The marks of an ancient hero (e.g., magical powers and miraculous birth) are replaced by marks of a modern hero. Hillel and the Pharisees become champions of the common people in an environment of black and white issues.

Hillel the Elder is not a study of religious tradition as history; it is a devotional work. A scheme of modern categories informs the ancient sources. For example, the sects are differentiated on ethical grounds, a matter of paramount importance to us but which certainly was subordinated in Late Antiquity to ritual considerations. Hopefully, *Hillel the Elder* will inspire in a student of Judaism in New Testament times a self-consciousness towards the material which he has already acquired in respect to the study of Christian beginnings.

In his bibliographic essay (see above), Judah Goldin makes two important points about "biographies" of ancient rabbinic leaders. First, the books are likely to be insensitive to questions about the historical reliability of their limited sources. Second, even granting the whole of the scattered tradition pointing to the men behind the revered names, there is no sure way to *arrange* the material. Narratives may be written, but insofar as development and maturation of the man's thinking cannot be discerned, these "biographies" must remain "collections." Louis Finkelstein's *Akiba: Scholar, Saint and Martyr* (New York: The World Publishing Company, 1936), a good collection of traditions about Akiba, depends heavily upon "presumably," "we gather," and "must have," to fill out its reconstruction of the sage's life.

In his *A Life of Rabban Yohanan Ben Zakkai* (Leiden: E. J. Brill, 1970), Jacob Neusner writes that in the absence of more knowledge about the transmission of the sources, he will not attempt a biography in the usual sense, but rather an "intellectual biography." Recognizing these limitations, Neusner presents the sayings attributed to and about Yohanan ben Zakkai, with digressions into his social and intellectual background. By allowing the sources to speak for themselves in extensive quotations, the outcome is a clear picture of a first-century religious leader.

The author views R. Yohanan as a historical phenomenon, not solely as a religious figure. The goal is an understanding of the sage's impact upon his own time and the occasions of his pronouncements. An apologia about the lasting value of his teachings is virtually absent. R. Yohanan's role in the formation of the rabbinic academy at Yavneh after the fall of the Second Temple makes him a central figure in Judaism in the New Testament period. Jews had to readjust their religious lives to take into account the loss of their center of worship. This, in turn, had meaning for Jewish attitudes toward heresy, and the attitudes of Jewish Christians toward their own position. A grasp of the way in which R. Yohanan and his colleagues rebuilt religious life around Torah is essential for an understanding of these other changes in outlook. One of the best treatments of Philo is found in Harry Wolfson's *Philo* (Cambridge: Harvard University Press, 1947). Wolfson wrote as a philosopher, not as a historian of religion. His equally well-known work, *The Philosophy Of Spinoza,* helped establish him as a scholar in the history of Western philosophy, and he comes to Philo with this perspective. Perhaps no other figure from Judaism in New Testament times yields so well to this sort of approach.

"The purpose of this book," Wolfson wrote, "'has been to delineate and depict the philosophy of Philo as it shaped itself in his own mind and in its own setting and to indicate briefly how in its main features it was the most dominant force in the history of philosophy down to the seventeenth century." The work was intended as one part of a series dealing with figures from Plato to Spinoza; consequently, Philo's links with Greek philosophy are emphasized. In Wolfson's eyes he was the first in a long line of thinkers to construct a synthesis between revealed religion and philosophy. At the same time, the author maintains that Philo was a loyal devotee of Palestinian Judaism.

The question, What sort of Jew was Philo? is taken up in other studies. Erwin Ramsdell Goodenough's *By Light, Light* (New Haven: Yale University Press, 1935) develops a thesis about two widely divergent styles of Judaism. He associates Philo with a mystical tradition which embraced Hellenistic mythological symbolisms. Samuel Sandmel's *Philo's Place in Judaism: A Study of Conceptions of Abraham in Jewish Literature* (Cincinnati: Hebrew Union College Press, 1956) is a more recent example of the careful, positivistic approach which has characterized scholarship on the subject. This book is a comparative study, focusing upon Philo's relation to rabbinism. Sandmel begins with a valuable survey of the history and issues of Philonic scholarship. He proceeds to a comparison of Philonic and rabbinic styles, terminologies, and outlooks, always with a keen awareness of problems with the historicity and chronology of the prime sources.

I have tried to mention many different scholarly approaches which focus upon individual figures from New Testament times. Biography can often bring out the human dimension of an age, a dimension missed in studies of great ideas and historical trends. Milton Steinberg takes another approach in the fictional *As a Driven Leaf* (New York: Behrman House Inc., 1939). The "central motivation" of this novel is "a historical personality of whose life ancient rabbinic literature records a limited number of incidents, some distressingly obscure." These few incidents are expanded into a Palestinian rabbi's lifelong search for intellectual certainty. In the course of this search, he plays a role in many of the dramatic events of the late first and early second centuries. The novel form allows liberties completely beyond the biography. and Steinberg takes advantage of these to present an engaging story. It would be interesting to study this book as a product of its own time. The characterizations of the great rabbis, the attitude towards Rome, and the dialogue between the Greek way and the rabbinic way are all potential inroads to an understanding of American Judaism between World Wars. As an entry in this bibliography, however, *As a Driven Leaf* is recommended for its excellent portrayal of rituals and festivals, the institution of discipleship, the operation of the rabbinic courts, and the daily life of Palestinian Jews of that era.

SPECIAL TOPICS

As examples of works on the interplay between first-century Judaism and the nascent Christian movement, I mention first W. D. Davies' *Christian Origins and Judaism* (Philadelphia: Westminster Press, 1962), and his *Paul and Rabbinic Judaism* (London: Cambridge University Press, 1948). The former surveys the state of recent New Testament scholarship, and then self-consciously renews the search for the facts of the life of Jesus. Davies proposes to establish his thesis by reference to the religious environment in first-century Palestine. He concentrates upon the office of ministry as it fell to Jesus and his followers, and finds a close link between this notion and contemporaneous ideas about the true remnant of the People of God. Davies' use of the Pharisaic and Dead Sea materials is essential to his argument.

Paul and Rabbinic Judaism is an excellent study of that apostle's brand of Pharisaism. The author compares Pauline and rabbinic writings on philological, theological, and historical grounds, in the course of examining similarities and differences. Paul's vision of Jesus as the New Torah bringing the advent of the Messianic Age, lies at the center of Davies' analysis. He is always sensitive to the support and opposition he finds in the work of other scholars, often digressing into discussions of other positions. This book deserves the serious attention it has received since its publication. As a further investigation into the problems under consideration in *Paul and Rabbinic Judaism,* see Davies' *Torah in the Messianic Age and/or the Age to Come* (Philadelphia: Society of Biblical Literature and Exegesis, 1952).

Wayne Meeks' *The Prophet King* (Leiden: E. J. Brill, 1967) is a model study dealing with the influence of the intellectual milieu in first-century Palestine upon Johannine Christology. The promise of a Mosaic prophet and the promise of a king to deliver Israel apparently collapsed into a Jewish expectation of one figure who would fulfill both roles. Meeks traces references to this figure through a wide range of sources, and examines the way in which the Johannine Jesus performs the signs required of the prophet-king.

Morton Smith has produced a meticulous study of similarities between the Tannaitic literature and the New Testament materials in *Tannaitic Parallels to the Gospels* (Philadelphia: Journal of Biblical Literature Monograph Series, Vol. VI, 1951). Smith examines parallels of vocabulary, idiom, meaning, and form. Pointing to peculiarities and shades of difference within parallel passages, he also comments on the intellectual and historical background which may account for the similarities. Paul's role in the reshaping of the form of Christian tradition is considered. Most frequently, however, Smith illuminates the parallels and omits speculation about their meaning for Jewish or Christian apologetics. Clear style and careful method make this book ideal for the study of the relationships between Jewish and Christian literature in the New Testament period.

An English work on the formation of Jewish liturgy is Abraham Zvi Idelsohn's *Jewish Liturgy and Its Development* (New York: Henry Holt and Company, 1932). The book consists of two parts, the first concerned with development of the liturgy, and the second with description of the liturgy itself. Unfortunately, the historical study is extremely brief; barely thirty pages are devoted to worship in the First and Second Temples. The early synagogue is covered, but also briefly. The descriptions in the second part contain scattered reference to historical events, and some of the appendices are relevant to New Testament times. The standard work on the subject of liturgy remains Ismar Elbogen's *Der jüdische Gottesdienst in seiner geschichtlichen Entwicklung* (Leipzig: G. Feck, 1913). For interesting studies on the influence of first-century Judaism upon Christian liturgy, see William Oscar Oesterley's *The Jewish Background of the Christian Liturgy* (London: Oxford University Press, 1925), and F. Gavin's *The Jewish Antecedents of the Christian Sacraments* (London: S.P.C.K., 1928).

Traditional Jewish apologetics have felt obliged to declare that the heroes of Late Antiquity in no way compromised the faith of their fathers to Hellenistic culture. The Hasidim adopted this attitude, then the Maccabees, then the Pharisees, and then the rabbis. A legend so old and revered will have its measure of truth. However, the question remains, How and to what degree did these religious men oppose Hellenistic inroads into their own style of Judaism? Two problems, distinct but related, have received a good deal of attention. They are, first, Hellenistic influence upon rabbinic writings, and second, the matter of the Second Commandment and iconography.

On the first topic, Saul Lieberman produced *Greek in Jewish Palestine* (New York: Jewish Theological Seminary of America, 1942), and *Hellenism in Jewish Palestine* (New York: Jewish Theological Seminary of America, 1950). The second, somewhat less technical work, is an investigation of rabbinic terminology and scholarly method. Lieberman's intention is to show, by comparison, commonalities of style and terminology between Jewish and Hellenistic writings. In addition, the author examines rabbinic attitudes to Greek wisdom, idolatry, and natural science. Finally there is a short, fascinating look at the Second Temple and its similarities to heathen temples. Lieberman argues convincingly that, consciously or otherwise, rabbinic Judaism absorbed much that was Hellenistic.

The issue over iconography arose when archaeology began to uncover many examples of Hellenistic art forms and symbols on Jewish tombs, synagogues, and amulets. The rabbinic writings could not have led us to expect the murals at Dura Europos, nor the zodiac floor at Bet Alpha. Now that they were before us, how were they to be reconciled with the rabbis' opposition to graphic religious symbols?

Erwin Goodenough's multivolumed *Jewish Symbols in the Greco-Roman Period* (New York: Pantheon Books, beginning 1953), includes excellent photographs and sketches of the artwork itself, as well as a full commentary and interpretation. To some extent, Goodenough modifies his hypothesis of the "two Judaisms," as he outlined it in *By Light, Light.* In the author's eyes, the placement and frequency of the art indicates that Hellenistic mythology and cosmology were real parts of the religious lives of the Jews who used these symbols. As a result, we should reappraise our view of the faith of rank-and-file Jews, and also understand that the power of the rabbis was still limited in the third century C.E.

Another interpretation which attempts to minimize the importance of the art is found in C. H. Kraeling's *The Synagogue (at Dura)* (New Haven: Yale University Press, 1956). Both these works contain fine bibliographical notes for students who wish to explore this topic further. I recommend that a student begin his reading on this subject with the single most comprehensive evaluation, Morton Smith's "Goodenough's *Jewish Symbols* in Retrospect," *Journal of Biblical Literature* (Vol. 86, No. 1, 1967, pp. 53–68). The interpretation of the synagogue art at Dura, with wide-ranging implications for the study of Judaism in Late Antiquity, has been greatly revised by Jonathan A. Goldstein in his book review, "Jewish Symbols in the Greco-Roman Period," *Journal of Near Eastern Studies* (July 1969, pp. 212–218). Goldstein rejects Kraeling's close reliance upon rabbinical literature, as well as Goodenough's use of Philonic categories of material and immaterial reality. He sees the Dura art in the context of rabbinic mysticism, and the central categories as temporal vs. eschatological reality.

The following are important works, some of which space would not permit me to include in detail.

PRIMARY SOURCES

Apocrypha, Revised Standard Version (New York: Thomas Nelson & Sons, 1952).

Apocrypha and Pseudepigrapha of the Old Testament, R. H. Charles (ed.) (Oxford: Clarendon Press, 1913).

Babylonian Talmud (London: Soncino Press, Rep., 1948).

Josephus, With an English Translation, H. St. J. Thackeray, R. Marcus, and L. H. Feldman, trans. (New York: G. P. Putnam's Sons, 1926–1965).

Midrash Rabbah (London: Soncino Press, Rep., 1948).

SECONDARY SOURCES

Abel, F. M., *Histoire de la Palestine* (Paris: Librairie Lecoffre, J. Gabalda, 1952).

Abrahams, Israel, *Studies in Pharisaism and the Gospels* (Cambridge: The University Press, 1924).

Anderson, J. G. C., "The Eastern Frontier from Tiberius to Nero," *Cambridge Ancient History,* Vol. X, 1934.

Angus, Samuel, *The Religious Quests of the Graeco-Roman World: A Study on the Historical Background of Early Christianity* (New York: Charles Scribner's Sons, 1929).

Baeck, Leo, *Judaism and Christianity* (Philadelphia: Jewish Publication Society of America, 1958).

———, *The Pharisees* (New York: Schocken Books, 1947).

Bamberger, B. J., "The Dating of the Aggadic Materials," *Journal of Biblical Literature,* LXVIII (1949), 115–123.

Baron, Salo W., *The Jewish Community* (Philadelphia: Jewish Publication Society of America, 1948).

———, and Blau, J. L., eds., *Judaism* (New York: The Liberal Arts Press, 1954).

———, *A Social and Religious History of the Jews,* Volume Two (New York: Columbia University Press, 1952).

Barrett, C. K., *Luke the Historian in Recent Study* (London: Epworth Press, 1962).

Bentwich, Norman, *Hellenism* (Philadelphia: Jewish Publication Society of America, 1943).

Bevan, E., *Jerusalem Under the High Priests* (London: E. Arnold, 1904).

Bickerman, Elias J., *Der Gott der Makkabäer* (Berlin: Schocken Verlag, 1937).

————, *Four Strange Books of the Bible* (New York: Schocken Books, 1967).

————, *From Ezra to the Last of the Maccabees* (New York: Schocken Books, 1962).

————, "The Historical Foundations of Postbiblical Judaism," in *The Jews: Their History, Culture and Religion,* edited by Louis Finkelstein (New York: Harper & Row, 1960).

Bloch, Joshua, *On the Apocalyptic in Judaism* (Philadelphia: Dropsie College for Hebrew and Cognate Learning, 1952).

Bokser, Ben Zion, *Pharisaic Judaism in Transition: R. Eliezar the Great and Jewish Reconstruction after the War with Rome* (New York: Bloch Publishing Co., 1935).

Box, G. H., *Judaism in the Greek Period* (Oxford: 1953); *Clarendon Bible,* Vol. V.

Brandon, S. F. G., *The Fall of Jerusalem and the Christian Church* (London: S.P.C.K., 1951).

————, *Jesus and the Zealots* (Manchester: University of Manchester Press, 1967; New York: Charles Scribner's Sons, 1967).

————, *The Trial of Jesus of Nazareth* (London: Batsford, 1968; New York: Stein and Day, 1968).

Braude, William G., *Jewish Proselytizing in the First Five Centuries of the Common Era* (Providence: Brown University Press, 1940).

————, *The Midrash on Psalms* (New Haven: Yale University Press, 1959).

Büchler, Adolph, *The Economic Conditions of Judea after the Destruction of the Second Temple* (London: Horace Hart at the Oxford University Press, 1912); Jewish College Publications, Vol. IV.

————, *Studies in Sin and Atonement in the Rabbinic Literature of the First Century* (London: Oxford University Press, 1929; New York: Ktav, 1967).

————, *Types of Jewish Piety from 70 B.C.E. to 70 C.E.* (London: Oxford University Press, 1922; New York: Ktav, 1968).

Burkitt, F. C., *Jewish and Christian Apocalypses* (London: Publications for the British Academy, by H. Milford, 1914).

Charles, R. H., *Religious Development Between the Old and New Testaments* (New York: Henry Holt and Co., 1914).

Christie, W. M., "The Jamnia Period in Jewish History," *Journal of Theological Studies,* Vol. XXVI, 1924–25, pp. 347–364.

Clark, Kenneth, "Worship in the Jerusalem Temple after A.D. 70," *New Testament Studies,* (1959–60).

Cohen, Gerson D., "The Talmudic Age," in *Great Ages and Ideas of the Jewish People,* edited by Leo Schwarz (New York: Random House, 1956).

Danby, H. (trans.), *The Mishnah* (London: Oxford University Press, 1933).

Daube, David, *The New Testament and Rabbinic Judaism* (London: Althone Press, 1956).

————, "Rabbinic Methods of Interpretation and Hellenistic Rhetoric," *Hebrew Union College Annual,* Vol. XIX (1949), pp. 239–264.

Davies, W. D., *Christian Origins and Judaism* (Philadelphia: Westminster Press, 1962).

————, *Paul and Rabbinic Judaism* (London: Cambridge University Press, 1948).

————, *The Setting of the Sermon on the Mount* (London: Cambridge University Press, 1964).

————, *Torah in the Messianic Age and/or the Age to Come* (Philadelphia: Society of Biblical Literature and Excgesis, 1952).

Drazin, N., *The History of Jewish Education from 515 B.C.E. to 220 C.E.* (Baltimore: Johns Hopkins Press, 1940).

Ebner, Eliezer, *Elementary Education in Ancient Israel During the Tannaitic Period (10–220 C.E.),* (New York: Bloch Publishing Co., 1956).

Elbogen, Ismar, *Der jüdische Gottesdienst in seiner geschichtlichen Entwicklung* (Leipzig: G. Feck, 1913).

Farmer, William, *Maccabees, Zealots and Josephus* (New York: Columbia University Press, 1956).

Feldman, Louis, *Recent Research on Josephus and Philo (1937–1962),* (New York: Yeshiva University Press, 1963).

Finkel, Asher, *The Pharisees and the Teacher of Nazareth* (Leiden: E. J. Brill, 1964).

Finkelstein, Louis, *Akiba: Scholar, Saint and Martyr (New York:* The World Publishing Co., 1936).

————, *The Pharisees: The Sociological Background of Their Faith* (New York: Jewish Publication Society of America, 1962).

Gavin, F., *The Jewish Antecedents of the Christian Sacraments* (London: S.P.C.K., 1928).

Gerhardsson, Birger, *Memory and Manuscript: Oral Tradition and Written Transmission in Rabbinic Judaism and Early Christianity* (Uppsala: C. W. K. Gleerup, 1961).

Ginzberg, Louis, *Legends of the Jews* (Philadelphia: Jewish Publication Society of America, 1946).

————, "The Mishnah Tamid," *Journal of Jewish Lore and Philosophy,* Vol. I, No. 33, Cincinnati: Hebrew Union College, 1919; reprinted New York: Ktav, 1969).

————, *On Jewish Law and Lore* (Philadelphia: Jewish Publication Society of America, 1955).

————, "The Religion of the Jews at the Time of Jesus," *Hebrew Union College Annual,* Vol. I, pp. 307–321. Cincinnati: Hebrew Union College, 1924; reprinted New York: Ktav, 1968).

Glatzer, Nahum N., *Hillel the Elder: The Emergence of Classical Judaism* (New York: Schocken Books, 1956).

Goldin, Judah (trans.), *The Fathers According to Rabbi Nathan* (New Haven: Yale University Press, 1955).

————, "Hillel the Elder," *Journal of Religion,* Vol. XXVI (1946), pp. 263–277.

————, (trans.), *The Living Talmud* (Chicago: University of Chicago Press, 1955).

————, "On a Selective Bibliography in English for the Study of Judaism," in *A Reader's Guide to the Great Religions,* edited by Charles A. Adams (New York: The Free Press, 1965), pp. 191–228.

————, "The Period of the Talmud," in *The Jews: Their History, Culture and Religion,* edited by Louis Finkelstein (New York: Harper & Row, 1960).

Goodenough, Erwin Ramsdell, *By Light, Light* (New Haven: Yale University Press, 1935).

————, *An Introduction to Philo Judaeus* (New Haven: Yale University Press, 1940).

————, *Jewish Symbols in the Greco-Roman Period* (New York: Pantheon Books, beginning 1953).

Grant, F. C., *Ancient Judaism and the New Testament* (New York: The Macmillan Co., 1959).

Grant, Robert M., *Gnosticism and Early Christianity* (New York: Columbia University Press, 1959).

Guignebert, C., *The Jewish World in the time of Jesus* (New York: University Books, 1959).

Guttmann, A., "Foundations of Rabbinic Judaism," *Hebrew Union College Annual,* Vol. XXII (1950), pp. 453–473.

Hadas, Moses, *Hellenistic Culture: Fusion and Diffusion* (New York: Columbia University Press, 1960).

Helfgott, Benjamin W., *Doctrine of Election in Tannaitic Literature* (New York: King's Crown Press, Columbia University, 1954).

Herford, Robert Travers, *Christianity in Talmud and Midrash* (London: Wms. & Norgate, 1903).

———, *Judaism in the New Testament Period* (London: Lindey Press, 1928).

———, *The Pharisees* (London: George Allen & Unwin Ltd., 1924).

Hoenig, S. B., *The Great Sanhedrin* (Philadelphia: Dropsie College for Hebrew and Cognate Learning, 1953).

Idelsohn, Abraham Zvi, *Jewish Liturgy and Its Development* (New York: Henry Holt & Co., 1932).

Jacobs, Louis, "Economic Conditions of the Jews in Babylon in Talmudic Times Compared with Palestine," *Journal of Semitic Studies,* Vol. II (1957), pp. 349–359.

The Jewish Encyclopedia (New York: Funk & Wagnalls, 1901–1906; reprinted New York: Ktav Publishing Co., 1967).

Johnson, N. B., *Prayer in the Apocrypha and Pseudepigrapha* (Philadelphia: Society of Biblical Literature and Exegesis, 1948).

Jones, A. H. M., *The Herods of Judea* (Oxford: The Clarendon Press, 1938).

Kadushin, Max, *Organic Thinking* (New York: Jewish Theological Seminary of America, 1938).

———, *Worship and Ethics: A Study in Rabbinic Judaism* (Evanston, Ill.: Northwestern University Press, 1964).

———, *The Rabbinic Mind* (New York: Jewish Theological Seminary of America, 1952).

Kaminka, A., "Hillel's Life and Work," *Jewish Quarterly Review,* Vol. XXX (1939), pp. 107–122.

Klausner, Joseph, *Jesus of Nazareth* (New York: The Macmillan Co., 1925).

———, *The Messianic Idea in Israel* (New York: The Macmillan Co., 1955).

Kraeling, C. H., *The Synagogue at Dura* (New Haven: Yale University Press, 1956).

Lauterbach, Jacob Z., *The Pharisees and their Teachings* (New York: Bloch Publishing Co., 1930).

———, *Rabbinic Essays* (Cincinnati: Hebrew Union College Press, 1951).

Lieberman, Saul, *Greek in Jewish Palestine* (New York: Jewish Theological Seminary of America, 1942).

———, *Hellenism in Jewish Palestine* (New York: Jewish Theological Seminary of America, 1950).

Mantel, Hugo, *Studies in the History of the Sanhedrin* (Cambridge: Harvard University Press, 1961).

Marcus, Ralph, *Law in the Apocrypha* (New York: Columbia University Press, 1927).

———, "Pharisees, Essenes and Gnostics," *Journal of Biblical Literature,* Vol. LXXIII (1954), pp. 157–161.

———, "Pharisees in the Light of Modern Scholarship," *Journal of Religion,* Vol. XXXII (1952), p. 153.

Marmorstein, Arthur, *The Old Rabbinic Doctrine of God, The Names and Attributes of God* (London: Jews, College Publications, 1927), X.

———, *Studies in Jewish Theology,* edited by J. Rabbinowitz and M. S. Lew (London: Oxford University Press, 1950).

Meeks, Wayne, *The Prophet-King* (Leiden: E. J. Brill, 1967).

Montefiore, Claude Goldsmid, and Loewe, Herbert M. (trans.), *A Rabbinic Anthology* (New York: Meridian Books, 1960).

———, *Rabbinic Literature and Gospel Teaching* (London: The Macmillan Co., 1930).

Moore, George Foot, "Christian Writers on Judaism," *Harvard Theological Review,* Vol. 14 (1921), pp. 197–254.

———, *Judaism in the First Centuries of the Christian Era: The Age of the Tannaim* (Cambridge: Harvard University Press, Vols. I–II, 1927; Vol: III, 1930).

———, "The Rise of Normative Judaism," *Harvard Theological Review,* Vol. 17 (1924), pp. 307–375; Vol. 18 (1925), pp. 1–39.

Morrison, W. D., *The Jews Under Roman Rule* (New York: G. P. Putnam's Sons, 1902).

Neusner, Jacob, *Fellowship in Judaism* (London: Vallentine, Mitchell, 1963).

———, *From Politics to Piety: Pharisaic Judaism in New Testament Times,* (Englewood Cliffs: Prentice Hall, 1972).

———, *History and Torah* (New York: Schocken Books, 1965).

———, *A History of the Jews in Babylonia,* Volume I (Leiden: E. J. Brill, 1965).

————, "Jews and Judaism Under Iranian Rule: Bibliographical Reflections," *History of Religions,* Vol. VIII (1968), pp. 159–177.

————, *A Life of Yohanan ben Zakkai, ca. 1–80* C.E. 2nd ed. completely revised. (Leiden: E. J. Brill, 1970).

————, ed., *Religions in Antiquity: Essays in Memory of Erwin Ramsdell Goodenough* (supplements to *Numen,* Vol. XIV, Leiden: E. J. Brill, 1968).

————, *There We Sat Down: Talmudic Judaism in the Making,* (New York: Abingdon Press, 1972).

Oesterley, William Oscar, *Judaism and Christianity* (New York: The Macmillan Co., 1937).

————, *The Jewish Background of the Christian Liturgy* (Gloucester, Mass.: P. Smith, 1965).

————, *The Jews and Judaism During the Greek Period: The Background of Christianity* (London: S.P.C.K., 1941; New York: The Macmillan Co., 1941).

Parkes, James W., *The Conflict of the Church and the Synagogue* (Cleveland: World Publishing Co., 1961).

————, *The Foundations of Judaism and Christianity* (London: Vallentine, Mitchell, 1960).

Perowne, Stuart, *The Later Herods* (New York: Abingdon Press, 1958).

Pfeiffer, Robert H., *History of New Testament Times with an Introduction to the Apocrypha* (New York: Harper & Row, 1949).

Podro, Joshua, *The Last Pharisee: The Life and Times of R. Joshua ben Hananyah* (London: Vallentine, Mitchell, 1959).

Radin, Max, *The Jews Among the Greeks and Romans* (Philadelphia: Jewish Publications Society of America, 1915).

Riddle, D. W., *Jesus and the Pharisees: A Study in Christian Tradition* (Chicago: University of Chicago Press, 1928).

Rosenblatt, S., "The Crucifixion of Jesus from the Standpoint of Pharisaic Law," *Journal of Biblical Literature,* Vol. LXXV (1956), pp. 315–321.

————, *The Interpretation of the Bible in Mishnah* (Baltimore: Johns Hopkins Press, 1935).

Rostovtzeff, Michael I., *Social and Economic History of the Hellenistic World* (Oxford: Clarendon Press, 1941).

————, *Social and Economic History of the Roman Empire* (Oxford: Clarendon Press, 1957).

Roth, Cecil, "A Debate on the Loyalty Sacrifices, A.D. 66," *Harvard Theological Review,* Vol. LIII, p. 93.

————, "The Zealots in the War of 66–73," *Journal of Semitic Studies,* Vol. IV (1959), pp. 332–355.

Sandmel, Samuel, *Herod: Profile of a Tyrant* (Philadelphia: Lippincott, 1967).

————, "The Jewish Scholar and Early Christianity," *Jewish Quarterly Review, 75th Anniversary Volume,* 1967.

————, *A Jewish Understanding of the New Testament* (Cincinnati: Hebrew Union College Press, 1956).

————, "Judaism, Jesus and Paul: Some Problems of Method in Scholarly Research," *Vanderbilt Studies in the Humanities,* Vol. I (1951).

————, "Myths, Genealogies and Jewish Myths and the Writing of Gospels," *Hebrew Union College Annual,* Vol. XXVII, New York (1956).

————, *Philo's Place in Judaism: A Study of Conceptions of Abraham in Jewish Literature* (Cincinnati: Hebrew Union College Press, 1956).

Schechter, Solomon, *Some Aspects of Rabbinic Theology* (New York: The Macmillan Co., 1923).

Schoeps, Hans J., *The Jewish-Christian Argument* (New York: Holt, Rinehart & Winston, 1963).

Scholem, Gershom, *Jewish Gnosticism, Merkabah Mysticism and Talmudic Tradition* (New York: Jewish Theological Seminary of America, 1960).

————, *Major Trends in Jewish Mysticism* (Jerusalem: Schocken Books, 1941).

Schürer, Emil, *A History of the Jewish People in the Time of Jesus* (Edinburgh: T. & T. Clark, 1885).

Silver, Abba H., *The History of Messianic Speculation in Israel* (New York: The Macmillan Co., 1927).

Smith, Morton, "The Common Theology of the Ancient Near East," *Journal of Biblical Literature,* Vol. LXXI (1952), pp. 135–147.

————, and Moses Hadas, *Heroes and Gods* (New York: Harper & Row, 1965).

————, "The Image of God," *Bulletin of the John Rylands Library* (March 1958), pp. 417–512.

————, "Palestinian Judaism in the First Century," in *Israel: Its Role in Civilization,* edited by Moshe Davis (New York: Harper & Row, 1956).

————, *Tannaitic Parallels to the Gospels,* Journal of Biblical Literature Monograph Series, Vol. VI (Philadelphia: 1951).

Strack, Hermann L., *Introduction to the Talmud and Midrash* (Philadelphia: Jewish Publication Society of America, 1945).

————, and Paul Billerbeck, *Kommentar zum Neuen Testament aus Talmud und Midrasch* (Munich: C. H. Beck, 1922–1956).

Tcherikover, Victor, *Hellenistic Civilization and the Jews* (Philadelphia: Jewish Publication Society of America, 1959).

Thackeray, M. St. J., *Josephus: The Man and the Historian* (New York: Jewish Institute Press, 1929).

Vermès, G., *Scripture and Tradition in Judaism* (Leiden: E. J. Brill, 1961).

Winter, Paul, *On the Trial of Jesus* (Berlin: De Gruyter, 1961).

Wolfson, Harry, *Philo* (Cambridge: Harvard University Press, 1947).

Zeitlin, Solomon, *The Rise and Fall of the Judean State* (Philadelphia: Jewish Publication Society of America, Vol. I, 1962; Vol. II, 1967).

RABBINIC SOURCES

by JOHN T. TOWNSEND

John T. Townsend, Associate Professor of Biblical Languages and New Testament on the faculty of Philadelphia Divinity School, spent his sabbatical doing research and study in Jerusalem. Dr. Townsend has written for many scholarly journals, including the *Harvard Theological Review,* the *Journal of Theological Studies,* and the *Anglican Theological Review,* among others.

INTRODUCTION

Most of the Rabbinic sources which have commonly been used to enlighten our knowledge of the early Christian era fall into three categories: *Targum, Talmud,* and *Midrash. Targum* (pl. *Targumim*) is a Hebrew word meaning "translation"; and, when used in a technical sense, the term designates one of several Aramaic paraphrases of Hebrew Scripture. Unfortunately, the different Targumim are often difficult to identify by name because of the inconsistent way in which various titles have been applied to them.

For the Pentateuch there are two main bodies of Targumim, Babylonian and Palestinian. The Babylonian Targum, which became the official pentateuchal Targum in the synagogue, is universally called *Targum Onqelos.* Although this Targum appears to have used Palestinian traditions, it was edited in Babylonia and used there before the end of the third century C.E. The *Palestinian Targum* to the Pentateuch appears in several recensions. What may be the earliest of these recensions is known as *Neofiti I,* a name adopted from the Vatican palimpsest on which it is written. A. Díez Macho, who first identified this Targum in December 1956, believes that the recension is as early as the first or second century C.E.; but his dating has been challenged by several scholars. (E.g., M. McNamara in *Revista Degli Studi Orientali* 41 [1966], pp. 1–15, argues that, while the basis of *Neofiti I* is very old, in its present state the recension comes from later, talmudic times.) Other relatively early recensions of the Palestinian Targum include what is known as the *Fragmentary Targum,* and various targumic fragments from the Cairo Genizah. The *Fragmentary Targum,* also called *Targum Yerushalmi* in the *Miqra'ot Gedolot* (below, I:D:1) or the *Palestinian Targum,* is found in five manuscripts representing two developments of this recension. The Genizah fragments appear to represent at least two other recensions. The latest recension in the Palestinian Targum tradition also has various titles. It is commonly called *Targum Yerushalmi* or the *Palestinian Targum.* After the fourteenth century it was erroneously called *Targum Jonathan,* as in the *Miqra'ot Gedolot* (below, I:D:1), and is now often referred to as the *Targum Pseudo-Jonathan.*

There are two Targumim to the Former and Latter Prophets. One is the *Targum Jonathan (ben 'Uzzi'el),* which gained acceptance in Babylonia during the third or fourth century C.E. The other, which stems from a later period, perhaps the latter part of the seventh century, is the *Targum Yerushalmi* or *Palestinian Targum* to the Prophets. The Targum Jonathan became the official Targum of the synagogue, but the Targum Yerushalmi is only extant in a few fragments.

Targumim to all the remaining Hebrew Scriptures still exist except for the Books of Ezra, Nehemiah, and Daniel. In fact, the Book of Esther has two Targumim known as *Targum Rishon* (First Targum) and *Targum Sheni* (Second Targum). Several of these Targumim appear to be more like commentaries than translations or paraphrases, and most of them come from a relatively late era. The Targumim on Psalms and Job were composed after the division of the Roman Empire, but the other Targumim in this group come from post-talmudic times, *i.e.,* from the sixth century or later.

Talmudic literature includes the *Mishnah,* the *Tosefta,* the *Talmud Bavli,* and the *Talmud Yerushalmi.* These works distinguish themselves by their similar arrangement. The Mishnah is divided into six main *sedarim* (or orders), each of which is subdivided into several *masekhtot* (or tractates). The Tosefta and the two Talmudim are arranged according to the *sedarim* and *masekhtot* of the Mishnah.

The word *mishnah* probably comes from the Hebrew verb *shanah,* which, in post-biblical times, meant "teach" or "study." Thus *mishnah* is what is taught or studied. Used as a title, Mishnah designates a collection of oral tradition taught and studied, in particular that which became the official Rabbinic compilation of this tradition. The compilation was the work of Rabbi Judah the Prince (= Rabbi Yehudah Hanasi) who died in 219/220.

The Tosefta, an Aramaic title usually defined as meaning "supplement," designates a compilation closely resembling the Mishnah in form; but the origin of this compilation is difficult to determine. The majority of traditional authorities agree that the Tosefta was in fact a "supplement" to the Mishnah compiled by one or more pupils of Rabbi Judah the Prince. This view, however, is not without problems. For example, it is difficult to understand the Tosefta simply as a supplement to the Mishnah. The relationship is more complex. Some of the Tosefta appears to explain the Mishnah text. The Tosefta records tradition that is not in the Mishnah, tradition that is opposed to what is in the Mishnah, and tradition that corresponds to the Mishnah in a greater or lesser degree. There is also much in the Mishnah, including whole tractates, that is not found in the Tosefta. No one theory concerning the origin of the Tosefta prevails today. In addition to the view that the Tosefta is essentially a Mishnah supplement, various other possible relationships between the two works have been suggested. Some view the Tosefta as an independent compilation using various sources (*e.g.,* Isaac Hirsch Weiss and Alexander Guttmann). For others the Tosefta preserves source material upon which the Mishnah is based (*e.g.,* A. Schwarz, B. Cohen, and B. de Vries). Moses Samuel Zuckermandel has even argued that the Tosefta represents the original mishnaic collection of Rabbi Judah, and that our Mishnah is a later Babylonian redaction. There is also wide disagreement concerning when the Tosefta was compiled. The dates suggested range from the early third century (*e.g.,* Zuckermandel) to the early sixth century (*e.g.,* Joseph Hirsch Dünner).

The two Talmudim comprise the Mishnah plus massive ampli-
fications of most tractates. The amplified sections in each Talmud
are called *gemara,* an Aramaic word derived from the verb *gemar,*
meaning "complete." Originally *gemara* designated the oral teaching that "completed" the written Pentateuch, and the word only
acquired its common technical meaning in post-talmudic times.
The *Talmud Yerushalmi* (= Jerusalem or Palestinian Talmud)
records. Palestinian tradition in its *gemara.* It ceased developing
about 425 C.E. when the Tiberian Patriarchate was abolished. The
Talmud Bavli (= Babylonian Talmud) records in its *gemara* the
developing tradition in Babylonia. It was essentially complete by
the end of the fifth century but continued to be supplemented until
as late as the ninth century.

References to talmudic literature include the name of the
tractate (usually abbreviated) and distinguish among Mishnah,
Tosefta, and Talmudim by the form in which the references appear.
Mishnaic references usually include merely the tractate name followed by numerals designating chapter and section within the
tractate, *e.g., Yevamot* 2:10. References to the Tosefta use the
same form preceded by the letter "T," *e.g., TYevamot* 2:6. References to the Talmud Yerushalmi consist of the tractate name preceded by the letter "y" (sometimes "j" or "p") and followed by
a reference to the part of the Mishnah that the *gemara is*
amplifying. In addition, it is common to add the folio number and
column from the Venice-Cracow-Krotschin edition (below, II:C:1),
e.g., yYevamot 2:12 (14b). References to the Talmud Bavli depend upon the fact that all editions of this work use standard
pagination. Such a reference usually consists of the tractate plus
the folio number and side, *e.g., Yevamot* 25b.

At the end of the fourth order *(Sedar Neziqin)* in the Talmud
Bavli, many editions add several treatises which are not part of
the Talmud proper. The number of these treatises varies. Seven
of them appear to have formed the first collection, but there are
fifteen in the Romm edition of the Talmud Bavli (below, II:D:1).
The earliest of these treatises is *Avot deRabbi Natan,* which is
an elaboration of the Mishnah tractate *Avot.* The rest are probably
all post-talmudic.

The word *midrash* comes from the Hebrew verb *darash,* which in post-biblical times meant "expound" or "interpret." Thus a midrash is a work which expounds or interprets Scripture. The earlier Rabbinic midrashim are commonly designated "tannaitic" because the interpretations they contain generally come from the *Tanna'im, i.e.* Rabbinic authorities from the period of the Mishnah. These works are also called "halakhic midrashim" because they are largely concerned with *halakhah* (or legal matter). The extant tannaitic midrashim include expositions on large portions of the last four books in the Pentateuch. They are generally known by the titles, *Mekhilta, Sifra,* and *Sifre. Mekhilta* usually denotes one of two commentaries on parts of Exodus; *Sifra,* also called *Torat Kohanim,* is a commentary on Leviticus; and *Sifre* designates commentaries on parts of Numbers and Deuteronomy.

Unfortunately the relatively early dating of all tannaitic midrashim can no longer be accepted without some question. Ben Zion Wacholder has recently challenged the traditional views on the two *Mekhiltot* in the *Hebrew Union College Annual,* 39 (1968), pp. 117–144. He argues that *Mekhilta deRabbi Yishma'el* stems from the eighth century and that this conclusion must also affect the closely related *Mekhilta deRabbi Shim'on bar Yoḥay.* A radically different emphasis, however, is the view of L. Finkelstein in his book, *New Light from the Prophets* (New York: Basic Books, 1969). According to him, parts of the tannaitic midrashim, as well as some of the earliest passages in the Mishnah and Tosefta, come from the time of the biblical prophets.

Later midrashim can generally be categorized as haggadic (or aggadic) in content since they are largely concerned with *Haggadah* (or non-legal material). By genre, these midrashim fall roughly into three categories: homiletic, exegetic, and narrative. Homiletic midrashim, as their name implies, are collections of sermons on the *sedarim* (or lections) in various synagogue lectionaries. Each homily generally begins with a discussion of some legal question or with a proem on an introductory text taken from outside the lection. Then follows the sermon proper which generally does not cover the whole lection but only the first few verses. Homiletic midrashim include *Pesiqta deRav Kahana* (below, V:A), *Pesiqta Rabbati* (below, V:B), and recensions of *Tan-huma* (below, V:C). Exegetic midrashim take the form of running commentaries, but they usually have some features of the homiletic style, such as the insertion of proems. Examples of exegetical midrashim are the *Midrash Rabbah* on Genesis and on Lamentations (below, V:D). Narrative midrashim are not commentaries but rather collections of legendary material about a central theme. Such works include *Pirqe deRabbi Eli'ezer* (below. V:P) and *Tanna deve Eliyahu* (below, V:Q).

It is common practice for students of Christian origins to make use of Rabbinic literature through secondary sources or through anthologies, such as those of Claude G. Montefiore and Herbert M. Loewe, *A Rabbinic Anthology* (Philadelphia: Jewish Publication Society of America, 1960), and by Hermann Leberecht Strack and Paul Billerbeck, *Kommentar zum Neuen Testament aus Talmud und Midrasch* (Munich: C. H. Beck, 1922–61). Those who wish to study the Rabbinic works themselves are often handicapped by not knowing Semitic languages and by a general unfamiliarity with the literature and its background. The problem of not understanding Hebrew and Aramaic can never be overcome entirely; however, there are translations of many Rabbinic works available in European languages. One can begin to overcome one's unfamiliarity with Rabbinic literature generally by the use of standard reference works such as: *The Introduction to the Talmud and Midrash*, by Hermann L. Strack (Philadelphia: Jewish Publication Society of America, 1931), and *The Jewish Encyclopedia* (New York: Funk & Wagnalls, 1900–1906; reprinted in New York; Ktav, 1967); in particular, the articles, "Midrash Haggadah," "Midrash Halakah," "Mishnah," "Talmud," and "Targum." Unfortunately these works are quite dated, especially in their references to editions, commentaries, translations, and the various technical tools. This bibliography aims to help fill this gap.

The bibliography includes listings for those Rabbinic works that come from the sixth century or earlier. Added to these are certain later works that tend to be cited by writers on Christian origins. Excluded are non-Rabbinic works and liturgical writings. In most cases the bibliography contains some indication of the date for each listing wherever the dating is not clear from this introduction.

The datings are given partly as a warning against the common practice of uncritically using medieval Rabbinic sources for depicting Judaism at the beginning of the Christian era. Many of these late sources, however, while of limited help to students of Christian origins, should be used more fully than at present by those working in later periods. For those who can read Hebrew or Aramaic the bibliography includes the best editions and concordances of the various sources along with some of the more important commentaries, lexicons, and other aids. For those who know little or no Hebrew and Aramaic, it includes the best English translations where they exist as well as many other European-language translations, particularly where English translations are lacking. Wherever there are duplicate listings of editions, translations, etc., for a given work, the order indicates the author's preference. The bibliography includes an introduction and selected secondary works. For those who need a fuller bibliography with greater emphasis on the post-talmudic periods, the author is now preparing such a work.

All Hebrew words have been transliterated into Roman characters. Transcriptions of titles, wherever possible, are taken from the particular books involved. Transcriptions of personal names generally follow the transcriptions of the Library of Congress, and transcriptions or translations of publishers' names usually follow the listings in international publisher lists. Other transcriptions follow the "broad transliteration-transcription" proposed by W. Weinberg, in the *Hebrew Union College Annual*, 40–41 (1969–1970), pp. 1–32 + charts.

In concluding these introductory remarks I wish to express my gratitude to the many scholars who have offered helpful criticism during the preparation of this bibliography. Particularly helpful have been the suggestions of Herbert Opalek and Svi Rin from the University of Pennsylvania, Morton Smith of Columbia University, and Jacob Neusner of Brown University.

I. TARGUMIM

A. TARGUMIM TO TORAH
  1. *Targum Onqelos*
     a. Critical editions:
        i. Sperber, A., *The Bible in Aramaic,* Vol. I: *The Penta-
           teuch according to Targum Onkelos* (Leiden: Brill,
           1959).
        ii. Berliner, A., *Targum Onkelos.* Herausgegeben und
            erläutert. 2 vols. in 1 (Berlin: Gorzelanczyk, 1884).
            Vol. 1: *Text, nach Editio Sabioneta V. J. 1557.* (Re-
            printed in Jerusalem: Makor, 1968/69).
            Some prefer this edition to that of Sperber. The text is
            pointed with the usual infralinear vowel signs.
     b. Translation:
        Etheridge, J. W., *The Targums of Onkelos and Jonathan ben
        Uzziel on the Pentateuch with Fragments of the Jerusalem
        Targum.* 2 vols. (London: Longman, Green, *et al.,* 1862–
        65; reprinted as one vol. in New York: Ktav, 1968).
     c. Concordances:
        i. Kasowski,[1] H. J., *Concordance to the Targum Onqelos.*
           5 vols. in 2; Hebrew (Jerusalem: Rabbi Kook Founda-
           tion, 1939–40).
        ii. Brederek, E., *Konkordanz zum Targum Onkelos.* Bei-
            hefte zur *ZAW, IX* (Giessen: Töpelmann, 1906).
            This work merely lists words with numerical refer-
            ences, and gives all the references only for words in-
            frequently used. More common words have but a few
            sample references.
  2. Palestinian Targum Tradition
     a. *Neofiti I.*
        i. *Editio princeps* with Spanish, French, and English trans-
           lations: Díez Macho, A., *Neophyti 1: Targum pales-
           tinense, Ms de la Biblioteca Vaticana,* Tomo I: *Génesis.*
           Edición príncipe, introducción general y versión cas-
           tellana. Traducciones cotejadas: francesa por R. Le
           Déaut; inglesa por M. McNamara y M. Maher. Textos
           y estudios 7 (Madrid: Consejo superior de investiga-
           ciones científicas, 1968).

---

[1] Often spelled Kassovsky.

The volumes for the rest of the Pentateuch have yet to appear. Unfortunately this volume contains no photographic reproductions, and the editor has corrected the text on numerous occasions without always indicating that he has done so. See the review of J. A. Fitzmyer in *Catholic Biblical Quarterly* 32 (1970), pp. 107–112.

ii. Edition of selected passages: Goshen-Gottstein, M. H., *Aramaic Bible Versions* (Jerusalem. Mif'al Hashikhpul [Hebrew Univ.], 1963).

This chrestomathy (with vocabulary) includes Gen. 3, Exod. 19, Num. 25, and Deut. 28 from *Neofiti I*.

iii. Edition of Deut. 1 with Spanish translation: Díez Macho, A., *Biblia Polyglotta Matritensia*, Series IV: *Targum Palaestinense in Pentateuchum, Adduntur Targum Pseudo-Jonatan, Targum Onqelos et Targum Palaestinensis Hispanica Versio*, I [iber] 5: *Deuteronomium, Caput I*. (Madrid: Consejo superior de investigaciones científicas, 1965).

The various recensions are arranged in parallel columns.

b. *Fragmentary Targum*

i. Edition: Ginsburger, M., *Das Fragmenthargum*. (Berlin: Calvary, 1899; reprinted in Jerusalem: [Makor], 1968/69).

This edition has many inaccuracies. M. C. Doubles (*Vetus Testamentum,* 15 [1965], p. 16) claims to have discovered about 2000 errors in Ginsburger's presentation of two mss. Doubles has prepared Ginsburger's text for republication.

ii. Translation: Etheridge (above, 1:b).

c. Cairo Genizah Fragments

i. Edition of Text: Kahle, P., *Masoreten des Westens,* II, 2. Texte und Untersuchungen zur vormasoretischen Grammatik des Hebräischen, IV (Stuttgart: W. Kohlhammer, 1930).

A new edition of the fragments, prepared mostly by G. Schelbert, was promised for one of the supplements to *Vetus Testamentum* by Paul Kahle in *The Cairo Geniza*. Second edition (Oxford: Blackwell, 1959) p. 205, n. 2.

       ii. Various other fragments have been published by: A. Díez Macho in *Sefarad,* 15 (1955), pp. 31–39; G. Schelbert in *Vetus Testamentum,* 8 (1959), 253–263; Y. Komlosh in *Sinai,* 45 (1959), pp. 223–228; and W. Baars in *Vetus Testamentum,* 11 (1961), pp. 340–342.

   d. *Targum Yerushalmi* (= *Targum Pseudo-Jonathan*).

       i. Edition: Ginsburger, M., *Targum Pseudo-Jonathan ben Usiël zum Pentateuch.* Nach der Londoner Handschrift Brit. Mus. add. 27031 (Berlin: Calvary, 1903; reprinted in Jerusalem: Makor, 1968/69).

         The edition has many errors.

       ii. Translation: Etheridge (above, 1:b).

B. Targumim to Former and Latter Prophets

   1. *Targum Jonathan*

     a. Critical edition: Sperber, A., *The Bible in Aramaic,* Vol. II: *The Former Prophets according to Targum Jonathan,* and Vol. III: *The Latter Prophets according to Targum Jonathan* (Leiden: Brill, 1959–62).

     b. Text and translation of Targum to Isaiah: Stenning, J. F., *The Targum of Isaiah* (Oxford: Clarendon, 1949; reprinted in 1953).

       Aramaic and English on opposite pages.

   2. *Targum Yerushalmi*

       Note that, while many of the fragments in the works listed below are labeled as coming from this Targum, others are not so identified. However, some of the unidentified fragments probably come from *Targum Yerushalmi* since a fragment unidentified in one ms. is ascribed to *Targum Yerushalmi* in another. See Stenning (above 1:b), pp. 227 f. on Isaiah 10:32.

     a. Fragments in *Codex Reuchlinianus:* Lagarde, P. A. de, *Prophetae Chaldaice.* E fide codicis Reuchliniani editit (Leipzig: Teubner, 1872; reprinted in Osnabrück, 1967).

       The fragments are scattered throughout the apparatus criticus, pp. VI–XLII. For a photocopy of *Codex Reuchlinianus,* see A. Sperber, *The Pre-Masoretic Bible,* Vol. I. *Codex Reuchlinianus* ("Corpus Codicum Hebraicorum Medii Aevi," II:I [Copenhagen: E. Munksgaard, 1956]).

     b. Fragments in *Codex Reuchlinianus* along with additional fragments from other mss: Sperber (above, 1:a) Vols. I and II.

The fragments are scattered throughout the apparatus criticus.

c. Fragments of the *Targum Yerushalmi* to Isaiah: Stenning (above, 1:b), pp. 88–105.

One fragment to Isaiah 10:32, found in British Museum Oriental Mss. 2211 and 1474, is translated.

C. TARGUMIM TO WRITINGS

1. Targum to Psalms, Proverbs, and Job.
   a. Edition: Lagarde, P. A. de, *Hagiographa Chaldaice* (Leipzig: Teubner, 1873; reprinted in Osnabrück, 1967).
   b. Text and partial translation of Targum to Job 1–3: Epstein, E. L., *A Critical Analysis of Chapters One to Twenty-six of the Targum to Job* (Chicago: University of Chicago, 1944).

      A translation is provided only where the Aramaic does not follow the Hebrew exactly. Unfortunately, the title is misleading since only the first three chapters are treated.

2. Targum to the Five Scrolls and to Chronicles.
   a. Editions:
      i. Lagarde (above, 1:a).
      ii. Sperber, A., *The Bible in Aramaic,* Vol. IV:A: *The Hagiographa* (Leiden: Brill, 1968).

         According to the author, "No attempt has been made in this volume to offer the texts published here in a critical edition, comparable to the first three volumes of this series." Targum to Ruth is based on the text of Jacob ben Chayim's Bible as reprinted by Lagarde (above, 1:a). The remaining four scrolls follow Brit. Mus. Or. Ms. 2375. Whereas Ben Chayim's Bible and Lagarde's edition have two Targumim to Esther, this ms. has but one Targum which follows sometimes the *Targum Rishon,* sometimes the *Targum Sheni,* and sometimes neither. In editing Chronicles, Sperber followed "the unique manuscript, which M. Steinschneider described *sub numero* 125 in his *Verzeichnis der hebräischen Handschriften* (in *Die Handschriften-Verzeichnisse der Königlichen Bibliothek zu Berlin;* II. Band, Berlin 1878)."
   b. Editions and translations of individual books:
      i. Song of Songs: critical edition: Melamed, R. H., *The*

Targum to Canticles (Philadelphia, 1921).

Translation: Gollancz, H., *Targum to the Song of Songs, the Book of the Apple, the Ten Jewish Martyrs, a Dialogue on Games of Chance.* (London: Luzac, 1908), pp. 1–4, 15–90.

ii. Ruth: translation: Saarisalo, A. "The Targum to the Book of Ruth," *Studia Orientalia,* 2 (1928), pp. 88–105.

iii. Lamentations: translation: Greenup, A. W., *The Targum on the Book of Lamentations* (Sheffield, 1893).

iv. Ecclesiastes: critical edition: Levy, A., *Das Targum zu Koheleth. Nach Südarabischen Handschriften* (Breslau: H. Fleischmann, 1905).

v. Ecclesiastes: translation: Ginsburg, C. D., *Coheleth, Commonly Called the Book of Ecclesiastes* (London: Longmans, Green, 1861), pp. 502–519.

vi. Esther:

(1) *Targum Rishon:* textual variants: Posner, S., *Das Targum Rishon zu dem biblischen Buche Esther* (Breslau: 1896), pp. 71 ff.

Text and Latin translation: Tayler [or Taylor], F., *Targum Prius et Posterius in Esteram* (1655).

(2) *Targum Sheni* (= *Targum Yerushalmi*): critical edition: David, M., *Das Targum Scheni zum Buche Esther.* Nach Handschriften herausgegeben und mit einer Einleitung versehen (Cracow: J. Fischer, 1898).

Other well-known editions are those of P. Cassel, *Zweites Targum zum Buche Esther* (Leipzig: W. Friedrich); and L. Munk, *Targum Scheni zum Buche Esther* (Berlin: 1876).

German translation: Sulzbach, A., *Targum Scheni zum Buch Esther* (Frankfurt a. M.: J. Kauffmann, 1920). Another German translation is that of P. Cassel, *Das Buch Esther* (Berlin: Bibliographisches Bureau, 1891), pp. 239–298.

vii. Chronicles: text and Latin translation:

Wilkins, D., *Paraphrasis Chaldaica in Librum Priorem et Posteriorum Chronicorum* (Amsterdam: J. Boom, 1715).

Beck, M. F., *Paraphrasis Chaldaica: Libri Chroni-*

corum. Hactenus inedita. 2 vols. (Augsburg: T. Goebelius, 1680).

D. COLLECTIONS OF BIBLICAL TARGUMIM

1. Text: *Miqra'ot Gedolot,* also called a Rabbinic Bible (Jerusalem: Schocken, 1958–59).

   An emended reprint of the Netter edition (Vienna, 1859). This Bible contains the Hebrew text and all Targumim except *Neofiti I,* the Geniza fragments, and the fragments of *Targum Yerushalmi* to the Prophets. In addition there are numerous traditional biblical commentaries, *e.g.,* the commentaries of Rashi, Nahmanides, and Ibn Ezra.

2. Text with Latin translation: Walton, B., *Biblia Sacra Polyglotta.* 6 vols. (4 for the Hebrew Scriptures). (London: T. Roycroft, 1657).

   All the great polyglots contain some Targum with Latin translation, but the Walton Polyglot is the most complete. This work contains all the Targumim printed in the *Miqra'ot Gedolot* (above, 1) except for the Targum to Chronicles and the *Targum Sheni* to Esther. Note that the *Targum Yerushalmi* (= *Pseudo-Jonathan*) and the *Fragmentary Targum* to the Pentateuch are printed as an appendix at the end of Vol. IV. In addition to the Hebrew text and Targumim, the Walton Polyglot also includes part or all of the following versions with their Latin translations: LXX with readings of Codex Alexandrinus, Old Latin, Vulgate, Syriac, Samaritan-Hebrew, Samaritan-Aramaic, Arabic, Ethiopic, and Persian.

II. TALMUDIC LITERATURE

A. MISHNAH

1. Editions with commentaries:

   a. Albeck, H., and H. Yalon, *Shishah Sidre Mishnah.* 6 vols. (Jerusalem: Bialik Institute, and Tel Aviv: Dvir, 1952–56).

      Each tractate of this useful edition is preceded by a survey of biblical references and an introduction to the subject matter. There are also two commentaries, a short explanation under the text in the spirit of the traditional commentaries, and an appendix to each volume of about 100 pages which deals with critical problems, etc. These introductions and commentaries, which are written in Hebrew, are the work of Albeck. The pointing is the work of Yalon and represents a new vocalization based on mss. rather than on later editions to the Mishnah in which the pointing is altered in conformity with the masoretic rules for biblical pointing.

b. Schachter, M., *The Babylonian and Jerusalem Mishnah Textually Compared* (Jerusalem: Rabbi Kook Foundation, 1959).

The two recensions appear in parallel columns with the differences between them indicated by italics. The notes must be used with caution as they contain several inaccuracies, but the texts are trustworthy.

2. Edition: Lowe, W. H., *The Mishnah on Which the Palestinian Talmud Rests*. Edited from a unique manuscript preserved in the University Library of Cambridge (Cambridge: University Press, 1883; reprinted in 1966).

A good text, but not what the title claims. Rather the text represents a mixed Jerusalem and Babylonian recension. Moreover, the ms. used is hardly unique. See E. Schürer, *Geschichte des jüdischen Volkes*. Third and fourth editions (Leipzig: Hinrichs, 1901–09), vol. I, p. 129.

3. Photocopies of mss.:

a. Beer, G., *Mischnacodex Kaufmann*. 2 vols. (Budapest: Der A. Kohut-Gedächtnisstiftung; reprinted in Jerusalem: Makor, 1969).

b. Katsch, A. I., *Ginze Mishna* (Jerusalem: Rabbi Kook Foundation, 1970).

Photocopy of Leningrad Mss. with a study of variant readings.

4. Edition with traditional commentaries: *Mishnayot . . . 'im Perush Rabbenu 'Ovadyah Bartinorah . . . Tosefot Yom Ṭov, wekhu. . . . we'im . . . Sheva' Wesheloshim Hosafot Ḥadashot* (Vilna: Romm, 1908).

This edition has twenty-one commentaries as well as the thirty-seven supplements mentioned in the title. The commentaries include all the traditional ones except those of Maimonides and Rashi, both of which are found in the Romm edition of the *Talmud Bavli* (below, D:1; but cf. next entry). Note that the publisher has emended the mishnaic text on the basis of manuscript variants recorded in *Tosefot Yom Ṭov*.

5. Edition of text with commentary of Maimonides (in Arabic and

Hebrew): Kafah, J. *Mishnah 'im Perush Rabbenu Mosheh ben Maymon: Maqor Wetargum* (Jerusalem: Rabbi Kook Foundation, 1963–68).

This edition of Maimonides' commentary is necessary because the Romm Talmud (below D:1) contains the work only in an imperfect Hebrew translation. This new edition contains the original Arabic text of the commentary in Hebrew letters along with a Hebrew translation in parallel columns under the Mishnah text. Note that there is another printing of this work which omits the Arabic text.

For a bibliography of critical editions, with Hebrew and some German translations to individual tractates of Maimonides' commentary, see A. Yaari, "Maimonides' Commentary on the Mishna, a Bibliography of Edited Parts," *Kirjath Sepher* 9 (1932/33), pp. 101–109, 228–235. See also *ibid.* 12 (1935/36), p. 129, and 29 (1953/54), p. 176.

6. Edition with commentaries of Maimonides and Obadiah of Bertinoro in Latin translation: Surenhusius, G., *Mischna . . . . cum Clarissimorum Rabbinorum Maimonidis et Bartenorae Commentariis Integris.* Quibus accedunt variorum auctorum notae ac versiones in eos quos editerunt codices. Latinitate donavit ac notis illustravit, 6 vols. Amsterdam, 1698–1703.

7. Editions with German translation, and commentary:

    a. Sammter, A., and D. Hoffmann (eds.), *Mishnayot: Die sechs Ordnungender Mischna (Berlin: Itzkowski,* 1887–1933; reprinted in Basel: Goldschmid, 1968—).

    The individual tractates are edited by various scholars, all Orthodox Jews. The German commentary is moderately full. The series has been praised by Schürer (above, 2), p. 129, and by H. Danby, "Presidential Address," *Journal Palestine Oriental Society,* 14 (1934), p. 174.

    b. Beer, G., O. Holtzmann, S. Krauss, H. K. Rengstorf, and L. Rost (eds.), *Die Mischna: Text, Übersetzung und ausführliche Erklärung.* Mit eingehende geschichtlichen und sprachlichen Einleitung und textkritischen Anhängen (Giessen and Berlin: Töpelmann, 1912—). Commonly known as "Giessen Mischna."

    The various tractates are in separate volumes and by different authors. To date the following volumes have been published: all of the first two orders except *Sheq., Ta'an..*

and *Ḥag.;* in the third order, only *Yev., Naz.,* and *Soṭah,* in the fourth order, *BQ, BM, San., Mak., Avot,* and *Hor.;* in the fifth order, *Tam., Mid., and Qin.;* and in the sixth order, *Parah, Zav., TY,* and *'Ukts.* Unfortunately the various volumes are of unequal merit. Several, in particular many of the early ones printed under the general editorship of Beer and Holtzmann, are open to much criticism. For a very critical review of some of these volumes, see C. Albeck in *MGWJ* 73 (1929), pp. 4–25. See also A. Goldberg, *JJS* 17 (1966), pp. 93–106.

8. Text with annotations and literal translation: Blackman, P., *Mishnayoth.* Third edition, revised, corrected, and enlarged. 6 vols. (New York: Judaica, 1965).

   On the supplement and index to this work, see below, IX:D:6. The text follows the traditional editions and is printed parallel to the translation. The annotations follow each *mishnah* (or section) and draw on the traditional commentaries. In general the work is intended as an aid to students of Mishnah more than as a scholarly contribution to the field of mishnaic studies.

9. Translation: Danby, H., *The Mishnah.* Translated from the Hebrew with introduction and brief explanatory notes (Oxford: Oxford University Press, 1933).

   Inexpensive and often reprinted. A good translation with an index and a few helpful notes interpreting the text along traditional lines.

10. Concordance: Kasowski, Ḥ. J., *Thesaurus Mishnae: Concordantiae Verborum quae in Sex Mishnae Ordinibus Reperiuntur.* Revised edition (Tel Aviv: Massada, 1967).

11. Index of proper nouns: Duensing, S., *Verzeichnis der Personennamen und der geographischen Namen in der Mischna* (Stuttgart: W. Kohlhammer, 1960; a reprint of the 1913 edition).

12. Variants and textual tools. For variants, see below, D 9 and 10. For an excellent history of how the Mishnah developed into its present form with much that is useful to the textual critic, see J. N. Epstein, *Mavo Lenosaḥ Hamishnah* (Jerusalem: Magnes, 1964).

13. Editions, annotations, etc. of series of tractates.

    a. Critical texts with various aids: Strack, H. L., in the series, "Schriften des Institutum Judaicum in Berlin" (Leipzig: Hinrichs, 1888–1915).

The following volumes were published: *Ber.* (1915), *Shab.* (1890), *Pes.* (1911), *Yoma* (1888), *San.* and *Mak.* (1910), *'AZ* (1888), *Avot* (1901). Several volumes were reprinted, and *Pirqê Aboth* was revised and published in the series "Ausgewählte Mischnatraktate" (Leipzig: Hinrichs, 1915).

b. German translation and commentary: Fiebig, P., *et al.* in the series "Ausgewählte Mischnatraktate in deutscher Übersetzung," edited by Fiebig (Tübingen: J. C. B. Mohr, 1905–12).

The following volumes were published: *Ber.*, by Fiebig (1906); *Shab.*, by G. Beer (1908); *Yoma,* by Fiebig (1905); *Meg.,* by J. W. Rothstein (1912); *San.* by G. Holscher (1910); *'AZ* by P. Krüger (1906); and *Avot,* by Fiebig (1906)

14. Editions, commentaries, etc., of individual tractates.

a. *Ber., Pe'ah,* and *Dem.:* text with substantial commentary in English: Herzog, J. D., *The Mishna: Berakoth, Peah, Demai.* Text with commentary of R. Obadiah of Bertinoro [in Hebrew], translation [of *Mishna* text], introduction and new commentary in English (Jerusalem: Harry Fischel Institute, 1945).

Unfortunately the Bertinoro commentary is not translated. In addition to the work of Herzog, there are variant readings and short exegetical notes in Hebrew by the fellows of the Harry Fischel Institute.

b. *Ber.:* Edition: Staerk, W., *Der Misnatraktat Berakhot.* In vokalisiertem Text mit sprachlichen und sachlichen Bemerkungen. Kleine Texte für theologische und philologische Vorlesungen und Übungen, 59 (Bonn: Weber, 1910).

c. *Meg.:* Edition, translation, and commentary: Rabbinowitz, J., *Mishnah Megillah* (Oxford: Oxford University Press, 1931).

The commentary is quite full and in English.

d. *Naz.:* Text, German translation, and commentary: Boertien, M., *Der Mishnatraktat Nazir.* Einleitung, Text, Übersetzung und Erklärung. Textkritischer Anhang. Diss. Amsterdam (Amsterdam: Niderlands Document Reproduktie, 1964).

This dissertation was also published in 1964 as part of the "Giessen Mischna" (above, 10) where it is one of the better volumes in the series.

e. *Qid.:* Text, German translation, and commentary: Stern, J.,

Der Mischnatraktat Qiddushin. Text, Übersetzung, und ausführlicher Kommentar. Diss. Zurich (Jerusalem: Gescher, 1948).

f. *BQ:* Text, translation, and commentary: Golden, H. E., *Mishnah Baba Kamma* (New York: Jordan, 1933).

g. *BM:* Text, translation, and commentary: Golden, H. E., *Mishnah Baba Mezia* (New York: Jordan, 1933).

h. *BB:* Text, translation, and commentary: Golden, H. E. *Mishnah Baba Batra* (New York: Jordan, 1933).

i. *San.:* Text with variants: Krauss, S., *The Mishnah Treatise Sanhedrin.* Semitic Study Series, XI. Edited with an introduction, notes, and glossary (Leiden: Brill, 1909).

j. *Avot:*

    i. Text, translation, and extensive commentary: Taylor, D., *Sayings of the Jewish Fathers.* Second edition (Cambridge: Cambridge University Press, 1897; reprinted New York: Ktav, 1969, with an introduction by J. Goldin).

    ii. Translation and commentary: Oesterley, W. O. E., *The Sayings of the Jewish Fathers.* Translations of Early Documents, III:1 (London: SPCK, 1919).

    iii. Text, translation, and commentary: Herford, R. T., *Pirke Aboth.* Third edition revised. (New York: Jewish Institute of Religion, 1945; reprinted often as "Schocken Paperback," SB 23, New York: Schocken, 1962—).

    iv. Translation with an English commentary extracted from traditional Rabbinic materials: Goldin, J., *The Living Talmud: The Wisdom of the Fathers* (New Haven: Yale, 1957; reprinted often as Mentor Book, MQ 1024, New York: New American Library, 1957—).

    v. Text, translation, and commentary: Hirsch, S. R., *Chapters of the Fathers* (New York: Feldheim for S. R. Hirsch Publication Society, 1967).

k. *Hor.:* Text, translation, and detailed commentary: Weis, P. R., and E. Robertson. *Mishnah Horayoth, its History and Exposition* (Manchester: Manchester University Press, 1952). Good for a critical commentary in English.

l. *Tam.:* Edition: Brody, A., *Der Misna-Traktat Tamid.* Text nach einer Vatikan Handschrift. Diss. Uppsala (Uppsala, 1936).

  m. *Ohol.:* Critical edition with Hebrew commentary: Goldberg,
  A., *The Mishna Treatise Ohaloth.* Diss. Heb. Univ. (Jerusalem: Magnes, 1955).

B. TOSEFTA

 1. Critical edition:
  a. Lieberman, S., *The Tosefta.* According to Codex Vienna
   and with variants from Codex Erfurt, Genizah Mss., and
   Editio Princeps (Venice, 1521) together with references to
   parallel passages in talmudic literature and a brief commentary [in Hebrew]. (New York: Jewish Theological Seminary of America, 1955—.)

    By far the best edition. To date three volumes have been
   published including the first two and a half orders (through
   Naz.)

 2. Commentary: Lieberman, S., *Tosefta ki-Fshutah.* A comprehensive commentary on the *Tosefta* (New York: JTSA, 1955—).

   This multivolumed commentary in Hebrew is appearing along
  with the critical edition of the Tosefta by the same author
  (above, 1). The eleven vols. printed to date complete the commentary through *Naz.*

 3. Critical edition and commentary: Lieberman, S., *Tosefot Rishonim.* 4 vols. (Jerusalem: Bamberger & Wahrmann, 1936/37–
  38/39).
   The best complete edition of the Tosefta.

 4. Critical edition: Zuckermandel, M. S., *Tosefta.* Based on the
  Erfurt and Vienna codices with parallels and variants. Second
  edition with supplement to the *Tosefta* by S. Lieberman (Jerusalem: Bamberger & Wahrmann, 1937).

   This edition is commonly used by scholars but is inferior to
  the editions of Lieberman (above, 1 and 3). Note that the reprint in Jerusalem: Wahrmann, 1963, lacks the Lieberman
  supplement. However, the same publisher has now made this
  supplement available in a separate volume.

 5. Critical edition, pointed and with commentary: Abramski, Y.,
  Ḥazon Yeḥezekel Vilna, London, and Jerusalem, 1925–63).
   Incomplete.

 6. Text with traditional commentary: Pardo, D. *Sefer Ḥasde David.*
  4 vols. (Leghorn: 1776–1790).

   The fourth volume of this work has been edited by S. Leiber-
  man (Jerusalem: JTSA, 1970).

7. Edition, German translation, commentary. Kittel, G., and K. H.
Rengstorf (eds.), *Die Tosefta.* Text, Übersetzung, Erklärung
(Stuttgart: W. Kohlhammer, 1933—).

   The several volumes represent the work of different authors.
To date, the following parts have been published: *Ber., Pe'ah*
(the beginning only), *Yev.* (all but part of the last chapter), and
all of the sixth order.

8. Text with Latin translation of thirty-one tractates: Ugolino, B.,
Thesaurus Antiquitatum Sacrarum, Vols. 17–20 (Venice: J. G.
Herthz, 1755–57).

   Text and translation are in parallel columns. The following
tractates are included: all of the first order in Vol. 20 (1757);
Shab., 'Eruv., Pes. in Vol. 17 (1755); the rest of the second
order in Vol. 18 (1755); and all extant tractates of the fifth
order in Vol. 19 (1756).

9. Concordance: Kasowski, H. J. *Thesaurus Thosephthae: Concordantiae Verborum quae in Sex Thosephthae ordinibus Reperiuntur.* 6 vols. in Hebrew (Jerusalem: Bamberger & Wahrmann, 1932–61).

   Vols. 5 and 6 are by M. Kasowski, the author's son.

10. Texts, translations, etc. of individual tractates:
    a. *Ber.:*
       i. Text, German translation, and commentary: Holtzmann,
          O., *Der Tosephtatraktat Berakot.* Text, Übersetzung,
          Erklärung. Beihefte zur *ZAW,* 23 (Giessen: Töpelmann,
          1912).

          According to H. L. Strack, *Introduction to the Talmud
          and Midrash* (Philadelphia: Jewish Publication Society of
          America, 1931), pp. 272 f., n. 13, this work is "quite
          unsatisfactory."
       ii. Translation and notes: Lukyn Williams, A., *Tractate
          Berakoth: Mishna and Tosephta.* Translations of Early
          Documents, III (London: SPCK, 1921).
    c. *Suk.:* Translation and notes: Greenup, A. W., *Tractate
       Sukkah: Mishna and Tosephta.* Translations of Early Docu-
       ments, III (London: SPCK, 1925).
    d. *Betsah:* Text, German translation, and commentary: Kern,
       M., *Der Tosefta-Traktat Yom Tob.* Einleitung, Übersetzung
       und Erklärung. Diss. Univ. Würzburg: (Würzburg: Schmer-
       sow, 1934).

Text and translation in parallel columns.

e. *Qid.:* Text, German translation, and commentary: Schlesinger, P., *Die Tosefta des Traktats Qiddusin.* Übersetzt und erklärt. Diss. Univ. Würzburg (Würzburg: 1926).

f. *San.:* Translation and notes: Danby, H., *Tractate Sanhedrin: Mishna and Tosefta.* Translations of Early Documents, III (London: SPCK, 1919).

C. TALMUD YERUSHALMI

1. Standard editions: Most references in modern works refer to the pagination of the edition printed by Bomberg in Venice (1523/24). The same pagination was followed by the later editions from Cracow (1609), and from Krotoschin (1866). For a good printing of this Talmud following the Venice-Cracow-Krotoschin edition, see *Talmud Yerushalmi* (New York: Shulsinger, 1948).

2. Edition with most of the traditional commentaries: *Talmud Yerushalmi o Talmud Hama'arav weyesh Qorin lo Talmud Erets Yisra'el.* Usevivo Perushim, Ḥiqre Halakhot, Girsa'ot, Wenusha'ot Shonot me'et Ge'one Yisra'el (Vilna: Romm, 1922; reprinted in New York: Talmud Yerushalmi Publishing Company and Otzar Hasefarim Turim Publishers, 1958–60).

3. Vocalized text with translation and commentary in English: Ehrman, A. (ed.), *The Talmud with English Translation and Commentary* (Jerusalem: El-'Am, 1965—).

Each volume of this massive work contains only one *pereq* (or chapter) of one tractate in the *Talmud Bavli* followed by the corresponding *pereq* in the *Talmud Yerushalmi.* Thus far the following have been published: *Ber.* 2a–15b, *Qid.* 2a–28a, *BM* 33b–48a, *yBM* 3:1–9 (8d–9b).

4. French translation: Schwab, M., *Le Talmud de Jérusalem.* 11 vols. (Paris: Maisonneuve, 1932–33; A reprint of the 1871–89 edition).

The translation contains a few gaps and is generally unreliable.

5. Text with Latin translation of twenty tractates: Ugolino, B. (above, B:8), Vols. 17–30 (Venice: Herthz, 1755–65).

Text and translations in parallel columns giving Mishnah as well as *Gemara* even though the tractates are labeled *Gemara.* The following tractates are included: *Ma'as., MS, Ḥal., 'Orl., Bik.* in Vol. 20 (1757); *Pes.* in Vol. 17 (1755); *Yoma, Sheq.,*

Suk., RH, Betsah, Ta'an., Meg., Ḥag., MQ in Vol. 18 (1755); *Soṭ., Ket., Kid.,* in Vol. 30 (1765); and *San., Mak.,* in Vol. 25 (1762).

6. Textual variants: Ratner, B., *Ahawath Zion we-Jeruscholaim: Varianten und Ergänzungen des Textes des jerusalemitischen Talmuds.* Nach alten Quellen und Handschriftlichen Fragmenten. 12 vols. (Vilna: Romm, 1901–17; reprinted in Jerusalem: 1964).

7. Genizah fragments: Ginzberg, L., *Seride ha-Yerushalmi: Yerushalmi Fragments from the Genizah,* Vol. 1, Texts and Studies of JTSA, 3 (New York: JTSA, 1909; reprinted in Jerusalem: Makor, 1969).

8. Commentary on difficult passages: Rabinowitz, Z. W., *Sha're Torath Eretz Israel* (Jerusalem: I. Rabinovitz, 1939/40).

9. Translations, commentaries, etc., on individual tractates.
   a. *Ber.:*
      i. Commentary: Goren, S., *Hayerushalmi Hameforash* (Jerusalem: Rabbi Kook Foundation, 1961).
      ii. English translation: Schwab, M. *The Talmud of Jerusalem,* Vol. I: *Berakhoth* (London, 1886; reprinted in New York: P. Feldheim, 1969).
      iii. 1:1 (2a)–5:4 (9c): Modern commentary in Hebrew: Ginzberg, L. *A Commentary on the Palestinian Talmud; A Study of the Development of the Halakah and Haggadah in Palestine and Babylonia.* 4 vols. Texts and Studies of the JTSA, 10, 11, 12, 21 (New York: JTSA, 1941–61).
   b. *Shab., 'Eruv., Pes.:* Commentary in Hebrew: Lieberman, S. *HaYerushalmi kiPhshuto: A Commentary.* Based on Manuskripts [sic] of the Yerushalmi, the works of the Rishonim and Midrashim in mss. and rare editions. Part I, Vol. I: *Sabbath Erubin Pesahim* (Jerusalem: Darom, 1934).
   c. *Betsah:* Commentary of Elazar Azkari (16th century) edited with references and notes: Francos, Y. *Talmud Yerushalmi: Massekhet Betsah 'im Perush . . . El 'azar Azkari* (New York: JTSA, 1966/67).
   d. *Ta'an.:* English translation: Greenup, A. W. *Talmud Yerushalmi: A Translation of the Treatise Taanith (on the Public Fasts) from the Palestinian Talmud* (London: Palestine House, 1918).

e. *Ned.:* German translation and commentary: Horowitz, C. *Nadarin* [jer.] *übersetzt und interpretiert* (Düsseldorf-Benrath: Kalima, 1957).

D. TALMUD BAVLI

1. Standard editions: References to this Talmud refer to the pagination of the edition printed by Bomberg in Venice (1520–23). The same pagination has been followed in later editions. The best of these later editions, in that it contains the most commentaries, is *Talmud Bavli* (Vilna: Romm, 1886).

2. Facsimile of Munich Ms.: Strack, H. L., *Talmud Babylonicum Codicis Hebraici Monacensis 95 Fautore Johanne Schnorr von Carlosfeld Arte Phototypica Depingendum Curavit* (Leiden: A. W. Sijthoff's uitgevers maatschappij, 1912).

3. Commentary of Don Solomon Vidal (= Menaheim ben Solomon Me'iri. 1249–1306): Schreiber, A., *et al.* (eds.), *Bet Habehirah* (Jerusalem: A Schreiber and the Institute for the Complete Israel Talmud, 1939—. Several vols. reprinted from earlier editions. Also published in New York).

   The various tractates represent the work of different editors. The *Bet Habehirah* is an important commentary which uses earlier sources and gives otherwise unknown textual variants.

4. Vocalized text with translation and commentary in English: Ehrman, A. (ed.) See above, C:3.

5. Standard text with English translation: Epstein, I. (ed.), *Hebrew-English Edition of the Babylonian Talmud* (London: Soncino, 1960—).

   The translation is that of the following entry arranged opposite pages of a standard edition. To date *Ber., Pes., Qid., BQ, BM,* and *San.* have appeared.

6. English translation and subject index:
   a. Epstein, I. (ed.), *The Babylonian Talmud* (London: Soncino, 1935–48).

      A good translation with notes and glossaries. References to the pagination of standard editions are given in the text, but the index volume refers to the pagination of this translation. Also, since the translators do not agree on translations of various Hebrew terms, references to them in the index often fall under several headings for each term.
   b. Rodkinson, M. K. *New Edition of the Babylonian Talmud.*

Original text edited, formulated, and translated into English (New York: New Talmud. Publ. Co., 1896–1903). Some vols. later revised by I. M. Wise.

The translation is free and heavily abbreviated. There is no Hebrew-Aramaic text. Moreover, it is difficult to find references in this work since the standard pagination is not indicated. A good work to avoid.

7. Standard text with variants and German translation: Goldschmidt, L. *Der Babylonische Talmud mit Einschluss der vollstaendigen Misnah.* Herausgegeben nach der ersten zensurfreien bombergschen Ausgabe (Venedig 1520–23) nebst Varianten der spaeteren von S. Lorja, J. Berlin, J. Sirkes u. AA. Revidirten. Ausgaben und der muenchener Talmud Handschrift, sinn- und wortgetreu uebersetzt und mit kurzen Erklärungen versehen (Leipzig: Harrassowitz [vols. 1, 5–6, 8], Berlin & Vienna: B. Harz [vols. 2–4, 7], and the Hague: M. Nijhoff [vol. 9], 1906–35). The original publication extended from 1896–1935.

The text and translation of this well-known work appear on the same page. Unfortunately the "kurzen Erklärungen" are very short indeed.

8. Text, Hebrew translation and commentary: Steinsalz, R., *The Babylonian Talmud* (Jerusalem: Israel Institute of Talmud Publications, [1969—]).

This work puts the Talmud within reach of anyone reading modern Hebrew. Thus far *Ber.* and *Shab.* have appeared.

9. Textual variants: Rabbinovicz, R. N. *Sepher Diqduke Sopherim: Variae Lectiones in Mischnam et in Talmud Babylonicum.* 16 vols. (Munich: 1867–97; Reprinted in New York: Edison Lithographing Corp., 1959/60.

10. Textual variants, supplemental volumes to the preceding entry:
    a. Hyman, M. A., *Diqduqe Soferim: Ne'erakh Wenisdar 'al Shete Massekhtot Nedarim weNazir* (Chicago, 1942/43).
       The texts of the Vilna edition and of the Munich Ms. appear in parallel columns.
    b. Feldblum, M. S., *Diqduqe Soferim: Tractate Gittin.* Annotated variant readings culled from mss. and Genizah fragments and talmudic commentaries from 750 C.E. to 1600 C.E. (New York: Horeb, 1966).

11. Commentary on difficult passages: Rabinowitz, Z. W.; *Sha'are*

Torath Babel. Edited by E. Z. Melamed (Jerusalem: JTSA, 1961).

12. Concordance: Kasowski, H. J. *Thesaurus Talmudis: Concordantiae Verborum quae in Talmude Babilonica Reperiuntur* (Jerusalem: Ministry of Education and Culture and JTSA, 1954—).

This multivolume concordance is now complete through *Kulhu.*

13. Subject concordance: Goldschmidt, L. *Subject Concordance to the Babylonian Talmud,* ed., R. Edelmann (Copenhagen: E. Munksgaard, 1959).

The listings are in Hebrew-Aramaic and the references give the pagination of both the Goldschmidt Talmud (above, 7) and the standard editions.

14. Editions, commentaries, etc. on individual tractates.

    a. *Ta'an.:*

       i. Critical edition: Malter, H., *The Treatise Ta'anit of the Babylonian Talmud.* Publications of the American Academy for Jewish Research, Vol. 1 (New York: American Academy for Jewish Research, 1930).

      ii. Critical edition, English translation, and notes: Malter, H., *The Treatise Ta'anit of the Babylonian Talmud.* Library of Jewish Classics (Philadelphia: JPSA, 1928; reprinted in 1967 with different pagination).

      This work uses the same text as the preceding entry, but the critical apparatus is abbreviated.

    b. *Nash.:* Halivni, D. (= Weiss, D.), *Sources and Traditions: A Source Critical Commentary on Seder Nashim,* in Hebrew (Tel Aviv: Dvir, 1968).

    This volume is the first in a projected series. For an English digest with scattered comments covering tractates *Ket., Qid.* and *Git.* see the articles of R. Goldenberg, S. Kanter, and D. Goodblatt, in *The Formation of the Babylonian Talmud,* ed., J. Neusner, (Leiden: Brill, 1970.), pp. 134–173.

    c. *Meg.:* Edition: Price, J. J., *The Yemenite Ms. of Megilla* [in the library of Columbia University]. Critically examined and edited (Toronto, 1916; reprinted in Jerusalem; Makor, 1970).

    d. *BM:* Text with German translation and commentary: Sammter, A. *Talmud Babylonicum, Tractat Baba Mezia.* Mit deutscher Übersetzung und Erklärung (Berlin: Benzian, 1876).

e. *BM* 2a–21a: text and commentary: Steinbach, A. W., Steinbach, R., and Steinbach, A. A., *Treatise Baba Mezia (Middle Gate), Order IV, Treatise, II, Chapter I.* Talmudic text annotated in English, punctuated and paragraphed. Rashi annotated in English and punctuated, etc. . . . (St. Louis, 1927).

f. *Mak.:* Critical edition: Friedmann, M., "Kritische Edition des Traktates Makkoth," *Verhandlungen des Siebenten Internationalen Orientalisten-Congresses, Semitische Section* (Vienna: 1888), pp. 1–78.

III. EXTRA-CANONICAL TRACTATES

A. Translation: Cohen, A. (ed.), *The Minor Tractates of the Talmud: Massektoth Ketannoth.* 2 vols. (London: Soncino, 1965).

The different treatises are the work of different translators. Each treatise has an introduction, but the introductions tend to be short on technical matters.

B. Editions, translations, etc., of separate treatises.

1. *Avot deRabbi Natan* (third or fourth century). The work is extant in two recensions. Recension A is the one found in *Talmud* editions and is translated in the Soncino translation (above, A). Recension B was printed for the first time by S. Schechter (next entry).

   a. Edition of both recensions: Schechter, S., *Aboth deRabbi Nathan* (Vienna, 1887; reprinted in New York: P. Feldheim, 1945).

   The two recensions appear in parallel columns.

   b. Translation of recension A: Goldin, J., *The Fathers According to Rabbi Nathan.* Yale Judaica Series, Vol. X (New Haven: Yale University Press, 1955).

2. *Soferim* (about the eighth century).

   a. Critical edition: Higger, M., *Massekhet Soferim* (New York: Debe Rabanan, 1937).

   b. Edition: Müller, J., *Masechet Soferim, der talmudische Traktat der Schreiber* (Leipzig: J. C. Hinrichs, 1878).

3. *Evel Rabbati, also called Semahot.* The work was known in the south of France in the twelfth century, but it contains earlier elements.

    a. Critical edition: Higger, M., *Treatise Semaḥot and Treatise Semaḥot of R. Ḥiyya and Sefer Ḥibbut haKeber and Additions to the Seven Minor Treatises and to Treatise Soferim II* (New York: Bloch, 1931).

    b. Edition and translation: Zlotnick, D., *The Tractate "Mourning" (Semaḥot)*. Translated from the Hebrew with introduction and notes. With an appendix: The Hebrew text of the tractate, edited from manuscripts [and] vocalized. Yale Judaica Series, Vol. XVII (New Haven: Yale University Press, 1966).

4. *Kalla and Kalla Rabbati.* In their present form both probably stem from the eighth century.

    a. Critical edition: Higger, M., *Massekhtot Kallah: Wehen Massekhet Kallah, Massekhet Kallah Rabbati* (New York: Debe Rabanan, 1936).

5. *Derekh Erets Rabbah* and *Derekh Erets Zuṭa* including *Pereq Hashalom.* These works, which appear in various recensions, are post-talmudic in their present form although individual sections are earlier.

    a. Critical edition and English translation with introductions in Hebrew and English: Higger, M., *The Treatises Derek Erez: Massektoth Derek Erez, Pirke ben Azzai, Tosefta Derek Erez* (New York: Debe Rabanan, 1935).

        Higger has rearranged the traditional order of the chapters along critical lines. Under "Derek Erez" he includes *Derek Erets Zuṭa,* chapters 1–9; and under "Pirke ben Azzai" he includes *Derek Erets Rabbah,* chapters, 3–9. The remaining chapters of both, including *Pereq Hashalom,* he adds under the general heading of "Supplement," or "Tosefta Derek Erez." For all but the "Supplement" Higger follows recension B (French). "Tosefta Derek Erez" depends on recension D (Italian) since recension B is lacking here. Variants from other recensions are in the apparatus.

    b. Edition following recension A (Gaonic): Higger, M., *Massekhtot Ze'erot* (New York: Bloch, 1928/29).

        This work contains six parts of *Derekh Erets Zuṭa* and *Rabbah* which Higger believes to represent early forms of the work. The six parts correspond to *DEZ* 1–4, 9; *DEZ* 5–8; *DER* 1; *DER* 2; *DEZ* 11 (= *Pereq Hashalom*) and a collection of all sections in *DEZ* and *DER* which begin "Gadol hashalom."

   c. Supplement to the preceding entry: Higger, M., *Hosafot Lemassekhtot Ze'erot* (Jerusalem: Merkaz, 1935).

6. Minor Extra-Canonical Tractates.

   a. Edition and translation: Higger, M., *Seven Minor Treatises: Sefer Torah, Mezuzah, Tefillin, Zizit, 'Abadim, Kutim, Gerim: And Treatise Soferim II.* Edited from manuscripts with an introduction, notes, variants and translation (New York: Bloch, 1929/30).

IV. TANNAITIC MIDRASHIM

A. *Mekhilta deRabbi Yishma'el* on Exodus.

1. Critical edition: Horovitz, H. S., and Rabin, A., *Mechilta d'Rabbi Ismael* (Frankfurt a. M.: J. Kauffmann, 1928–31; reprinted in Jerusalem: Bamberger & Wahrmann, 1960).

   The best edition available. Other well-known editions, in addition to the next entry are those of M. Friedmann (Vienna: 1870) and of J. H. Weiss (Vienna: 1865).

2. Critical edition with English translation: Lauterbach, J. Z., *Mekilta de-Rabbi Ishmael.* A critical edition on the basis of manuscripts and early editions with an English translation, introduction and notes. 3 vols. Library of Jewish Classics (Philadelphia: JPSA, 1933–35; reprinted in 1949).

   The last volume contains a "page concordance" (= table of cross references) to the Friedman, Weiss, and Horovitz-Rabin editions (above 1). The first volume of this edition and translation has been reprinted by M. Kadushin, *A Conceptual Approach to the Mekilta* (New York: JTSA, 1969), appendix.

3. Concordance: Kosovsky, B., *Otzar Leshon haTannaim: Concordantiae Verborum quae in Mechilta d'Rabbi Ismael Reperiuntur.* 4 vols. (Jerusalem: JTSA, 1965–66).

4. Concordance of personal names including names of tribes and places named for people: Kosovsky, B. *Thesaurus Nominus* [sic] *quae in Mechilta d'Rabbi Ismael Reperiuntur* (Jerusalem: JTSA, 1965).

B. *Mekhilta deRabbi Shim'on bar Yohay.* This midrash on Exodus was extracted from *Midrash Hagadol* (below, VI:A:1) by D. Hoffmann and published in the periodical, *Hapeles,* from 1901 through 1904. Hoffmann later published the work in one volume with the help of twelve leaves from the Cario Genizah under the title, *Mechilta de-Rabbi Simon b. Jochai* (Frankfurt a. M.: J. Kauffmann, 1905; the work has been reprinted in Tel Aviv: Zion, 1967/68).

1. Critical edition: Epstein, J. N., and E. Z. Melamed, *Mekhilta d'Rabbi Sim'on b. Yochai.* Fragmenta in Geniza Cairensi reperta digessit. Apparatu critico, notis, praefatione instruxit (Jerusalem: Mekitze Nirdamim, 1955).

2. Supplement to preceding entry: Sarfatti, G., "Qeta' mitokh Mekhilta deRabbi Shim'on," *Lesonenu,* 27–28 (5723–24 [= 1962–64]), p. 176.

   The fragment of nine lines, from Ms. 3205 in the JTSA Library, belongs at the end of *Yitro* (= Exodus 18–20) and corresponds to p. 157, lines 5–11, of the Epstein-Mclamed edition (above, 1).

C. *Sifra* (= *Torat Kohanim*) on Leviticus.

1. Facsimile of Codes Assemani LXVI in the Vatican Library: Finkelstein, L., *Sifra or Torat Kohanim according to Codex Assemani LXVI.* With a Hebrew introduction (New York: JTSA, 1956).

2. Edition with traditional commentary: Koleditzky, S., *Sifra or Torat Kohanim and the Commentary by Rabbenu Hillel ben R. Eliakim* (Jerusalem: Hatchiya Press, 1960/61).

3. Edition with commentary of Abraham ben David of Posquières: Weiss, I. H., *Sifra deve Rav: Hu Sefer Torat Kohanim* (Vienna: J. Schlossberg, 1862; reprinted in New York: Om, 1946).

4. Edition of the beginning of *Sifra* with commentary in Hebrew. Friedmann, M., *Sifra, der älteste Midrasch zu Levitikus.* Nach Handschriften neu herausgegeben mit Anmerkungen bis 3:9. Schriften der Gesellschaft zur Förderung der Wissenschaft des Judentums (Breslau: M. & M. Marcus, 1915).

5. German translation: Winter, J., *Sifra: Halachischer Midrasch zu Leviticus.* Schriften der Gesellschaft des Judentum, 24. (Breslau: Munz, 1938).

   This translation follows the Friedmann edition (above, 4) where available and elsewhere, the Weiss edition (above, 3).

6. Text with Latin translation: Ugolino, B. *Thesaurus Antiquitatum Sacrarum,* Vol. 14 (Venice: Herthz, 1752).

   The translation is unreliable.

7. Concordance: Kosovsky, B., *Otzar Leshon haTannaim: Con-*

cordantiae Verborum quae in Sifra aut Torat Kohanim Re-
periuntur. 4 vols. (Jerusalem: JTSA, 1967–69).
D. Sifre on Numbers and Deuteronomy
    1. Edition: Friedmann, M., *Sifrè debè Rab: Der älteste halachische*
        und hagadische Midrasch zu Numeri und Deuteronomium
        (Vienna, 1864; reprinted in New York and again in 1968 with-
        out any indication of the place of publication).
    2. Edition with commentary of Rabbenu Hillel Ben R. Eliakim:
        Koleditzky, S., *Sifre Lehatanna Ha'elohi Rabbi Shim'on ben*
        Yoḥay (Jerusalem: Rabbi Kook Foundation, 1947/48).
    3. Text with Latin translation: Ugolino, G., *Thesaurus Antiquitatum*
        Sacrarum, Vol. 15 (Venice: Herthz, 1753).
    4. *Sifre* on Numbers alone
        a. Critical edition: Horovitz, H. S., *Siphre de'be Rab,* Fasciculus
            primus: *Siphre ad Numeros adjecto Siphre zutta.* Schriften,
            herausgegeben von der Gesellschaft zur Förderung der Wis-
            senschaft des Judentums: Corpus Tannaiticum, 3:3:1 (Leip-
            zig: G. Fock, 1917; reprinted in Jerusalem: Wahrmann,
            1966).
            The best edition available.
        b. German translation with commentary and the variants from
            the Horovitz edition (above, a): Kuhn, K. G., *Der tan-*
            naïtische Midrasch Sifre zu Numeri. Rabbinische Texte,
            zweite Reihe: Tannaitische Midraschim, 3 (Stuttgart: W.
            Kohlhammer, 1959).
            The work is based on a draft translation by J. Winter
            and notes of H. Windisch.
        c. English translation of selected passages: Levertoff, P. P.
            Midrash Sifre on Numbers. Translations of Early Docu-
            ments, Series III: Rabbinic Texts (London: SPCK, 1926).
    5. *Sifre* on Deuteronomy alone.
        a. Critical edition: Finkelstein, L., and Horovitz, H. S., *Siphre*
            d'be Rab, Fasciculus alter: *Siphre ad Deuteronomium.* Cor-
            pus Tannaiticum, 3:3:2 (Berlin: Gesellschaft zur Förderung
            der Wissenschaft des Judentums, 1939; reprinted in New
            York: JTSA, 1969).
            The best edition available. The reprinting of this edition
            by JTSA is especially welcome because the Nazis had de-
            stroyed nearly all of the original printing.
        b. German translation and commentary: Ljungman, H., *Sifre*

> *zu Deuteronomium.* Übersetzt und erklärt. Rabbinische Texte, zweite Reihe: Tannaitische Midraschim, 4 (Stuttgart: W. Kohlhammer, 1964—).
>
> The translation is only completed through § 31 (= Deut. 6:4).

   c. Translation with notes of *Sifre* Deut. §§ 1–54 (= through Deut. 11:28): Kittel, G., *Sifre zu Deuteronomium* (Stuttgart: W. Kohlhammer, 1922).

E. *Sifre Zuṭa,* a midrash on Numbers extracted from *Yalquṭ Shim'oni* (below, VI:A:2). This work contains teachings from unknown or relatively unknown tannaitic authorities as well as otherwise unknown disputes between Bet Hillel and Bet Shammai. For a recent detailed study of this work (in Hebrew) see S. Lieberman, *Siphre Zutta (the Midrash of Lydda)* [and] *II: The Talmud of Caesarea* (New York: JTSA, 1968).

   1. Edition: Horovitz (above, D:4:a), pp. xv–xxi, 225–336.

     Horovitz had previously published the work separately under the title, *Der Sifre Sutta, nach dem Jalkut und anderen Quellen* (Breslau; 1910).

   2. Edition with commentary and the Horovitz introduction translated into Hebrew. Joskowicz, J. Z., *Sifre Zuṭa Lesefer Bemidbar Hayemuḥas Lehatanna Rabbi Yishma'el.* . . . 2 vols. (Lodz, 1929 [vol. 1], n.d. [vol. 2]; reprinted in Bene Baraq, Israel, 1966/67).

   3. Edition with commentary: Garbuz, E. Z., *Sifre Zuṭa 'al Sefer Bemidbar* (Jerusalem, 1946/47).

F. *Midrash Tanna'im* on Deuteronomy, formerly known as *Mekhilta on Deuteronomy.* This midrash was originally extracted from the *Midrash Hagadol* (below, VI:A:1) by D. Hoffmann and published under the title, *Neue Collectaneen aus einer Mechilta zu Deuteronomium* (Jahres-Bericht des Rabbiner-Seminars zu Berlin 1895 und 1896 (Berlin: 1897).

   1. Edition: Hoffmann, D. *Midrash Tannaim zum Deuteronomium* (Berlin: M. Poppelaver, 1908–09).

     This edition uses Geniza fragments published by S. Schechter in the *Jewish Quarterly Review* 4 (1904), pp. 446–452, 695–697.

G. *Midrash Zuṭa* on Deuteronomy, extracted from *Yalquṭ Shim'oni* (below, VI:A:2).

   1. Edition: Buber, S. *Liqqutim Mimidrash Elleh haDevarim Rabbah*

[i.e. *Zuṭa*] *Hanimtsa'im baYalqut* (Vienna: 1885; reprinted in Jerusalem: 1966/67).

In addition to the *Yalquṭ* excerpts (pp. 1–10), the book contains a recension of the *Midrash Rabbah* on Deut. 1:1–3:23 differing from the other printed editions (below, V:D). It is taken from Cod. Munich Heb. 229.

V. LATER MIDRASHIM

A. *Pesiqta deRav Kahana,* a homiletic collection stemming from some-time in the seventh–ninth centuries.
  1. Critical edition: Mandelbaum, B., *Pesikta de Rav Kahana.* According to an Oxford manuscript with variants from all known manuscripts and genizoth fragments and parallel passages with commentary and introduction, in Hebrew and English. 2 vols. (New York: JTSA, 1962).
  2. Older edition: Buber, S., *Pesikta: Die älteste Hagada redigirt in Palästina von Rab Kahana* (Lyck: Vereins Mekize Nirdamim, 1868; reprinted in Vilna, Romm: 1925, in New York: Om, 1948/49, and in Jerusalem: 1962/63).
  3. German translation: Wünsche, A., *Bibliotheca Rabbinica,* IV:2: *Pesikta des Rab Kahana.* Nach der buberschen Textausgabe (Leipzig: O. Schulze, 1885; reprinted in Hildesheim: Olms, 1967).
  4. English translation: One has been almost completed by W. G. Braude and will probably soon be published in New Haven, Yale, or in Philadelphia: Jewish Publication Society of America.
B. *Pesiqta Rabbati.* This homiletic midrash is commonly dated after the middle of the ninth century although parts are earlier, *e.g., Pes. R.* 15–18 and 33 since they are taken from *Pes. K.* 5–8 and 19. Furthermore over half of the Homilies begin in the name of R. Tanḥuma, who lived at the beginning of the fifth century.
  1. Edition: Friedmann, M., *Pesikta Rabbati: Midrasch für den Fest-Cyclus und die ausgezeichneten Sabbathe* (Vienna: 1880; reprinted in Tel Aviv: 1962/63).
  2. Edition with Hebrew commentaries: *Pesiqta Rabbati de Rav Kahana 'im Arba'ah Perushim* (Warsaw: 1913. Reprinted in New York: Menorah, 1958/59).
  3. English translation: Braude, W. G., *Pesikta Rabbati: Discourses for Feasts, Fasts, and Special Sabbaths* 2 vols. Yale Judaica Series, 18 (New Haven: Yale University Press, 1968).

4. Critical edition, German translation, and commentary of § 26: Prijs, L., *Die Jeremiah-Homilie, Pesikta Rabbati, Kapitel 26* (Stuttgart: W. Kohlhammer, 1966).

C. *Midrash Tanḥuma* (= *Midrash Yelammedenu*). The work exists in three recensions. Two recensions were known to the author of the *Yalqut* (below, VI:A:2), recension A, which he called *Tanḥuma*, and recension B, which he called *Yelammedenu*. Apart from fragments recension B is lost, but there exists a third recension (C) which drew on both recension A and recension B. This midrash is the oldest commentary on the whole Pentateuch, and according to S. Buber recension A is even older than Genesis Rabbah (below, D:7:a), which comes from the fourth or fifth century.

1. Recension A.
   a. Critical edition: Buber, S., *Midrash Tanchuma: Ein agadischer Commentar zum Pentateuch von Rabbi Tanchuma ben Rabbi Abba.* Zum ersten male nach Handschriften aus den Bibliotheken zu Oxford, Rom, Parma und München herausgegeben. Kritisch bearbeitet, commentirt und mit einer ausführlichen Einleitung [auf Hebräisch] versehen (Vilna: Romm, 1885; reprinted in Vilna, 1912/13, in New York, 1946, and in Jerusalem: Ortsel 1963/64).

2. Recension B. (= *Yelammedenu*) fragments.
   a. Jellinek, A., *Bet ha-Midrasch* (below, VI:B:1:a). vol. 6, pp. 79–105.
   b. Neubauer, A., "Le midrasch Tanchuma et extraits du Yélamdénu et petits midraschim," *Revue des études juives*, 13 (1886), pp. 224–238; 14 (1887), pp. 92–113.
   c. Grünhut, S., *Sefer Haliqqutim,* Vols: IV–VI (Frankfurt: J. Kauffmann, 1900–1903).
   d. Ginzberg, L. *Genizah Studies in Memory of Doctor Solomon Schechter,* Vol. I: *Midrash and Haggadah.* Texts and Studies of JTSA, VII (New York: Jewish Theological Seminary of America; reprinted in New York: P. Feldheim, 1969).

3. Recension C.
   a. Selected editions with the commentaries of Enoch Zundel:
      i. *Midrash Tanḥuma 'al Ḥamishah Ḥummeshe Torah* (Stettin: E. Schrentzel, 1863/64; reprinted in New York: Horeb, 1924).
      ii. *Midrash Tanḥuma* (Warsaw: N. D. Süssberg, 1875).
   b. Text and German translation (Genesis only):

Singermann, F., *Midrash Tanhuma 'al Ḥamishah Ḥummeshe Torah*. Mit verbessertem hebräischem Texte, übersetzt und erläutert (Berlin: Lamm, 1921).

4. German translations of selections from all three recensions: Winter, J., and A. Wünsche. *Die jüdische Literatur seit Abschluss des Kanons,* Erster Band: *Die jüdisch-hellenistische und talmudische Literatur* (Trier: S. Mayer, 1894), pp. 411–432.

D. *Midrash Rabbah*. The title denotes a collection of midrashim on the Pentateuch and the Five Scrolls from various centuries. The dates when several of these midrashim were compiled are disputed, but the following datings are typical: Genesis in the fourth or fifth century, Exodus as early as the seventh century but perhaps as late as the twelfth century, Leviticus from the seventh through the ninth century, Numbers in the eleventh or twelfth century, and perhaps even later, Deuteronomy in the tenth century, Song of Solomon in the seventh century or later, Ruth from the seventh to the tenth century, Lamentations in the fifth century, Ecclesiastes in the seventh century, and Esther in the fifth century but perhaps in the tenth century or later.

1. Critical edition for the Pentateuch: Halevi, E. E. (= Epstein, E.), and Y. Toporovski, *Midrash Rabbah*. Meforash [we]menuqqad (Tel Aviv: Machbarot Lesifrut, 1956–63).

   The critical apparatus is not extensive, and all the Aramaic passages are given in Hebrew translation.

2. Edition with traditional commentaries: *Midrash Rabbah 'al Ḥamishah Ḥummeshe Torah weḤamesh Megillot* (Vilna: Romm, 1884–87).

3. Edition with Hebrew commentary: Mirkin, M. A., *Midrash Rabbah,* 9 vols. (Tel Aviv: Yavneh, 1956–64).

4. Edition with Hebrew commentaries: Yadler, I. Z., *Sefer Midrash Rabbah*. 'im pe. *Matnot Kehunah* we 'im pe. ḥadash *Tif'eret Tsiyyon* . . . (Tel Aviv: Lipa Fridman, 1958–63).

5. English translation and index: Freedman, H. and M. Simon (eds.), *Midrash Rabbah*. Translated into English with notes, glossary, and indices. 10 vols. (London: Soncino, 1939; reprinted in 1951 and 1961).

6. German translation: Wünsche, A., *Bibliotheca Rabbinica*. 5 vols. (Leipzig: O. Schulze, 1880–85. Vols. I–III, IV:1, 3, 4, and V:1, 2, 4; reprinted in Hildesheim: Olms, 1967).

Do not overlook the notes and emendations by J. Fürst at the ends of the various sections.

7. Concordance (the beginning of one): Horovitz, A. M., *Thesaurus Midrase Rabbae: Concordantiae Verborum* (Jerusalem: Otsar Leshon Hamidrash, 1939—).

Only one volume, covering part of the letter *alef,* ever appeared.

8. Editions, commentaries, etc., on the separate midrashim.

   a. *Gen. R.:* Theodor, J., and Ch. Albeck, *Midrash Bereshit Rabba.* Critical edition with notes and commentary [in Hebrew]. 3 vols. 2nd printing corrected (Jerusalem: Wahrmann, 1965).

   A superb edition and commentary.

   b. *Lev. R.:* Margulies, M., *Midrash Wayyikra Rabba.* A critical edition based on manuscripts and genizah fragments with variants and notes. 5 vols. (Jerusalem· Ministry of Education and Culture, L. M. Epstein Fund, American Academy for Jewish Research, 1953–60).

   c. *Deut. R. in a new recension:* Lieberman, S., *Midrash Debarim Rabbah.* Edited for the first time from the Oxford Ms. no. 147 with an introduction and notes [in Hebrew]. 2nd ed. with additions and corrections (Jerusalem: Wahrmann, 1964/65).

   d. *Lam. R.:* Buber, S., *Midrasch Echa Rabbati: Sammlung agadischer Auslegungen der Klagelieder.* Kritisch bearbeitet, commentirt und mit einer Einleitung versehen (Vilna: Romm, 1899; reprinted in Tel Aviv, 1963/64, and in Hildesheim: G. Olms, 1967).

E. *Midrash Aggadah,* a relatively late commentary on the Pentateuch that derives its material mainly from Tanḥuma, recension A. (above, C:1).

   1. Edition: Buber, S., *Agadischer Commentar zum Pentateuch.* Nach einer Handschrift aus Aleppo (Vienna: A. Fanto, 1894; reprinted in New York: Sinai, 1959/60).

F. *Aggadat Bereshit,* a collection of homilies on Genesis from a relatively late date.

   1. Edition: Buber, S., *Agadath Bereshith: Midraschische Auslegungen zum ersten Buche Mosis.* Nach den ältesten Druckwerken in Vergleichung mit einer Oxforden Handschrift, Cod. 2340 (Cracow: J. Fischer, 1902; reprinted in Vilna: Romm, 1925, and in New York: Menorah, 1958/59).

G. *Bereshit Rabbati,* a late midrash not to be confused with the earlier
   Bereshit Rabbah (= *Gen. R.,* above, D).
   1. Edition: Albeck, Ch. *Midras Beresit Rabbati ex libro R. Mosis
      Haddarsan* [11th century] (Jerusalem: Mekize Nirdamim, 1940;
      Reprinted in Jerusalem: Rabbi Kook Foundation, 1966/67).
H. *Midrash Samuel* (= *Aggadat Shermu'el*). This work was compiled
   in Palestine perhaps during the eleventh century. In the editions
   of Zolkiev (1800) and of Lemberg (1808 and 1850) it is erroneously named *Shoher Ṭov.*
   1. Edition: Buber, S., *Midrash Shemu'el weyesh Qorin lo Aggadat
      Midrash Shemu'el o Aggadat Shemu'el o Aggadat deShemu'el.*
      2nd edition, emended (Vilna: Romm, 1925). The first edition
      (Cracow: J. Fischer, 1893) has been reprinted in Jerusalem,
      1964/65, along with the Midrash on Proverbs.
   2. German translation: Wünsche, A., *Aus Israels Lehrhallen,* V.
      Band (1. Hälfte): *Der Midrasch Samuel* (Leipzig: E. Pfeiffer,
      1910; reprinted in Hildesheim: Olms, 1967).
I. *Midrash on Psalms* (= *Midrash Tehillim* = *Shoher Ṭov*). This
   midrash was probably composed in Palestine during the ninth
   century or even later, although the nucleus may be considerably
   earlier (2nd–4th century). There is manuscript evidence that the
   section on Psalms 119–150 comprise a later addition.
   1. Edition: Buber, S., *Midrasch Tehillim (Schocher Tob): Samm-
      lung agadischer Abhandlungen über die 150 Psalmen.* Heraus-
      gegeben nach Handschrift aus der Bibliothik zu Parma . . . mit
      Vergleichungen der Lesarten anderer . . . Handschriften . . .
      kritisch bearbeitet, commentirt, und mit . . . Einleitung versehen
      (Vilna: Romm, 1891; reprinted in New York, 1947, and in
      Jerusalem, 1965/66).
      The best edition but full of errors.
   2. English translation: Braude, W. G., *The Midrash on Psalms.*
      Translated from the Hebrew and Aramaic. 2 vols., Yale
      Judaica Series, 13 (New Haven: Yale, 1959).
      In order to make this wonderfully accurate translation with
      notes and indices, the author revised the inaccurate Buber edi-
      tion (above, 1) although he did not print any text.
   3. German translation: Wünsche, A., *Midrasch Tehillim, oder
      Haggadische Erklärung der Psalmen.* Nach der Textausgabe
      von Solomon Buber [above, 1] zum ersten Male ins Deutsche
      übersetzt und mit Noten und Quellenangaben versehen. 2 vols.

(Trier: S. Mayer, 1892–93; reprinted in Hildesheim: Olms, 1967).

J. *Midrash* on Proverbs (= *Midrash Mishle*). The work was compiled sometime before the first half of the eleventh century when it is mentioned by name. In the edition of Zolkiev (1800) it is erroneously named *Shober Tov*.

   1. Edition: Buber, S., *Midrasch Mischle: Samlung* [sic] *agadischer Auslegung der Sprüche Salomonis* (Vilna: Romm, 1893; reprinted in Jerusalem, 1964/65, along with the midrash on Samuel).

   2. German translation: Wünsche, A., *Bibliotheca Rabbinica*, V:3: *Der Midrasch Mischle* (Leipzig: O. Schulze, 1885; reprinted in Hildesheim: Olms, 1967).

K. Midrash on Job.

   1. Edition of fragments: Wertheimer, S. A., *Midrash Iyyov* (Jerusalem: S. Zuchremann, 1921).

L. *Midrash Megillot Zuṭa*. The midrash on the Song of Solomon in this collection seems to come from about the tenth century.

   1. Edition: Buber, S., *Midrasch Suta: Haggadische Abhandlungen über Schir ha-Schirim, Ruth, Echah und Koheleth nebst Jalkut zum Buche Echah* (Berlin: Vereins Mekize Nirdamim, 1894; reprinted in Vilna: Romm, 1925, and in Tel Aviv, 1963/64).

     For a severe criticism of this work, see S. Schechter in the *Jewish Quarterly Review*, 8 (1895/96), pp. 179–184.

   2. *Song of Solomon Zuṭa* (= *Shir hashirim Zuṭa* = *Aggadat Shir Hashirim*): edition: Schechter, S., *Agadath Shir Hashirim*. Edited from a Parma manuscript (Cambridge: D. Bell, 1896).

     First published in the *Jewish Quarterly Review*, 6 (1893/94), pp. 672–697; 7 (1894/95), pp. 145–163; 8 (1895–96), pp. 298/320.

M. *Midrash* Song of Solomon (neither *Rabbah* nor *Zuṭa*). This work was first used by writers in the eleventh century and was found written on a manuscript dated 1147.

   1. Edition: Grünhut, L., *Midrasch Schir ha-Schrim*. Zum ersten Male nach ei[n]er in Egypten aufgef[u]nden Hs. edirt kritisch untersucht mit Quellenangabe und einer Einleitung versehen (Jerusalem: W. Gross, 1896/97).

N. Selected midrashim on Esther.

   1. *Midrash Abba Gorion, Midrash Panim Aherim,* and the Midrash on Esther found in *Leqaḥ Tov* (a midrash on the

Pentateuch and Five Megillot written by Tobiah ben Eliezer in 1079 and revised in 1107–8): edition: Buber, S., *Sammlung agadischer Commentare zum Buche Esther* (Vilna: Romm, 1886).

2. *Aggadat Ester* (at least as late as the fourteenth century): edition: Buber, S., *Agadische Abhandlung zum Buch Esther* (Cracow: J. Fischer, 1897; reprinted with additions in Vilna, 1925 and in Jerusalem, 1963/64).

O. *Midrash of the Thirty-Two Rules.* This work was believed to be tannaitic by H. G. Enelow, who first published it; but, although it contains tannaitic material, the midrash is probably post-talmudic. According to M. Zucker, in *Proceedings of the American Academy for Jewish Research,* 23 (1954), pp. 1–39 (Hebrew section), the author was R. Samuel ben Hofni Gaon (d. 1034), who relied heavily on R. Saadya Gaon (882–942).

1. Edition: Enelow, H. G., *The Mishnah of Rabbi Eliezer, or, The Midrash of Thirty-Two Hermeneutic Rules* (N.Y.: Bloch, 1933)

P. *Pirqe deRabbi Eli'ezer.* In its present form the work comes from a time as late as the eight or ninth century.

1. Edition: Higger, M., "Pirqe Rabbi Eli'ezer," *Horeb* 8 (1944), pp. 82–89; 9 (1946), pp. 94–166; 10 (1948), pp. 185–294.

2. English translation with notes: Frielander, G., *Pirke deRabbi Eliezer* (London: 1912; reprinted in England by Hermon Press, 1965, and in the United States by M. Vallentine, 1967).

Q. *Tanna deve Eliyahu (= Seder Eliyahu Rabbah + Seder Eliyahu Zuṭa + Pseudo-Seder Eliyahu Zuṭa).* In its present form the work comes from the ninth or tenth century, but it contains *baraitot* from a time as early as the third century. On the critical problems connected with this work, see Kadushin, M., *The Theology of Seder Eliahu* (New York: Bloch, 1932), pp. 6–16.

1. Edition of *Seder Eliyahu Rabbah* and *Zuṭa:* Friedmann, M., *Seder Eliahu rabba und Seder Eliahu Zuṭa (Tanna d'be Eliahu).* (Jahresbericht der israelitisch-theologischen Lehranstalt in Wien VII, Vienna: 1900.)

2. Edition of *Pseudo-Seder Eliyahu Zuṭa:* Friedmann, M., *Pseudo-Seder Eliahu Zuṭa (Derech Ereç und Pirke R. Eliezer).* (Vienna: 1904).

3. Combined reprint of the two Friedmann editions (above, 1 and 2): Friedmann, M., *Seder Eliahu rabba and Seder Eliahu Zuṭa (Tanna d'be Eliahu); Pseudo-Seder Eliahu Zuṭa* (Jerusalem: Bamberger & Wahrmann, 1960; reprinted in Jerusalem: Wahrmann, 1969).

VI. MIDRASHIC COLLECTIONS AND ANTHOLOGIES

A. MEDIEVAL

The following two works provide the sources in which fragments from earlier, lost midrashim have been found. See above, IV:B, F, G, and V:C:(2).

1. *Midrash Hagadol* on the Pentateuch. The work was compiled in Yemen after Maimonides (d. 1204).

   a. Critical editions of individual books:
      i. Genesis: Margulies, M., *Midrash Haggadol on the Pentateuch, Genesis* (Jerusalem: Rabbi Kook Foundation, 1946/47).
      ii. Exodus: Margulies, M., *Midrash Haggadol on the Pentateuch, Exodus* (Jerusalem: Rabbi Kook Foundation, 1955/56).
      iii. Leviticus: Rabinowitz, N. E., *Midrash Hagadol 'al Ḥamishah Ḥummeshe Torah, Sefer Wayiqra* (New York, 1929/30).
      iv. Numbers:
         (a) Fisch, S., *Midrash Haggadol on the Pentateuch, Numbers* (London: Sepher & Sivan Press, 1957–63).
         (b) Rabinowitz, Z. M., *Midrash Hagadol on the Pentateuch, Numbers* (Jerusalem, Rabbi Kook Foundation, 1967).
      v. Deuteronomy: Hasida, N. Z., *Midrash Haggadol on the Pentateuch, Deut. i–xiii* (Jerusalem: Rabbi Kook Foundation, 1934–42).

2. *Yalqut Shim'oni* on the whole Hebrew Bible. The collection was compiled in Germany in the first half of the thirteenth century.

   a. Edition: *Yalqut Shim'oni, Midrash 'al Torah, Nevi'im, uKhetuvim* (New York: *Horeb*, 1925/26; reprinted in Jerusalem: Lewin-Epstein, 1951/52).

B. MODERN

1. Editions:
   a. Jellinek, A., *Beth ha-Midrasch*. Sammlung kleiner Midrashim und vermischter Abhandlungen aus der älteren jüdischen Literatur. 6 vols. (Leipzig: C. W. Vollrath, 1853–77; reprinted in Jerusalem: Wahrmann, 1967).

      The work contains a hundred small midrashim and recensions.
   b. Horowitz, Ch. M., *Sammlung kleiner Midrashim* (Berlin:

H. Itzkowski, 1881; reprinted in Jerusalem, 1966/67).

c. Grünhut, L., *Sefer ha-Likkutim: Sammlung älter Midrashim und wissenschaftlicher Abhandlungen* (Jerusalem: Ha-Meassef, 1894/95; reprinted in Jerusalem, 1966/67).

d. Eisenstein, J. D., *Ozar Midrashim: A Library of Two Hundred Minor Midrashim* (New York, 1915).

e. Wertheimer, S. A., *Batei Midrashot.* Twenty-five midrashim published for the first time from manuscripts discovered in Genizot of Jerusalem and Egypt with introductions and annotations. 2nd edition enlarged and amended (Jerusalem: Rabbi Kook Foundation, 1950–53; reprinted in Jerusalem: Ktab Waspher, 1967/68).

2. Collections in German translation.

a. Wünsche, A., *Bibliotheca Rabbinica.* Eine Sammlung alter Midraschim zum ersten Male in Deutsche übertragen (Leipzig: O. Schulze, 1880–85; reprinted in Hildesheim: Olms, 1967).

The collection contains the *Midrash Rabbah,* the *Midrash on Proverbs,* and *Pesiqta deRav Kahana.*

b. Wünsche, A., *Aus Israels Lehrhallen* (Leipzig: E. Pfeiffer, 1907–09; reprinted in Hildesheim: Olms, 1967).

The texts for the sixty-two midrashim translated here can generally be found in Jellinek (above, 1:a).

3. Collection in Latin: Ugolino, B., *Thesaurus Antiquitatum Sacrum Complectens Selectissima Clarissimorum Virorum Opuscula in quibus Veterum Hebraeorum Mores, Leges, Instituta, Ritus Sacri et Civiles Illustrantur* (Venice: J. G. Herthz, 1744–69).

VII. COLLECTIONS OF EARLY PIECES OF TRADITION

A. COLLECTIONS IN HEBREW:

1. Melamed, E. Z., *Halachic Midrashim of the Talmud Babli,* Vol. I. [Halachic midrashim of the Tanna'im in the Talmud Bavli.] (Jerusalem: Rabbi Kook Foundation, 1943).

2. Higger, M., *Otsar Habaraytot.* 10 vols. (New York: Debe Rabanan, 1938–43).

3. Stiglitz, M. *Die zerstreuten Baraitas der beiden Talmuds zur Mischna Berachot* (Frankfurt a. M., 1908).

B. COLLECTIONS IN ENGLISH TRANSLATION:

1. Neusner, J. *Development of a Legend: Studies on the Traditions concerning Yoḥanan ben Zakkai* (Leiden: Brill, 1970).

2. Neusner, J., *The Rabbinic Traditions on the Pharisees before 70.*
   3 vols. (Leiden: Brill, 1971–73[?]).
   Neusner's work on these volumes is substantially complete.

VIII. CHRONICLES AND RELATED WORKS

A good collection of the works listed here, plus other chronicles all with a critical apparatus, is that of A. Neubauer, *Medieval Jewish Chronicles and Chronological Notes* (Oxford: Clarendon, 1887–95).

A. *Fasting Scroll* (= *Megillat Ta'anit*), a calendar of festivals. Much of the Aramaic text of this work comes from as early as 66 C.E. with additions until the time of Hadrian. The Hebrew scholia are generally from the talmudic period but contain early traditions.
   1. Edition: Lichtenstein, H., "Die Fastenrolle, eine Untersuchung zur jüdisch-hellenistischen Geschichte," *Hebrew Union College Annual,* 8–9 (1931–32), pp. 257–351.
   2. Edition of the Aramaic only with vocabulary and commentary: Dalman, B., *Aramäische Dialektproben Unter dem Gesichtspunkt neutestamentlicher Studien.* 2nd edition, enlarged (Leipzig: J. C. Hinrichs, 1927), pp. 1–3, 41–45. Reprinted in Darmstadt: Wissenschaftliche Buchgesellschaft, 1960, along with the author's *Grammatik des jüdisch-palästinischen Aramäisch.*
   3. Edition of Aramaic only with English translation: Zeitlin, S., *Megillat Taanit as a Source for Jewish Chronology and History in the Hellenistic and Roman Periods.* Diss. Dropsie College (Philadelphia: 1922; printed in England at Oxford University Press), pp. 65–70.
   4. Text with Latin translation: Meyer, J., *Tractus de Temporibus Sacris et Festis Diebus Hebraeorum . . .* (Amsterdam: 1724).
   5. English translations of Aramaic only:
      a. Edersheim, A., *The Life and times of Jesus the Messiah.* 8th edition revised (New York: Longmans, Green, and Co., Ltd., 1905), vol. II, pp. 698–700.
      b. Zeitlin, S., *The Rise and Fall of the Judaean State* (Philadelphia: JPSA, 1967), Vol. II, pp. 363–365.

B. *Seder 'Olam* [*Rabbah*], a chronology listing events and dates from Adam to the Bar Kokhba revolt (132–135 C.E.). The work is traditionally ascribed to R. Yose ben Halafta (died c. 160), but it was probably compiled in early Amoraic times (i.e., after 219/220.)
   1. Edition: Ratner, B., *Seder Olam Rabba: Die Grosse Weltchronik Nach Handschriften und Druckwerken herausgegeben, mit*

kritischen Noten und Erklärungen versehen (Vilna: Romm, 1894–97; reprinted in New York: Talmudical Research Institute, 1966).

2. Edition and German translation of chaps. 1–10: Marx, A., *Seder Olam (Kap. 1–10)*. Herausgegeben, übersetzt und erklärt (Berlin: Itzkowski, 1903).

3. Text and Latin translation: Meyer, J., *Chronicon Hebraeorum Majus et Minus* (Amsterdam, 1699).

C. *Seder 'Olam Zuṭa,* a chronology extending from Adam through the death of R. Ḥatsuv (d. 800).

1. Edition: Grosberg, M., *Seder 'Olam Zuṭa and Complete Seder Tannaim v'Amoraim.* With introduction and notes (London: 1910).

2. Text and Latin translation: Meyer, J. (above, B:3).

D. *Letter of R. Sherira Gaon* (= *Iggeret Rav Sherira Ga'on*).

1. Edition: Lewin, B. M., *Iggeret R. Scherira Gaon* (Haifa: 1921). French and Spanish recensions appear in parallel columns.

2. A new edition is being prepared by H. Opalek with a translation and introduction in English.

IX. ENCYCLOPEDIAS AND DICTIONARIES

A. ENCYCLOPEDIAS AND SIMILAR WORKS:

1. Berlin (Bar-Ilan), M., S. J. Zevin and J. Hunter (eds.), *Entsiqlopediah Talmudit* (= *Talmudic Encyclopedia*) (Jerusalem: Rabbi Herzog World Academy and Jerusalem Talmudic Encyclopaedia Institute, 1955—).

   13 vols. through *Ḥazaqa*) of this important work have now appeared. For an English version, see the following entry.

2. Epstein, I., and H. Freedman. *Encyclopedia Talmudica* (Jerusalem: Rabbi Herzog World Academy and Jerusalem Talmudic Encyclopaedia Institute, 1969—).

   This work is an English translation of the preceding entry. Only one volume has appeared to date. Unfortunately the translation is inferior to the Hebrew original. Cf. A. M. Fuss in the *Jewish Quarterly Review,* 60 (1970), p. 356: "This translation is inept. . . . The English is poor, the translations are imprecise."

3. Kasher, M. M., *Torah Shelemah.* A talmudic and midrashic encyclopaedia to the Pentateuch (New York: American Biblical Encyclopedic Society, 1949—).

The 23 volumes of this work which have appeared complete Genesis and Exodus.

4. Hyman, A. *Sefer Torah Haketuvah Wehamesurah 'al Torah, Nevi'im, u'Khetuvim.* 3 vols. (Tel Aviv: Dvir, 1964/65. A reprint of the 1936–39 edition).

B. TECHNICAL DICTIONARIES:

1. Schachter, J., *Otsar ha-Talmud* (Tel Aviv: Dvir, 1963).

   An excellent one-volume dictionary of technical terms in Hebrew. The definitions are short enough for anyone with a minimal knowledge of Hebrew to use.

2. Bacher, W., *Die Exegetische Terminologie der jüdischen Traditionsliteratur.* Zwei Teile (Leipzig: 1899–1905; reprinted in Darmstadt: Wissenschaftliche Buchgesellschaft, 1965).

3. Umánski, J., *Ḥakhme haTalmud: Reshimat Kol Hatanna'im Weha'amora'im Shebetalmud.* . . . 2 vols., one for each Talmud (Jerusalem: Rabbi Kook Foundation, 1948/49–1951/52).

C. LEXICONS:

1. Jastrow, M., *A Dictionary of the Targumim, the Talmud Babli and Yerushalmi, and the Midrashic Literature.* 2 vols. (New York: G. P. Putnam, 1895–1903; reprinted in New York: Pardes, 1950).

2. Levy, J., *Chaldäisches Wörterbuch über die Targumim und einen Grossen Theil des Rabbinischen Schriftthums* (Leipzig: Baumgärtner, 1867–68; reprinted as one volume in Cologne: J. Melzer, 1959).

3. Levy, J., *Wörterbuch über die Talmudim und Midraschim.* 4 vols. (Darmstadt: Wissenschaftliche Buchgesellschaft, 1963; a reprint of the 2nd edition, Berlin and Vienna: 1924).

4. Krauss, S., *Griechische und latinische Lehnwörter in Talmud, Midrasch und Targum* (Berlin: Calvary, 1898–99).

D. DICTIONARIES FOR RABBINIC ABBREVIATIONS:

1. Heilprin, M., *Hanotriqon, Hasammanim Wehakinnuyim* (Vilna: 1912; reprinted in 1930).

2. Ashkenazi, S. and D. Jarden. *Ozar Rashe Tevot: Thesaurus of Hebrew Abbreviations.* 3rd printing (Jerusalem: R. Mass., 1969).

3. Ashkenazi, S., *Mefa'neah Ne'elamim* (Jerusalem: Shila, 1969).

   This work supplements the preceding entry with 4000 abbreviations.

4. Bader, G., *Cyclopedia of Hebrew Abbreviations* (New York: Pardes, 1951).
5. Stern, A., *Handbuch der Hebräischen Abbreviaturen* (Sighetul-Marmatiei, 1926).

   A useful handbook.
6. Blackman, P., *Mishnayoth,* Vol. VII. *Supplement & Index.* 2nd edition, revised, corrected, enlarged (New York: Judaica, 1964). Pp. 47–54 contain a key to some of the more important abbreviations.

JUDAISM ON CHRISTIANITY: CHRISTIANITY ON JUDAISM

by FRANK TALMAGE

Frank Talmage is a member of the Department of Near Eastern Studies, University of Toronto, and an expert in medieval polemics and exegesis. He has contributed to the *Harvard Theological Review, Judaism,* and other periodicals.

THE IMAGE OF CHRISTIANITY IN JUDAISM

The following list, comprised of source collections, historical and theological works, polemical writings, etc., represents the two-thousand-year development of the image of Christianity in the eyes of Judaism and that of Judaism and the Jews in the view of Christianity. The material is organized wherever possible by period (late antiquity, Middle Ages, modern times) although a number of works overlap and may be mentioned more than once. Works are cited in the text by author and title only, with full bibliographic information provided in the numbered list at the end. A supplementary list of titles not discussed in the text is appended.

A. VIEWS OF JESUS

1. *Rabbinic and Medieval Periods*

References or alleged references to Jesus, New Testament figures, or Christians in Talmud and Midrash have been the object of prolonged speculation and controversy among both Jewish and Christian scholars. The problem was rendered more complex by the fact that much of this material, sufficiently obscure in itself, was censored out of the printed editions by Church authorities. The best known and classic attempt to sift through and organize this material is Travers Herford's *Christianity in Talmud and Midrash* (32) in which all the relevant passages are collected in the original Hebrew and Aramaic, translated, and carefully annotated. Herford set himself a twofold task. He first attempted to identify those passages actually referring to Jesus on the basis of philological analysis, from which he proceeded to an examination of the material concerning the minim, whom he generally identifies with early Jewish Christians. A correction of certain technical failings in Herford such as mistranslations and inadequate use of manuscripts was essayed by Morris Goldstein in *Jesus in the Jewish Tradition* (28). This volume has the advantage of having the passages sorted by period and classified into the three categories of authentic references to Jesus, references incorrectly identified with Jesus (e.g. others by the name of Yeshu, Ben Stada, etc.), and indirect allusions. Possible references to Christianity and Christian doctrine are examined with the constant awareness that "with regard to . . . [our positive identifications], too, we deal with probabilities." In addition to the rabbinic material, the author adds an English rendition of one of the medieval Hebrew "biographies" (*Toledot Yeshu*) of Jesus and a review of the medieval polemical literature. The fairly thorough bibliographic treatment is helpful.

Although not as conveniently arranged as Goldstein, the most technically competent and thorough treatment of the subject is Jacob Zallel Lauterbach's essay "Jesus in the Talmud" in his *Rabbinic Essays* (40). In his effort to show that the rabbinic material has no historical value whatsoever for a study of Jesus and Christian origins, Lauterbach is even more conservative than his predecessors in admitting rabbinic references to Jesus of Nazareth. Especially important is his reexamination of the historical background of the passages in which a number of long-accepted interpretations are dismissed, though in some instances they are replaced by others equally conjectural.

2. *The Modern Period*

Modern Jewish interest in Jesus may be traced from the early nineteenth-century writers, who, out of apologetic motives, frequently sought to couple a "reclamation" or "re-judaization" of Jesus with a negative evaluation of Christianity, through more recent scholarship which interests itself in Jesus as a historical and religious figure within the framework of the history of Judaism. A most exhaustive and erudite literary history of this problem is Gösta Lindeskog's *Die Jesusfrage im neuzeitlichen Judenthum*

(41) which covers the period from the Emancipation to the outbreak of World War I. The author first surveys the literature from the period of the *Wissenchaft des Judentums* through the writings, historical, theological, and belletristic, of the thirties. Then topically, he treats, in addition to the major questions of Jewish attitudes towards the religion of Jesus and its relation to Judaism, the problems of historiography of the intertestamental period, the person and role of Jesus, the trial and crucifixion, and the founding of Christianity. Each chapter is well endowed with full bibliographic annotation including references to works written in Hebrew.

A much smaller volume in English, Thomas Walker's *Jewish Views of Jesus* (68) ably summarizes the views of selected Jewish thinkers still significant at the time of writing (1931), allowing them insofar as possible to speak for themselves. These include two orthodox writers (Paul Goodman, Gerald Friedlander), two liberal thinkers (Claude G. Montefiore, Israel Abrahams), and two "portraits" (Joseph Jacobs, Joseph Klausner).

An actual example of the kind of writing done by the liberal-apologetic school of the late nineteenth and early twentieth centuries is Ernest R. Trattner's *As a Jew Sees Jesus* (67). Without real scholarly merit, the work is of some interest in its reflection of prevailing attitudes. Of some value is the extensive bibliography (pp. 200–208) of books, tracts, and articles in English by Jewish writers on the subject of Jesus.

Joseph Klausner's *Jesus of Nazareth* (38) remains the classic work from the Jewish nationalist point of view. Highly dependent upon liberal Protestant scholarship (it was roundly condemned in Roman Catholic circles), the chief significance of the work lies less in its advancement over previous scholarship than in the fact that it clearly marked the transition from the liberal-apologetic approach to that of historical criticism. Indicative of this, in part, is the fact that the author wrote the volume in Hebrew intending it for members of the *Yishuv* (Palestinian Jewish community). Klausner's view of Jesus is one that perceives him as a nationalist whose goal was the redemption of his people, but who rendered a disservice to Judaism instead by sapping it of its peculiarly

Jewish content and abstracting it into an ethico-religious system. Seeing himself as the awaited redeemer, Jesus was frustrated in his approach to the people who refused to recognize him because of his failure to provide a concrete plan of redemption. A similar approach is found in the chapter on Christianity in another Hebrew work, Yehezkel Kaufmann's *Golah ve-nekhar* (36). Kaufmann brings a heavily documented account of Jesus' unswerving faithfulness to the *halakhah* on the one hand and his deviation from Judaism, on the other, in his role as apocalyptic Messiah.

Less a study of Jesus than of first-century Palestinian Judaism is Robert Aron's *Jesus of Nazareth: The Hidden Years* (1), an exploration of the kind of life Jesus probably led in the years between his early youth and ministry, concerning which the Gospels are silent. In setting Jesus against his Jewish background, Aron presents Jewish life and institutions (despite certain anachronisms) in a way which should prove enlightening for the Christian reader. Of special interest is the chapter on language in which the author points out the influence of Semitic linguistic structure and modes of thinking on Jesus' thought and preaching.

The most recent critical study of Jesus by a Jewish scholar is David Flusser's *Jesus* (27). Succinct, but highly eloquent, Flusser brings to bear on the work his considerable erudition in both New Testament scholarship and Christian origins on the one hand, and in Rabbinic Judaism on the other. According to the author, "the main purpose of this book is to show that it is possible to write the story of Jesus' life." In doing so, he employs the method of isolating the old Markan account and the logia from the later revisions in the Synoptics. This plus his recoveries of Hebrew idiom behind the Greek lead him to his attempted restoration of Jesus' role and mission as he himself understood it.

Among popular or semi-popular writings, most deserving of mention is *Jésus et Israël* (33) by the Franco-Jewish writer Jules Isaac. Isaac presents a Jesus who loves and is loyal to his people and with consummate irony contrasts his own words as found in the Gospels with the attitudes towards the Jews expressed by the Church Fathers and Christian theologians up to the twentieth century. The material so presented attains a particular poignancy when it is recalled that he is writing in the aftermath and as a result of the Nazi holocaust. "This interesting book," writes David Flusser, "which is not written by a professional scholar and which is the product of apologetic enthusiasm deserves to be read by specialists because of the author's acumen and the penetrating analyses of his sources."

Two other semi-popular studies are worthy of mention. Samuel Sandmel's *We Jews and Jesus* (58) contains useful reviews of nineteenth- and twentieth-century New Testament scholarship and an analysis of the Jewish background of the Gospels. Written for Jews as a sort of *praeparatio dialogica,* the author firmly rejects any attempt to reclaim Jesus. Schalom Ben-Chorin's *Bruder Jesus* (9) is, as the title indicates, inspired by Martin Buber's picture of Jesus. The author sets himself the task of portraying Jesus as his Jewish brother in order to demonstrate to Christians how "the belief of Jesus unites us . . . but the belief in Jesus separates us."

3. *The Crucifixion*

The most sensitive topic in the discussion of Jesus' life and ministry is undoubtedly that of the trial and crucifixion. The charge, a major factor in the development of anti-Semitism, has been sounded by Christian theologians and historians from antiquity through to the twentieth century. With the perhaps naive hope that a demonstration of the lack of Jewish, or at least of popular Jewish, complicity in Jesus' death would lead to an amelioration of Christian attitudes, a number of writers in the nineteenth and twentieth centuries began the work of compiling apologies on the subject. While few of these works are of especial interest in themselves any longer, the account of their development is. This has been charted by Lindeskog in his *Jesusfrage* (41). Lindeskog distinguishes between this first apologetic stage and a second phase, the historical, which was still no doubt prompted by apologetic motives, but is characterized by critical evaluation of the sources. Representative of the prevalent point of view is Joseph Klausner, in *Jesus of Nazareth* (38), who advances the basic theory of a Sadducee-controlled Sanhedrin, concerned over Jesus as a possible political revolutionary, and who hand him over to the Romans to prevent the situation from getting out of control. A refinement of this position came with the development of the two-Sanhedrin theory, which originated with Adolph Büchler but was most ably articulated by Solomon Zeitlin, in *Who Crucified Jesus?* (71). As in other writings, Zeitlin notes that two different types of organizations appear to be spoken of in contemporary Hebrew literature, on the one hand, and in Greek literature, on the other. On the basis of this and other observations, he posits the existence of two bodies, a religious Sanhedrin, the *Bet Din,* composed of scholars and authorized to deal with "religious" matters, and a separate organization of a political nature. It was the latter body composed of the Sadducee minority which tried Jesus in league with the Roman authority. Although the subject of Jesus' death is dealt with only tangentially, the treatment in Hugo Mantel's *Studies in the History of the Sanhedrin* (42) is well worth the reader's attention because of the new light shed on it by his detailed and careful review of previous scholarship and his own critical reexamination of the problem.

The most recent major study in this area written by a Jew is a work of considerable scholarly sophistication, Paul Winter's *On the Trial of Jesus* (70). Winter follows the fruitful method of combining literary with historical analysis. Allowing the Gospel materials less credibility than is customary, he attempts to isolate the historical event from the primary report as found in the Gospels and the secondary tradition of the editors. This leads him to distinguish between reasonably certain facts, probable facts, and issues which must remain unanswered. To the first group belong Jesus' arrest by the Romans, his trial by a Jewish administrative authority during the night, his sentencing by the procurator, and his execution according to Roman procedure. Of high probability are the interrogation by the high priest's representatives and the derision of the Roman soldiers. Points which cannot be determined are the immediate cause of Jesus' arrest, the identification of those who initiated this action, and the deeds that Jesus performed to provoke action against himself.

This most sober treatment of the subject may finally be contrasted with the rather novel approach taken by Haim Cohn of the Israel Supreme Court in his *Reflections on the Trial and Death of Jesus* (16). Attacking the problem from the point of view of the legal historian, the author rejects the two-Sanhedrin theory and sees the night meeting of the Sanhedrin, an investigative body conducted under Sadduceean Law, as an eleventh-hour attempt to save Jesus by acquitting him before Pilate. According to Cohn, the attempt proved abortive because of Jesus' refusal to cooperate.

B. Views of Christianity

1. *The Middle Ages*

The Middle Ages saw a continuous output of anti-Christian polemical literature, both in the form of protocols of compulsory disputations, such as those of Barcelona and Tortosa, and of textbooks for combating Christian missionaries or for the dissuasion of potential apostates. Several of these texts have been made available in English translation. Oliver S. Rankin's *Jewish Religious Polemics* (54) presents a selection of polemical texts of several literary genres including the midrashic *Chronicle of Moses* (narrative), *The Book of Contention* of Rabbi Yom Tov Lippman Muelhausen (poetry), the "Letters" of Rittangel and the Jew of Amsterdam (epistolary), and the disputation of Nahmanides with Pablo Christiani (debate). Each of these texts is put into context with a thorough historical and literary introduction and extensive annotation. In addition to these, the three classic medieval disputations of Paris, Barcelona, and Tortosa are presented in Morris Braude's *Conscience on Trial* (13).

A comprehensive study of medieval Jewish polemic remains a *desideratum*.[1] In addition to the older studies of Isidore Loeb (41a, 41b), Salo Baron's treatment in his *Social and Religious History* (4) will serve as the best introduction to the subject. Two chapters, one devoted to the mechanics of the public disputations and the other to literary polemics, take into account the socioreligious factors and consequences of these controversies. Of special value are the bibliographic annotations which, in themselves, read as a literary history of the material. A briefer thematic study of the material is to be found in Hans Joachim Schoeps'

[1] A comprehensive bibliography of this literature has been prepared by J. Rosenthal in *Areshet* II, pp. 130–179; III, pp. 433–437.

lucid *Jewish-Christian Argument* (59). In his chapter on the medieval polemic, he indicates the place of such central issues as the election of Israel, Law and faith, the destruction of the Temple, and the messiahship of Jesus.

The Bible was no doubt the major battleground of the Jewish-Christian argument, and biblical commentaries frequently contained polemical excursuses. An indication of the exegetical procedures and of such motifs as the status of Israel and the nations in the divine economy, christological interpretations, etc., may be found in my "R. David Kimḥi as Polemicist" (65), a study of the thirteenth-century Provençal exegete.

The Christian assertions of the degenerate character of Judaism and the negation of its right to exist, certainly brought forth responses in kind on the part of the Jews. Nevertheless, certain major theoreticians of the Jewish faith accorded to Christianity and its founder a rather high status in their view of the religious development of mankind. The interesting views of the most distinguished of medieval Jewish thinkers, Moses Maimonides, are expanded in Gershon Tchernowitz's brief Hebrew work *The Relation between Israel and the Gentiles According to Maimonides* (66), which also reviews his attitudes towards Islam. Rabbi Menaḥem ha-Meiri declared unequivocally that Christianity was in no sense to be classed as an idolatrous religion and was to be esteemed for its "practical" ethical norms. Ha-Meiri's ideas are very competently discussed in Jacob Katz's Hebrew study, "Religious Tolerance in the Halakhic and Philosophical System of Rabbi Menahem ha-Me'iri" (35) which appeared with an English summary in *Zion*.

2. *The Modern Period*

Treatments of Christianity by European Jewish writers in the nineteenth and twentieth centuries have generally followed the pattern set by Christian interpreters of Judaism which may be characterized as a typological approach. According to this, Judaism would be seen as the embodiment of the finest ideas of Western culture, with Christianity viewed as a poor imitation falling somewhat short of the mark. This trend, which may be said to have begun with Moses Mendelssohn and to have reached a turning point of sorts in the writings of Franz Rosenzweig, is surveyed in two works which commend themselves to the reader. The first is the above mentioned *Jewish-Christian Argument* (59) by Schoeps which gives a brief history of these discussions. The second is the far more exhaustive and highly competent treatment of Jacob Fleischmann, *The Problem of Christianity in Modern Jewish Thought* (Hebrew: [26]). The work analyzes the thought of ten representative Jewish thinkers of the modern period—Mendelssohn, Ascher, Salvador, Formstecher, Hirsch, Steinheim, Geiger, Benamozegh, Cohen, and Rosenzweig. The attempt on the part of all of these to define Judaism in terms of, or at least vis-à-vis, Christianity may be followed throughout the work to its conclusion in the important discussion of Rosenzweig. In his view of Judaism as the Life and of Christianity as the Way, Rosenzweig tried to abandon the apologetic approach and establish a corelationship with Christianity which would affirm the necessity of each. Much of Rosenzweig's approach to Christianity, if not his fully developed doctrine, has recently been made available in *Judaism Despite Christianity* (55), the English translation of his correspondence with Eugen Rosenstock-Heussy, the editor of the volume. Of great interest is the tone of immediacy in which the correspondence is couched, revealing one of those very rare instances of genuine preparedness for dialogue. The volume is enhanced by the illuminating introductions of the editor, of Dorothy Emmett, and of Professor Alexander Altmann.

Two twentieth-century theologians not mentioned by Fleischmann who are concerned with the relative characterization of Judaism and Christianity are Leo Baeck and Martin Buber. Baeck's effort to distill the "essence" of Judaism in response to Harnack's definition of the essence of Christianity led to the famous formulation of Judaism as the classical religion and Christianity as the romantic religion which came to expression in his *Judaism and Christianity* (2). For an analytical approach to Baeck's writings concerning Christianity, the reader may consult Reinhold Mayer's detailed *Christentum und Judentum in der Schau Leo Baecks* (44). Christianity is considered in many places throughout Martin Buber's work, but the central discussion is to be found in his *Two Types of Faith* (14), where faith as trust (Judaism) and faith as *pistis,* the belief *that* something is true (Christianity), are contrasted. An analysis of Buber's views on the subject together with his evaluations of Jesus and Paul are found in an essay, "The Jewish Jesus and the Christ of Faith," in Malcolm Diamond's *Martin Buber: Jewish Existentialist* (18). Of some interest is the reply to Buber from a Roman Catholic point of view in Hans Urs von Balthasar's *Martin Buber and Christianity* (3).

Once again from the "nationalist"-historical point of view, Joseph Klausner continued his examination of Christian origins in his sequel to *Jesus of Nazareth, From Jesus to Paul* (37). The work was able to arouse the enthusiasm of no less a critic than Arthur Darby Nock who was moved to comment that "Klausner has written with a scholar's depth and prophet's passion of issues which for him are never bloodless abstractions. The result is a piece of religious history as well as a study of it." Klausner surveys the history of the first and second centuries to provide the background for his analysis of the role and thinking of the apostle Paul. As in *Jesus of Nazareth,* Klausner's concerns are Jewish-oriented and the object of his effort is to answer the question why Pauline Christianity could never have been accepted by the Jews. Yehezkel Kaufmann in *Golah ve-nekhar* (36) procedes from his evaluation of Jesus to a critique of Christianity. While his interpretation may not be altogether original, it is forcefully and boldly stated. Kaufmann sees in the Christian emphasis on ethics and love a "great deception" in that, unlike Judaism, Christianity created an illusion of spirituality and other-wordliness by "secularizing" its law and ritual. The success of Christianity lies not in its innovations but in its continuing the task of Judaism, viz., the combating of paganism.

Christian interest in "dialogue" with the Jewish people in the wake of the Christian ecumenical movement has evoked a re-evaluation of the temper of the Jewish stance towards Christianity on the part of a number of Jewish thinkers. Still operative, of course, is the traditional apprehensiveness that any overtures on the part of Christians towards Jews are a cover for missionary ambitions. Such concerns are the subject of an essay by Leo Baeck—"Some Questions to the Christian Church from the Jewish Point of View" —in Göte Hedenquist's *The Church and the Jewish People* (31) in which the very premises of Christian evangelism are questioned. Martin Buber's essay "The Two Foci of the Jewish Soul" which appeared in *Israel and the World* (15), is to be commended to any Christian interested in undertaking a program of dialogue. Written shortly after World War II, it is one of the most eloquent responses to the concept of the mission to the Jews.

In addition to this traditional concern, other fundamental questions have been raised with respect to the possibility and desirability of the dialogical enterprise. At issue here are not only attitudes but actions, with the consensus being that the bi-millenial history of Christian complicity in or, at best, indifference to Jewish suffering provides a poor background for conversation at this time. In an essay included as a "Jewish contribution to a Christian-secularist dialogue" in *Quest for Past and Future* (24), Emil Fackenheim raises and examines the charge that "throughout the long struggle for Jewish human rights the secularist liberal has usually fought alongside the Jew, while the established Christian forces were—on the whole, but with very notable exceptions—ranged against him." That this is so, and that no fundamental change in this situation has been brought about, has been noted too by Eliezer Berkovits. In an article entitled "Judaism in the Post-Christian Era" in *Judaism* XV (10) Berkovits ascribes any apparent softening in Christian attitudes to the fact that Christianity realizes itself to be only one world force among many and, of these, not the most powerful. Because of the events of recent history which represent the culmination of Christian traditions of persecution, the Jew could not at this time emotionally face the prospect of Jewish-Christian dialogue. Rather, he suggests, stress should be placed on an "inter-human," non-theological type of dialogue. Stevens S. Schwarzschild, in "Judaism, Scriptures, and Ecumenism" in *Judaism XIII* (61) couples similar reservations with the traditional mistrust of Christian motivations as discussed above. Schwarzschild, in rejecting contemporary ecumenism speaks instead of an eschatological ecumenism implying a loyalty to Scriptures at the end of time. The event which created the heaviest impact on Jewish attitudes towards the question of dialogue was, of course, the 1967 Israel-Arab war. The general silence of the churches in the face of what appeared to be the imminent destruction of the Jewish state, coming as it did only twenty-five years

after a similar silence concerning the Jews of Europe, caused many
to feel a loss of optimism "in the hope that the long age of Christian triumphalism over Judaism is truly being superseded by an
age of Jewish-Christian dialogue." Emil L. Fackenheim, writing
in *Commentary* XLVI ("Jewish Faith and the Holocaust") (23)
states that the Christian "failed to recognize the danger of a second
Holocaust because he has yet to recognize the fact of the first."
This he cannot do because "he knows that as a Christian he should
voluntarily have gone to Auschwitz where his own Master would
have been dragged . . . and he is racked by a sense of guilt the
deeper the less he has cause to feel it." The shift in mood created
by the Six Day War is poignantly expressed, too, in the two letters
of Jacob Neusner in *Judaism* XV (47), one written before and the
other after the war, in reaction to the Berkovits article cited above
(10).

In conjunction with these statements, it is of profit to examine
a closely aligned Christian point of view, A. Roy Eckardt's "Can
There Be a Jewish-Christian Relationship?" in the *Journal of Bible
and Religion* XXXIII (19). For such reasons as the lack of contrition on the part of the church, the failure of the church to root
out anti-Semitic ideology, and the refusal to see anti-Semitic elements in the Gospels, there cannot yet be a relationship "of human
equality and justice" between Jews and Christians.

More positive points of view are to be found of course. Representative of these is Abraham Joshua Heschel's "No Religion is an
Island" (32a) which calls for the ordering of an association of
religions on the model of the United Nations. While the autonomy
of each religion would be respected (again an answer to missionary
claims), one would "regard a divergent religion as His Majesty's
loyal opposition," conceding that "one truth comes to expression
in many ways of understanding." Interreligious cooperation is
needed for, among other things, finding "ways of helping one
another in the terrible predicament of here and now." A similar
optimistic—yet nonconciliatory—attitude towards the future of
Jewish-Christian dialogue may be seen in the address of Arthur
Gilbert (27a) to the Consultation on the Church and the Jewish
People sponsored by the World Lutheran Federation at Logum-
kloster, Denmark in 1964. Rabbi Gilbert's views are expressed with
a full consciousness of and perhaps despite the strong currents of
opposition to interfaith confrontation at the time.

THE CHRISTIAN VIEW OF JUDAISM

The principal document which was to shape and mold Christian attitudes towards the Jews is, of course, the New Testament and any statements made by Christians forever after on this topic are in the nature of a commentary upon it. However, in this survey our main concern is not what the New Testament itself says concerning the Jews, a subject which would form the basis of a bibliography of New Testament exegesis, but rather what Christians from antiquity to the present believed it or declared it to say. This section will therefore begin with the period of the Fathers and the Middle Ages.

A. THE PATRISTIC AND MEDIEVAL PERIODS

The missionary overtones behind A. Lukyn Williams' *Adversus Judaeos* (69) do not vitiate its usefulness as a compendium of the anti-Jewish polemic of the patristic period and the high Middle Ages. No systematic arrangement of the material is presented. Rather the anti-Jewish works of each author, listed under one of the rubrics, Latin, Greek, Syriac, or Spanish, are outlined and summarized. Both subject and scriptural indices make the work a particularly valuable tool in researching the literature. An excellent collection of texts is Solomon Grayzel's *The Church and the Jews in the XIIIth Century* (29). This source book presents statements of attitude and policy on the part of the ecclesiastical hierarchy of the period in both the original Latin and in English translation. *Aphrahat and Judaism: The Christian-Jewish Argument in Fourth Century Iran* (47a) by Jacob Neusner includes a translation of this early Christian monk's "Demonstrations" plus studies of pertinent issues.

For a good introductory survey to the literature of the period, one would do well to consult George Foot Moore's very competent essay "Christian Writers on Judaism" (45) in the *Harvard Theological Review*. Approaching the subject from the point of view of literary history, the author traces the anti-Jewish polemic as it develops into the Middle Ages.

In terms of more detailed analysis of the material of this period, three major works may be cited. James Parkes' well-documented *Conflict of the Church and the Synagogue* (50) is devoted to an

examination of the relationship between the stance and teachings
of Christianity with respect to the Jews and anti-Semitism. The
work begins with a discussion of the rise of Christianity and Jewish
resistance towards it and then moves into the topic of the relationship of the Church to the Jews in Rome and Byzantium. Marcel
Simon's *Verus Israel* (62) is a somewhat more systematic treatment of Jewish-Christian relations in the Roman Empire. The
patristic polemic against the Jews is discussed both methodologi-
cally and topically. The author evaluates the chief uses of the
polemic, viz., the status of Israel under the new dispensation, the
law, etc. Of particular importance, especially for an understanding of later phenomena, is his analysis of the implications of Christian theology for Christian anti-Semitism. Bernhard Blumenkranz's
excellent *Juifs et Chrétiens dans le monde occidental. 430–1096*
(11) does the same for the medieval period through the eleventh
century. Blumenkranz deals with the theological issues—the mission to the Jews, polemics, use of the Bible, the questions of the
crucifixion, election of the gentiles, etc.—against the background
of the legal and political status of the Jews, their social position,
and their religious life.

A particular aspect of the status of Judaism in the eyes of the
early and medieval church is the relationship of Christianity to rabbinic literature. Louis Ginzberg's investigation of *Die Haggada bei
den Kirchenvätern* (27b) and Ch. Merchavia's recent comprehensive study of the treatment of Talmud and Midrash by patristic
and medieval Christianity from 500–1248 (44a) are additional
volumes in which the rather ambivalent stance of the church towards this literature may be traced. On the one hand, it was condemned for being blasphemous and anti-Christian while on the
other, it was carefully combed for any possible "proofs" of Christianity which it might contain.

Three highly significant volumes, two by Roman Catholics and
one by a Jew, deal with the materials discussed in the above works
from the point of view of their influence upon the development of
modern anti-Semitism. Malcolm Hay, a Scottish historian, had
interested himself early in his career in correcting popular mis-
conceptions and "chains of error" in British history. Following his
experience in World War II which made him acquainted with the

Jewish problem, he saw fit to study yet another "chain of error," the anti-Semitic tradition in Christian theology. Hay's *Foot of Pride* or *Europe and the Jews* (30), the result of his research, is a spirited and provocative work which makes its points by juxtaposing medieval and modern texts and accounts and demonstrating thereby how all the stereotypes of both modern Christian and non-Christian anti-Semitism are direct metamorphoses of earlier attitudes. Edward H. Flannery's *Anguish of the Jews* (25) complements Hay's work in that it follows a chronological rather than a thematic arrangement, starting with pre-Christian anti-Semitism and proceeding century by century until modern times. The evolution of modern anti-Semitic attitudes from Christian teachings, finally, is the subject of Jules Isaac's *Teaching of Contempt* (34). As does Hay, Isaac arranges his material topically and follows the method used in *Jésus et Isräel* (*Jesus and Israel*) of allowing the sources to speak for themselves. A wide range of materials, especially from the French scene, is used.

One may conclude this section with a reference to an article surveying the subject of "Luther and the Jews" (62a) which appeared in *Lutheran World*. Aarne Siirala presents this well-known saga from both the non-Lutheran and Lutheran perspectives. The former sees the negative turn in Luther's thinking as a result of frustration in his failure to convert the Jews; the latter, as being rooted in his exegesis of Scripture. Siirala raises questions concerning both the assumptions of the latter approach and some of the larger implications of this approach for Lutheranism in general. Of considerable interest in this connection is Haim Hillel Ben Sasson's study of Jewish awareness of and reaction to Lutheran initiatives in *Harvard Theological Review* LIX (9a).

B. THE MODERN PERIOD

The writings of Hay, Flannery, and Isaac trace the continuity of thought patterns and prejudicial attitudes from the patristic and medieval periods into modern anti-Semitism in both its Christian and non-Christian varieties. A number of studies have been done, attempting to evaluate the effect of Christian preaching and teaching on the attitudes of parishioners towards the Jews, which generally measure the relationship of prejudicial attitudes to degrees

of orthodoxy. *Christian Beliefs and Anti-Semitism* (27b), a study
by two sociologists, Charles Y. Glock and Rodney Stark, records
the results of their survey of the "religious roots of anti-Semitism"
and establishes "religious particularism" as a direct cause of anti-
Jewish prejudice. Bernhard Olson's excellent study, *Faith and
Prejudice* (49) remains one of the best of all these studies, however, in that it does not rely on analyses of responses to black-
and-white form questions but rather examines the catechetical
literature of four basic theological viewpoints: fundamentalist,
conservative, neo-orthodox, and liberal. Its analysis demonstrates
that an attempt to establish a direct correlation between orthodoxy
and anti-Semitic belief must be branded as simplistic. An important
deficiency, however, in the Olson work, which has been corrected
in the Glock-Stark study, is the failure to assess properly the role
of Christian teachings to reinforce and foster anti-Semitic attitudes. This is particularly significant at a time when an increasing
number of Christian theologians are becoming aware that anti-
Semitism cannot be seriously combated without coming to grips
with this problem. The reader is referred too to A. Roy Eckardt's
penetrating study "The Theology of Anti-Semitism" (22) in
Religion in Life XXXI. The author concludes that doctrinal modifications in themselves, except where such doctrines be overtly
anti-Semitic, is not the solution to anti-Semitism. Rather the
emphasis should be on the correction of distortions of doctrine
stemming from subconscious mechanisms. (See below, "Zionism
and the State of Israel.") Finally, Alfred de Quervain's *Das
Judentum in der Lehre und Verkundigung der Kirche Heute* (53)
in the series *Theologische Existenz Heute* discusses the current
situation in this area on the European scene, and the Lutheran
perspective is presented in Rudolph Pfisterer's "Judaism in the
Preaching and Teaching of the Church," in *Lutheran World* (52a).

The legacy of the patristic and medieval periods had its influence, of course, not only on the pulpit and on popular attitudes,
but in the academy as well. Recasting the old attitudes into a new
mold, nineteenth-century scholarship waged a new polemic against
Judaism in its efforts to stress the advance of Christianity over the
parent religion. George Foot Moore's essay, "Christian Writers
on Judaism" (45) which has been mentioned above, traces the

techniques and themes of this polemic which centered around the contrast between Christian piety and Jewish legalism on the one hand, and the theme of the impassable transcendental Jewish view of the Diety on the other.[2] Moore singled out for criticism one work which had and has been most influential in shaping Christian ideas of Judaism, viz., Emil Schürer's *A History of the Jewish People in the Time of Jesus* (60). While the history of the second commonwealth could not be gainsaid, Moore rejected what he felt were Schürer's attempts to prove "that the strictures on Judaism in the Gospels and the Pauline epistles are fully justified." There were, to be sure, correctives to the work of Schürer and similar investigators, written by Christians, notably, Travers Herford, James Parkes, and Moore himself. Worthy of special mention in this regard is the latter's *Judaism in the First Centuries of the Christian Era: The Age of the Tannaim* (46), a work which gave Christian readers a view of rabbinic theology disembarrassed of prejudicial distortions.

An outstanding study of the fruits of the medieval and patristic legacies is Uriel Tal's *Christians and Jews in the "Second Reich" (1870–1914): A Study in the Rise of German Totalitarianism* (Hebrew; 64a). With a preference for middle-brow writers such as students, the "man in the street," and the average intellectual, Tal presents a careful analysis of the dilemma in which the Jews (especially the liberals) found themselves in their double striving after integration into German society and preservation of their identity as Jews. On the one hand, one encounters the opposition of Christian conservatives who did not trust the Jews to be good Germans since, by rejecting their own nationhood, they had not been good Jews. On the other hand, the very similarity and proximity of liberal Judaism to liberal Christianity provoked the Christion liberals to reject the logic of a separate existence for the Jew. The author treats in detail the development from Christian anti-Semitism to racial anti-Semitism which, in itself, becomes anti-

---

[2] This survey has been brought up to date in the first chapter of E. E. Urbach's *ḤaZal Pirke Emunot ve-De'ot* (Jerusalem: Magnes Press, 1969), pp. 1–14. See also L. H. Silberman, "Judaism and the Christian Theologian," *Journal of Religion* XXXVII (1957), 246–53 in which the author shows "the dangers involved in assuming the 'possibilities of man's present understanding of existence' have a point-to-point correspondence with the 'phenomena of past history' and in then dealing with the past as though it were the present."

Christian. One sees the latter's theoreticians employ traditional Christian critiques of Judaism as a weapon against Christianity itself in their effort to show that the latter was right in trying to extirpate Judaism but wrong in not going far enough. Christianity had to be purged of its Jewish elements—its universalism; its soppish ethics; its squelching of the *joie de vivre* and spontaneity of natural man; its failure to carry the equation "God equals man" to the conclusion that Jesus become the Aryan and the Kingdom of Heaven the German State. In this analysis, the line from the invective of the Second Reich to the slaughter of the Third is clearly traced.

The one event in our time which had the greatest potential for causing a rethinking of Christian attitudes towards the Jews was of course the European Holocaust. In 1948, three years after the end of World War II, the World Council of Churches, meeting in Amsterdam, promulgated a statement concerning the Jews which, while decrying anti-Semitism and expressing similar appropriate sentiments, showed little evidence of a modification of attitudes on basic questions. The report is available in the anthology edited by Göte Hedenquist, *The Church and the Jewish People* (31), a collection of essays by Jews and Christians on contemporary Judaism and the stance of the Church toward it. Most of the essays explore the theological status of the Jewish people as primarily a subject for evangelization, and the discussions center around the proper approach to take to achieve this end, especially in the new State of Israel.

Of roughly the same vintage and the same line is Karl Barth's best known essay on the Jewish question, "The Jewish Problem and the Christian Answer" (5). He too laments the events of the recent past, denounces anti-Semitism, and even gives lip service to Jewish nationalism although rejecting the meaning of Jewish nationhood unless it fits Christian categories of thought. Remarkable is his hypothesis that anti-Semitism stems from the Gentile's resentment of Israel's election when viewed in the light of his failure to mention at all the influence of Christian anti-Jewish teachings. While evangelism is not advocated, the unredeemed character of the Jewish people is made evident as Barth celebrates the mystery of Israel's blindness. One still hears the echo of Frederick the Great's pastor who, on being asked for a proof of Christianity, replied, "Your Majesty, the Jews." Barth's other writings and statements concerning the Jews have been analyzed in detail in *Die Entdeckung des Judentums für die christliche Theologie* (43) by Friedrich Wilhelm Marquardt.

A formal Roman Catholic statement on the Jews took much longer in coming than the report of the World Council of Churches. When it did come in the form of the Vatican II "Declaration on Non-Christian Religions," many among the Jewish people anticipated that it would herald a dramatic change in Jewish-Christian relations while others regarded it with apathy or even indignation. The central issue was, of course, the "deicide" question and the appropriateness of an "exoneration" of the Jews by the Church, again without the slightest hint of contrition for the injustices of two millennia, was held in question. As it turned out, even this "exoneration" was attenuated, and the declaration, in other areas, also, fell short of its anticipated aims. The text of the document with an extensive commentary is found in *The Church and the Jewish People* (8) by Augustine Cardinal Bea, one of the chief and most liberal architects of the schema. The reader is here advised not to read between the lines but beneath them for the footnotes frequently contain revealing *apologiae* for discrepancies between the original and final drafts.

The Church and the Jewish People as a blueprint for action points in the direction of dialogue. Yet the direction and tone which Vatican II-inspired dialogue might take may vary widely as two recent publications would indicate. The one is that of the New Testament scholar Father Jean Daniélou entitled *Dialogue with Israel* (17), a collection of brief essays dealing with a variety of themes, e.g., early Judaism and Christianity, some Jewish views of Jesus, anti-Semitism, and so forth. Although it is, as the title indicates, intended as a contribution to dialogue, the book is a clear example of the kind of impasse reached in an understanding of Judaism when approached by a rigid traditionalist. Of interest is the appended response of Rabbi Jacob B. Agus to several excesses of the work. Dialogue would seem to take on a very different meaning in Father Gregory Baum's "The Doctrinal Basis for Jewish-Christian Dialogue" (7) which appeared in the journal *Dialog*.

The author probes the possibilities of a reevaluation of Judaism in Roman Catholic theology and concludes that the "destiny" of Judaism is not to disappear and give way to Christianity. Judaism continues to exercise a positive role in God's "plan of salvation."

This concession, which radically alters the notion of the Church's mission with respect to the Jews has been as rarely heard in Protestant circles as in Roman Catholic. To be sure, there are important Protestant theologians who have decried attempts at evangelization such as Reinhold Niebhur ("Christians and Jews in Western Civilization" in *Pious and Secular America* [48] and Markus Barth *(The Broken Wall: A Study of the Epistle to the Ephesians* [611]*)*. Yet their point of view may be far from that of Baum's. Niebuhr, for example, claims that the two faiths, despite differences, are sufficiently alike for the Jew to find God more easily in terms of his own religious heritage than by subjecting himself to the hazards of guilt feelings involved in "conversion to a faith which, whatever its excellencies, must appear to him as a symbol of an oppressive majority culture. . . ." This, coupled with his praise in *Christianity and Crisis* (48a) for "Vatican II's ignoring Pauline authority and thereby satisfying the demand of a Jewish minority for a recognition of its authentic autonomy" indicates that he has little sensitivity to what the "autonomy" demand by the Jews really means. (See the strictures of Steven S. Schwarzschild in "Judaism, Scriptures, and Ecumenism" cited above [61]; also G. Harder, "Christian/Jewish Conversation" in *Lutheran World* XI (1964), 326–336. Harder's remarks are put into perspective through a comparison with K. H. Rengstorf's "The Place of the Jew in the Theology of the Christian Mission," in the same issue (pp. 279–295).

The finest expression of a Protestant Christian recognition of the legitimacy of Judaism and of Israel's existence is A. Roy Eckardt's *Elder and Younger Brothers* (20). Eckardt reviews the theological implications of the role of Jews as the consenting people in the "unbroken Covenant God has made with Israel." He shows that "the messiahship of Jesus is both grounded in and yet discontinuous with the salvation-history of Israel. The existence of the Christian Church in no way annuls Israel's abiding meaning and independent destiny" (from the dust jacket). In a different formulation, James Parkes ("A Reappraisal of the Christian Attitude Toward Judaism" in *Journal of Bible and Religion* XXIX [52]), affirms Judaism's existence in his thesis that both Judaism and Christianity are needed as complements in that Christianity stresses man as a person while Judaism sees man as a member of a natural community. Finally, Krister Stendahl ("Judaism and Christianity: Then and Now" in *New Theology No. 2* [63]) calls for a reexamination of the relationship between Judaism and Christianity seen as "peoples" rather than "religions," and on the basis of a new scholarly understanding of both Testaments, the contribution of Paul, etc.

C. CHRISTIANITY AND THE STATE OF ISRAEL

A subject worthy of special treatment is the attitude of Christianity towards Zionism and the establishment and existence of the Jewish state. The loss of Jewish national independence early in the Christian era and the stateless condition of the Jewish people became for the Church a cardinal proof of the truth of Christianity. The Jew, who never lost hope in the eventual return, wrote often of the folly of Muslims and Christians who believed that Eretz Israel had become their possession, although he was to wait many centuries before his own hopes could be realized. Although there were notable exceptions, Christianity as such showed little sympathy and considerable scorn for Zionist aspirations. Judah Rosenthal has traced the history of this relationship in two essays, "The State of Israel and the Christian Church" (56) and "The State of Israel in the Light of Christian Theology" (57) which have appeared most recently in his Hebrew *Texts and Studies*. The essays chart the development and significance of the idea of Israel's eternal exile and wandering in Christian theology and document the attitudes and pronouncements of ecclesiastical leaders, both Catholic and Protestant, from the inception of modern Zionism through the establishment of the State. The material in these studies sheds a great deal of light on the indifference or even hostility displayed towards the State of Israel on the part of certain North American churches, especially at the time of the 1967 war. No full study of this problem is available in English, but much of the material is fortunately to be found in Hay's *Foot of Pride*

(30) which analyzes the posture of Europe and America towards the emergence of the State of Israel against this theological background. Of interest too is the material in Pinchas Lapide's *Three Popes and the Jews* (39) which outlines the historical hostility of the papacy (with the exception of Benedict XV) toward the Zionist movement.

Perhaps ironically, Christian fundamentalism, which is often most vocal about the unredeemed character of the Jewish people tends to be most enthusiastic about the State of Israel, seeing in it a fulfilment of biblical prophecy and a sign of the imminent return of Christ. It comes as less of a surprise, then, to discover that at the opposite end of the theological spectrum the situation may find itself reversed.

In *The Crime of Christendom: The Theological Sources of Christian Anti-Semitism* (12), Fred Gladstone Bratton presents a Unitarian-Universalist version of the writings of Hay and Flannery. The work seems less an attempt to heal the wounds of the Jews than to scourge orthodox Christology. The author sees in the latter the principal cause of anti-Semitism which, he claims, will persist until the churches radically revise (or abandon) creed. What follows may suitably be described by what Niebuhr has termed "provisional tolerance." The author stipulates that in order to benefit from an amelioration of Christian attitudes, the Jews will have to abandon their own form of particularism, viz., Zionism, and in effect subscribe to a Jewish counterpart of Unitarian-Universalism. In this context, the following remarks of A. Roy Eckardt are especially relevant: "Is it not conceivable that traditional forms of faith may possess greater insight into the perversity of men, into the bond between inhuman behavior and inhuman idolatry, and into the mysteries of God's work than do less traditional and more rationalistic views? Is it really the case that religious liberals know more or do more about social maladies as discrimination against Jews than traditionalists know or do?" (The Theology of Anti-semitism," *Religion in Life* XXXI [1962], p. 566.)

Thus do we find on the part of certain representatives of more conservative churches greater sympathy in this regard. Long known is James Parkes' *History of Palestine from 135 A.D. to Modern Times* (51) in which he sets as his task the tracing of the unsevered connection of the Jewish people with the Holy Land throughout the centuries of the dispersion. A. Roy Eckardt closes his *Elder and Younger Brothers* (20) with a supplement, originally published in *Christian Century,* entitled "Again, Silence in the Churches." The essay reproves the churches for their silence during the Six Day War and advances the case for the State of Israel from a Christian point of view. In this regard, see his *Midstream* article, "Eretz Israel: A Christian Affirmation" (21), in which the author explains his commitment on "Christian grounds to bespeak the integrity of Israel among Jews as among Christians," and his latest volume, *Encounter With Israel: A Challenge to Conscience,* (22a) written in collaboration with his wife. Krister Stendahl's "Judaism and Christianity II; After a Colloquium and a War" (64) in the *Harvard Divinity Bulletin* is a continuation of his discussion of the article in *New Theology No. 2* (63) in the light of the Harvard Jewish-Christian Colloquium of 1966 and the 1967 Israel-Arab war. Of particular interest is the author's position concerning the desirability of a united Jerusalem from a Christian standpoint.

PUBLICATIONS CITED IN TEXT

(1) Aron, Robert, *Jesus of Nazareth: The Hidden Years,* trans. F. Frenaye (London: H. Hamilton, 1962).

(2) Baeck, Leo, *Judaism and Christianity,* trans. W. Kaufmann (Philadelphia: Jewish Publication Society of America, 1961).

(3) Balthasar, Hans Urs von, *Martin Buber and Christianity,* trans. A. Bru (London: Harvill Press, 1961).

(4) Baron, Salo W., *A Social and Religious History of the Jews* (New York: Columbia University Press, 1965), Vol. IX, chapters XXXIX, XL.

(5) Barth, Karl, "The Jewish Problem and the Christian Answer," in *Against the Stream,* trans. E. M. Delacour (London: SCM Press, 1954, 193–202).

(6) Barth, Markus, *The Broken Wall: A Study of the Epistle to the Ephesians* (Chicago: Judson Press, 1959).

(7) Baum, Gregory, "The Doctrinal Basis for Jewish-Christian Dialogue," *Dialog* VI (1967), 200–209.

(8) Bea, Augustine, S. J. *The Church and the Jewish People,* trans. P. Loretz, S. J. (New York: Harper & Row, 1966).

(9) Ben-Chorin, Schalom, *Bruder Jesus: Der Nazarener in Jüdischer Sicht* (Munich: Paul List Verlag, 1967).

(9a) Ben Sasson, Haim Hillel, "Jewish-Christian Disputation in the Setting of Humanism and Reformation in the German Empire," *Harvard Theological Review* LIX (1966), 369–390.

(10) Berkovits, Eliezer, "Judaism in the post-Christian Era," *Judaism* XV (1966), 74–84.

(11) Blumenkranz, Bernhard, *Juifs et Chrétiens dans le monde occidental, 430–1096* (Paris: Mouton, 1960).

(12) Bratton, Fred Gladstone, *The Crime of Christendom: The Theological Sources of Christian Anti-Semitism* (Boston: Beacon Press, 1969).

(13) Braude, Morris, *Conscience on Trial* (New York: Exposition Press, 1962).

(14) Buber, Martin, *Two Types of Faith,* trans. N. P. Goldhawk (London: Routledge and Paul, 1951).

(15) ———, "The Two Foci of the Jewish Soul," in *Israel and the World* (New York: Schocken Books, 1948).

(16) Cohn, Haim H., *Reflections on the Trial and Death of Jesus* (Jerusalem: Israel Law Review Association, 1967; reprint from *Israel Law Review* II [1967], 279–332).

(17) Daniélou, Jean, *Dialogue with Israel,* trans. J. M. Roth (Baltimore: Helicon, 1968).

(18) Diamond, Malcolm, *Martin Buber: Jewish Existentialist* (New York: Oxford University Press, 1960); chapter 7: "The Jewish Jesus and the Christ of Faith."

(19) Eckardt, A. Roy, "Can There Be a Jewish-Christian Relationship?" *Journal of Bible and Religion,"* XXXIII (1905), 122–130.

(20) ———, *Elder and Younger Brothers: The Encounter of Jews and Christians* (New York: Charles Scribner's Sons, 1967).

(21) ———, "Eretz Israel: A Christian Affirmation," *Midstream* XIV (1968), 9–12.

(22) ———, "The Theology of Anti-Semitism," *Religion in Life* XXXI (1962), 552–62.

(22a) ——— and Alice L., *Encounter with Israel: A Challenge to Conscience* (New York: Association Press, 1970).

(23) Fackenheim, Emil L., "Jewish Faith and the Holocaust," *Commentary* XLVI (1968), 30–36.

(24) ———, *Quest for Past and Future* (Bloomington: Indiana University Press, 1968); chapter 16.

(25) Flannery, Edward H., *The Anguish of the Jews: Twenty-three Centuries of Anti-Semitism* (New York: The Macmillan Company, 1965).

(26) Fleischmann, Jacob, *The Problem of Christianity in Modern Jewish Thought,* in Hebrew (Jerusalem: Magnes Press, 1964).

(27) Flusser, David, *Jesus,* trans. R. Walls (New York: Herder and Herder, 1969).

(27a) Gilbert, Arthur, "The Mission of the Jewish People in History and in the Modern World," *Lutheran World* XI (1964), 296–310.

(27b) Ginzberg, Louis, *Die Haggada bei den Kirchenvätern* (Berlin: A. Calvary, 1900).

(27c) Glock, Charles Y. and Rodney Stark, *Christian Beliefs and Anti-Semitism* (New York: Harper & Row, 1966).

(28) Goldstein, Morris, *Jesus in the Jewish Tradition* (New York: The Macmillan Company, 1950).

(29) Grayzel, Solomon, *The Church and the Jews in the XIIIth Century* (New York: Hermon Press, 1966).

(30) Hay, Malcolm, *The Foot of Pride: The Pressure of Christendom on the People of Israel for 1900 Years* (Boston: The Beacon Press, 1950; republished under the title *Europe and the Jews,* 1960).

(31) Hedenquist, Göte (ed.), *The Church and the Jewish People* (London: Edinburgh House Press, 1954).

(32) Herford, R. Travers, *Christianity in Talmud and Midrash* (London: Williams and Norgate, 1903).

(32a) Heschel, Abraham J., "No Religion is an Island," *Union Theological Quarterly Review* XXI, January, 1966, pp. 117–134.

(33) Isaac, Jules, *Jesus and Israel,* trans. S. Gran (New York: Holt, Rinehart and Winston, 1971).

(34) ———, *The Teaching of Contempt,* trans. H. Weaver (New York: Holt, Rinehart and Winston, 1964).

(35) Katz, Jacob, "Religious Tolerance in the Halakhic and Philosophical System of Rabbi Menahem ha-Me'iri" (Hebrew), *Zion* XVIII (1953), 15–30.

(36) Kaufmann, Yehezkel, *Golah ve-nekhar* (Tel Aviv: Dvir, 1954).

(37) Klausner, Joseph, *From Joseph to Paul,* trans. W. F. Stinespring (Boston: Beacon Press, 1961).

(38) ———, *Jesus of Nazareth: His Life, Times and Teaching,* trans. H. Danby (New York: The Macmillan Company, 1945).

(39) Lapide, Pinchas E., *Three Popes and the Jews* (New York: Hawthorn Books, 1967).

(40) Lauterbach, Jacob Z., "Jesus in the Talmud," in *Rabbinic Essays* (Cincinnati: Hebrew Union College Press, 1951).

(41) Lindeskog, Gösta, *Die Jesusfrage im neuzeitlichen Judenthum* (Uppsala: Almqvist & Wiksells Boktryckeri-a.-b., 1938).

(41a) Loeb, Isidore, "La Controverse religieuse entre les Chrétiens et les Juifs au Moyen Age," *Revue de l'Histoire des Religions* XVII–XVIII (1888), 133–156, 311–337.

(41b) ———, 'Polémistes chrétiens et juifs," *Revue des Études Juives* XVIII (1889), 43–70, 219–42.

(42) Mantel, Hugo, *Studies in the History of the Sanhedrin* (Cambridge, Mass.: Harvard University Press, 1961).

(43) Marquardt, Friedrich-Wilhelm, *Die Entdeckung des Judentums für die christliche Theologie: Israel in Denken Karl Barths* (Munich: Chr. Kaiser Verlag, 1967).

(44) Mayer, Reinhold, *Christentum und Judentum in der Schau Leo Baecks* (Stuttgart: W. Kohlhammer, 1961).

(44a) Merchavia, Ch., *Ha-Talmud bi-re'i ha-natsrut* (Jerusalem: Bialik Institute, 1970).

(45) Moore, George Foot, "Christian Writers on Judaism," *Harvard Theological Review* XIV (1921), 197–254.

(46) ———, *Judaism in the First Centuries of the Christian Era: The Age of the Tannaim* (Cambridge, Mass.: Harvard University Press), Vols. I-II, 1927, Vol. III, 1930.

(47) Neusner, Jacob, Correspondence, *Judaism* XV (1966), 223–226; XVI (1967), 363.

(47a) ———, *Aphrahat and Judaism: The Christian-Jewish Argument in Fourth Century Iran* (Leiden: E. J. Brill, 1967).

(48) Niebuhr, Reinhold, *Pious and Secular America* (New York: Charles Scribner's Sons, 1958); Chapter 7: "Christians and Jews in Western Civilization."

(48a) ———, "The Unsolved Religious Problem in Christian-Jewish Relations," *Christianity and Crisis* XXVI (1966), 279–83.

(49) Olson, Bernhard E., *Faith and Prejudice* (New Haven: Yale University Press, 1963).

(50) Parkes, James, *The Conflict of the Church and the Synagogue*, (Philadelphia: Jewish Publication Society of America, 1961).

(51) ———, *A History of Palestine from 135 A.D. to Modern Times* (London: Oxford University Press, 1949); revised edition: *Whose Land? A History of the People of Palestine* (Baltimore: Penguin, 1970).

(52) ———, "A Reappraisal of the Christian Attitude toward Judaism," *Journal of Bible and Religion* XXIX (1961), 299–307.

(52a) Pfisterer, Rudolf, "Judaism in the Preaching and Teaching of the Church," *Lutheran World* XI (1964), 311–328.

(53) Quervain, Alfred de, *Theologische Existenz Heute: Das Judentum in der Lehre und Verkundigung der Kirche Heute* (Munich: Chr. Kaiser Verlag, 1966).

(54) Rankin, Oliver S., *Jewish Religious Polemics of Earlier and Later Centuries* (Edinburgh: University Press, 1956).

(55) Rosenstock-Huessy, Eugen, *Judaism Despite Christianity* (Alabama: University of Alabama Press, 1969).

(56) Rosenthal, Judah, "The State of Israel and the Christian Church" (Hebrew), in *Mehkarim* (Jerusalem: Rubin Mass, 1966), 578–586.

(57) ———, "The State of Israel in the Light of Christian Theology" (Hebrew), *op. cit.,* 556–577.

(58) Sandmel, Samuel, *We Jews and Jesus* (New York: Oxford University Press, 1965).

(59) Schoeps, Hans Joachim, *The Jewish-Christian Argument: A*

History of Theologies in Conflict, trans. D. S. Green (New York: Holt, Rinehart, and Winston, 1963).

(60) Schürer, Emil, *A History of the Jewish People in the Time of Jesus* (Edinburgh: T. & T. Clark, 1885).

(61) Schwarzschild, Steven S., "Judaism, Scriptures, and Ecumenism," *Judaism* XIII (1964), 259–273.

(62) Simon, Marcel, *Verus Israel* (Paris: E. de Boccard, 1964).

(62a) Siirala, Aarne, "Luther and the Jews," *Lutheran World* XI (1964), 337–347.

(63) Stendahl, Krister, "Judaism and Christianity: Then and Now," in Marty, Martin E., *New Theology No. 2* (New York: The Macmillan Company, 1965, 153–164).

(64) ———, "Judaism and Christianity II: After a Colloquium and a War," *Harvard Divinity Bulletin,* N.S. I (1967), 2–8.

(64a) Tal, Uriel, *Christians and Jews in the "Second Reich" (1870–1914): A Study in the Rise of German Totalitarianism,* in Hebrew (Jerusalem: Magnes Press-Yad Vashem, 1969).

(65) Talmage, Frank, "R. David Kimḥi as Polemicist," *Hebrew Union College Annual* XXXVIII (1967), 213–235.

(66) Tchernowitz, Gershon, *The Relation between Israel and the Gentiles according to Maimonides,* in Hebrew (New York: Bitsaron, 1950).

(67) Trattner, Ernest R., *As a Jew Sees Jesus* (New York: Charles Scribner's Sons, 1931).

(68) Walker, Thomas D., *Jewish Views of Jesus* (London: Allen and Unwin, 1930).

(69) Williams, Arthur Lukyn, *Adversus Judaeos* (Cambridge: Cambridge University Press, 1935).

(70) Winter, Paul, *On the Trial of Jesus* (Berlin: Walter de Gruyter, 1961).

(71) Zeitlin, Solomon, *Who Crucified Jesus?* (New York: Bloch Publishing Company, 1964).

SUPPLEMENTARY BIBLIOGRAPHY

Baron, S. W., "John Calvin and the Jews," in *Harry A. Wolfson Jubilee Volume* (Jerusalem: American Academy for Jewish Research, 1965), English section, 141–163.

——, "Medieval Heritage and Modern Realities in Protestant-Jewish Relations," *Diogenes* XLI (1968), 32–51.

Barth, Markus, *Theologische Existenz Heute: Israel und die Kirche im Briefe des Paulus an die Epheser* (Munich: Chr. Kaiser Verlag, 1952).

Ben-Chorin, Schalom, "Jesus der Jude" in *Das Judentum in Ringen der Gegenwart* (Hamburg: Herbert Reich, 1965).

Fackenheim, Emil, "Samuel Hirsch and Hegel: A Study of Hirsch's *Religionsphilosophie der Juden (1842),*" in A. Altmann (ed.), *Studies in Nineteenth Century Jewish Intellectual History* (Cambridge, Mass.: Harvard University Press, 1964, 171–201).

Fasman, Oscar Z., "An Epistle on Tolerance by a 'Rabbinic Zealot,' " in Jung, Leo (ed.), *Judaism in a Changing World* (New York: Oxford University Press, 1939).

Federici, Tommaso, *Israele vivo* (Turin: Edizioni Missioni Consolata, 1962).

Goldschmidt, Dietrich, *Der ungekündigte Bund* (Stuttgart: Kreuz-Verlag, 1962).

Isaac, Jules, *Génèse de l'antisémitisme* (Paris: Calmann-Lévy, 1956).

———, *Has Anti-Semitism Roots in Christianity?,* trans. D. and J. Parkes (New York: N.C.C.J., 1961).

Israël en de Kerk (The Hague: Lecturbureau der Nederlands Hervormde Kerk, 1959).

Lohse, Eduard, *Israel und die Christenheit* (Göttingen: Vandenhoek & Ruprecht, 1960).

Maritain, Jacques, *Le Mystère d'Israël* (Paris: Desclée, De Brouwer, 1965).

Meisels, Misha, *Mahashava ve-'emet* (Tel Aviv: Mizpeh, 1938–39), Vol. 2.

Oesterreicher, John M. (ed.), *The Bridge: A Yearbook of Judaeo-Christian Studies* (New York: Pantheon Press, 1955, 1956, 1958, 1962).

Rylaarsdam, J. Coert, "Common Ground and Difference," *Journal of Bible and Religion* XLIII (1963), 261–170.

Schultz, Hans Juergen (ed.), *Juden-Christen-Deutschen* (Stuttgart: Kreuz Verlag, 1961).

Synan, Edward A., *The Popes and the Jews in the Middle Ages* (New York: The Macmillan Company, 1965).

Tillich, Paul, *Die Judenfrage: Ein christliches und ein deutsches Problem* (Berlin: Gebrüder Weiss Verlag, 1953).

Weiss-Rosmarin, Trude, *Judaism and Christianity: The Differences* (New York: Jonathan David, 1953).

Wilpert, Paul (ed.), *Judentum im Mittelalter, Beiträge zum Christlich-Jüdischen Gespräch,* Miscellanea Mediaevilia 4, (Berlin: Walter de Gruyter, 1966).

MODERN JEWISH THOUGHT

---

by FRITZ ROTHSCHILD
and SEYMOUR SIEGEL

Fritz Rothschild, Associate Professor of the Philosophy of Religion at the Jewish Theological Seminary of America, has lectured extensively in the United States, Canada and South Africa. Dr. Rothschild is the author of *Between God and Man: An Interpretation of Judaism from the Writings of A. J. Heschel,* and has contributed to various journals.

Seymour Siegel is Professor of Theology, Ethics and Rabbinic Thought at the Jewish Theological Seminary of America. He has written for *Judaism, Conservative Judaism* and *Union Seminary Quarterly Review,* among other publications, and has lectured widely. Dr. Siegel is an editor of the *Encyclopedia Judaica.*

113

I.

INTRODUCTION

The following essay attempts to provide bibliographical information on modern Jewish thought. For our purposes we define this area as works which were written since the second half of the eighteenth century. It was Moses Mendelssohn (1729–1786) who ushered in the era of emancipation and acculturation which brought European Jewry (first in Central and Western Europe, and subsequently also in Eastern Europe) into the world of modern European culture. Faced with the challenges of this culture, a variety of Jewish thinkers had to reconsider the meaning, value and relevance of their ancestral traditions. The changing role of Jews who had left the self-enclosed world of the ghetto, the development of scholarly investigation of the Jewish past and its literary creations (the so-called *Wissenschaft des Judentums*), and the onslaughts of modern secular thought on traditional religion gave rise to questions which engaged the minds of Jewish theologians and philosophers.

At about the same time that Mendelssohn, in Germany, inaugurated the entry of the Jews into the political and intellectual mainstream of Western civilization, Israel Baal Shem Tov (c. 1700–1760), in Podolia, founded a popular pietistic movement, know as Hasidism, which swept large parts of Eastern Europe and clashed not only with the traditional rabbinic establishment of the time, but also came into conflict with the adherents of the *Haskalah* (Enlightenment) in the nineteenth century.

The inroads of assimilation, the granting of civic rights to Jews in the nineteenth century, and the rise of anti-Semitism in various

European countries, were followed by the Nazi extermination of six million Jews and the reestablishment of a Jewish sovereign state in 1948 after almost 2000 years of exile.

Reacting to some of these developments, Reform, Orthodox, and Conservative Judaism arose in the religious sphere, while Zionism and Jewish socialism came into being as political movements for Jewish renewal and survival.

Although our paper will concentrate on Jewish religious thought and thus will focus on theology and religious philosophy, we have found it impossible to omit such secular and quasi-secular movements as Zionism and Jewish socialism. To show how indispensable their understanding is for the serious student we may point, by way of example, to Martin Buber, perhaps the best-known Jewish thinker of the twentieth century. Although a religious philosopher, his return to Judaism was sparked by his involvement in the nascent Zionist movement, and his thought was influenced as much by his rediscovery of Hasidism as by his study of the Bible.   [F.A.R.]

To avoid confusion and to enable the reader to find his way in the field of modern Jewish thought, we have divided this essay into these sections:

I.   Introduction
II. Surveys, Anthologies and Histories of Jewish Thought
III. Handbooks on the Jewish Religion
VI. Movements in Judaism: Reform, Conservative, Orthodox (including Hasidic and Musar), Zionist, Jewish Socialist
V.   Jewish Thinkers from Mendelssohn to the Present
VI. Bibliographic Listing.

II.

SURVEYS, ANTHOLOGIES AND HISTORIES OF JEWISH THOUGHT

Unfortunately, no complete history of modern Jewish thought has been written in English. The most complete work which has appeared to date is Julius Guttmann's *Philosophies of Judaism* (1964), the standard history of Jewish philosophy. It is available in an English translation and covers its subject from biblical times to Franz Rosenzweig.[1] It is a scholarly and valuable work, but makes considerable demands on the reader's philosophical knowledge. It does not cover Buber and such contemporary philosophers as Mordecai Kaplan and Abraham Heschel. Professor Nathan Rotenstreich of the Hebrew University in Jerusalem published a Hebrew volume in 1950 which has appeared in an English translation under the title *Jewish Philosophy in Modern Times* (1968). It is much more detailed than Guttmann's work and covers all major figures from Mendelssohn to Rosenzweig, including Moritz Lazarus and Samuel David Luzzatto (nineteenth century), and the mystical thought of Rav Kook (twentieth century) not treated in Guttmann. Again the reader is expected to have some familiarity with philosophical literature, and the "translation English" does not make his task easier. However, no serious student can dispense with these two books which are scholarly and reliable.

For the beginner, Samuel H. Bergman's little book *Faith and Reason: An Introduction to Modern Jewish Thought* (1961) is highly recommended. It is popular, yet trustworthy, and may be read as a prelude to the standard works noted above. (Unlike them it also contains a chapter on Buber.) Jacob B. Agus' pioneer study in English, *Modern Philosophies of Judaism* (1941), although written almost three decades ago, is a very useful survey of Jewish thinkers beginning with Abraham Geiger and ending with Martin Buber. It contains good, clear expositions and is especially valuable on Hermann Cohen, Rosenzweig, and Kaplan.

Another book by the same author, *The Evolution of Jewish Thought from Biblical Times to the Opening of the Modern Era* (1959) treats Hasidism and Enlightenment in chapters eleven and twelve, but is written in a more popular style and with less detailed analyses. Joseph L. Blau's *Story of Jewish Philosophy* (1962), devotes the last two chapters (ca. 50 pages) to the period from Mendelssohn to Kaplan, and thus can give only brief, but useful, summaries of their works. Mordecai M. Kaplan, himself a major contemporary Jewish philosopher, presents an interesting history of modern Jewish thought in his work, *The Greater Judaism in the*

---

[1] The original German edition was published in 1933. The Hebrew enlarged, revised edition, on which the translation is based, was published in 1953.

Making: A Study of the Modern Evolution of Judaism (1960). After chapters on "traditional" and "medieval" Judaism, he discusses the major movements in modern Judaism (Reform, Orthodoxy, Conservatism, Zionism) and concludes with an exposition of his own approach, Reconstructionism, which he advocates as the Judaism for our times. Although written from the standpoint of his own ideology and not the work of an "objective" historian of Jewish thought, Kaplan's treatment of the various movements in modern Judaism is informative and valuable even for those who do not share his views.

Great Jewish Thinkers of the Twentieth Century (1963), edited by Simon Noveck, contains essays by various authors on ten thinkers. Of these, three are devoted to East European figures (Ahad Ha-Am, A.D. Gordon, A.I. Kook), four to German Jews (H. Cohen, Leo Baeck, F. Rosenzweig, M. Buber) and three to American Jews (K. Kohler, M. Kaplan, J. Soloveitchik). A companion volume, *Contemporary Jewish Thought: A Reader* (1963) contains selections from the works of these thinkers (except Soloveitchik). These two volumes are valuable and popularly written and provide a useful introduction to the field. It is to be regretted that Abraham Heschel, the best-known contemporary Jewish thinker in America, was not included in either of these two volumes.

Bernard Martin edited *Great 20th Century Jewish Philosophers: A Reader in Jewish Existentialism* (1970), containing well-written essays on and selections from Lev Shestov, Franz Rosenzweig and Martin Buber.

Arthur A. Cohen's *The Natural and Supernatural Jew* (1962) bears the subtitle "An Historical and Theological Introduction" and attempts to give a survey of Jewish thought from the sixteenth century to the present. It deals with most major figures from Mendelssohn to Will Herberg, but is uneven and highly coloured by the author's own theology which he states in the form of "five existential dogmas." Where he likes a thinker (as in the case of Herberg) he proves a good expositor, but where he feels out of sympathy (as in the case of Kaplan and Heschel) he is less than fair and informative. Cohen is also the editor of a collection of contemporary Jewish essays *Arguments and Doctrines: A Reader of Jewish Thinking in the Aftermath of the Holocaust* (1970). In his introduction he admits that his anthology is highly subjective and that his selections reflect his own attitude, a supernaturalist, existentialist, non-Zionist, eschatological outlook. Thus the problems of Jewish law and observance, the meaning of the State of Israel, etc. are not covered. Each selection is prefaced with an introduction which reflects the editor's own viewpoint. Although this makes the anthology less than a fair reflection of the whole range of contemporary Jewish thought, it contains enough important essays by such important authors as Emil Fackenheim, Will Herberg, Gershom Scholem, Yeheskel Kaufmann, et al., to make it a useful resource for the student of contemporary religious thought. [F.A.R.]

III.

HANDBOOKS ON JEWISH RELIGION

"Handbooks" of Jewish thought and practice, written for the intelligent layman, are usually straightforward presentations of Jewish religion and life. They do not as a rule present the historical background and development of the ideas of Judaism, but are written to acquaint the Jew and the non-Jew with the foundations of Jewish faith.

Though written more than twenty years ago, the most popular presentation of Jewish thought is still Milton Steinberg's *Basic Judaism* (1947), a brief, eloquent, and comprehensive discussion of the fundamentals of Judaism as seen from the perspective of a gifted rabbi who was a part of the liberal wing of Conservative Judaism. Steinberg presents the principles of Judaism both from what he calls the "traditionalist" as well as the "modernist" viewpoint.

The Beliefs and Practices of Judaism (1952) by Louis Finkelstein, Chancellor of the Jewish Theological Seminary, includes a compact presentation of the traditional views of Judaism on God, man and the world, as well as a brief, though thorough, description of the practices of Judaism. The book originally appeared as part of *The Jews* (1949) edited by Finkelstein, which contains important articles on such topics as the meaning of Jewish mysticism, the role of Judaism in the formation of world philosophy, and articles on the historical periods of Jewish creativity. For a scholarly and thoroughly annotated analysis, Louis Jacobs' *The Principles of the Jewish Faith* (1964) is extremely valuable. It is built around the thirteen principles of Jewish faith enunciated by Moses Maimonides in the twelfth century. Jacobs summarizes the views of Jewish thinkers throughout the ages on the problems of religion and Jewish faith. His bibliographical excursus will be useful to the student. Jacobs is a Conservative rabbi in England.

A short, paperback introduction to Judaism and its history, good for college classes in comparative religion and as an introduction to Judaism, is provided by Jacob Neusner in *The Way of Torah* (1970). This volume is part of Dickenson Press, "The Religious Life of Man" Series. Neusner has also included useful bibliographical essays. *Judaism: A Historical Presentation* (1959) by the late British scholar, Isadore Epstein, traces the beliefs and doctrines of Judaism. It is written from a basically Orthodox point of view. He has also published a longer, more detailed work, *The Faith of Judaism* (1954). Both should be useful for the beginning student wishing to read a balanced, learned presentation of Judaism. *Judaism: Religion and Ethics* (1953), by Meyer Waxman, consists of two parts. The first half deals with beliefs and practices; the second half, with the ethics of Judaism. The author tends toward the Orthodox viewpoint. It is written in the style of a handbook with short, rather dogmatic statements on the principal aspects of Judaism. Impressionistic is Leon Roth's *Judaism: A Portrait* (1961) in which he sharply sketches in the outlines of the history of Jewish religion and the meaning of some of its basic concepts. It is not the usual handbook covering the conventional theological topics, but is lively as well as learned.

Long a standard handbook has been *The Jewish Religion* (1891) by Michael Friedländer (1833–1910), who was the principal of Jews' College, London. The book is divided into two parts: creed and duties. The presentation is Orthodox in spirit and non-apologetic. It is somewhat outdated and does not, of course, deal with such problems as the state of Israel and the New Morality. Widely used is the pocket volume, *What Is a Jew?* (1960) by Rabbi Morris Kertzer. In a question-and-answer format, he tries to answer some of the important questions about Jews and Judaism.

The presentation is from a liberal point of view and can be used when a short rather simple explication of Judaism is required.

Image of the Jew: Teachers' Guide to Jews and Their Religion (1970) includes the texts of seven television lectures on the American Jew, what Jews believe, worship and the Jewish year, and the life cycle of Jews, plus additional exposition, bibliography, etc., by Ruth Selden. The book is the outcome of a teacher-education television series jointly developed by the Catholic Archdiocese of New York and the Anti-Defamation League. (Films of these lectures are available.)

Scholar and rabbi, Robert Gordis, has written *A Faith for Moderns* (1960), a theological exposition of the principles of religion in general, and Judaism in particular. The outlook is traditional but not Orthodox. Written in non-technical language, this will be read with profit by those interested in knowing what the arguments are for maintaining traditional Jewish concepts in the modern world.

Where Judaism Differed (1957) by Abba Hillel Silver (1893–1963) contrasts the beliefs of Judaism with other religions, especially Christianity. Silver, who was one of America's leading (Reform) rabbis and Zionist spokesmen, writes with verve to magnify the differences in theology between Judaism and the other religions.

Eternal Faith, Eternal People (1962) by Leo Trepp, a lucid and interesting presentation of the principles and history of Judaism, discusses rather briefly some of the principle philosophies and thinkers of contemporary Judaism. *Judaism: A Profile of a Faith* (1963) by Ben Zion Bokser, which portrays the Jewish heritage of faith and its conception of man, God and the universe, is a balanced presentation by a Conservative rabbi.

Although technically not a handbook, *What Is This Jewish Heritage?* (1954) by the late novelist and literary critic Ludwig Lewisohn, is an impassioned plea for a return to basic Jewish values and principles. Lewisohn, who had been distant from Jewish life, is a powerful voice calling back the alienated. Though written before the current revolution in morals and outlook, this book is an eloquent statement of what being a Jew means in the modern world. In *This is My God* (1959), novelist Herman Wouk, an

Orthodox Jew, presents his version of Judaism with grace and conviction. Though not a scholar, he does make use of the standard works on Judaism.

Mention should also be made of Arthur Hertzberg's anthology of classic Jewish sources, *Judaism* (1962). Of special interest is *Commentary's* "Symposium on the State of Jewish Belief" (August 1966), which includes the views of some thirty rabbis representing the different wings of Judaism. This is an interesting document on the principles espoused by the leaders of American Jews' spirituality.   [s.s.]

IV.

MOVEMENTS IN JUDAISM

Several important ideologies and movements were created to cope with the problem of adjusting Judaism to the New World. With but one exception (Reconstructionism) they had their genesis in Europe and were transplanted to the New World. The ideologies are primarily religious, but even when the patterns of thought were not explicitly religious in form and content (as in Zionism and Jewish socialism), they are included in our discussion because it may be said that any structure of thought and action which deals with Jewish identity can be considered part of Judaism. In what follows we will mention the important works which explain the origins and ideologies of modern Judaism.

General Surveys:

The standard histories of the Jewish people deal with the rise of the ideologies which serve contemporary Judaism. The classic work by Heinrich Graetz, *The History of the Jewish People* (1648–1870) (Volume V), and *A Century of Jewish Life* (1940) by Ismar Elbogen, contain excellent chapters of the rise of movements and ideologies in Judaism. Likewise, Howard Morley Sachar's *The Course of Modern Jewish History* (1958) describes developments within modern Jewry. Sachar also has a fine bibliography in this book which will guide the student into the literature about our subject. Useful, too, is David Rudavsky's *Emancipation and Ad-*

justment (1967), a study of contemporary Jewish religious movements. A convenient well-written account is Joseph Blau's *Modern Varieties of Judaism* (1966) which analyzes the ideologies of Reform Judaism, Neo-Orthodoxy, Conservative Judaism and Zionism. Blau sees all of these in the light of the impact of emancipation upon modern Judaism.

Reform Judaism:

Reform Judaism was the first of the movements in modern Judaism which attempted to meet the challenge of the new discoveries and approaches of science, philosophy, and politics. It sought to reinterpret Judaism in the light of the new philosophy—especially German idealism—and asserted its authority to modify Jewish traditional practice and ritual in the light of modern needs and conditions. In the beginning at least, it tended to deny the importance of Jewish nationhood and saw Judaism as essentially a religious communion.

The movement began in the early nineteenth century and struck roots in America. A standard history is that of David Philipson (1862–1949), *The Reform Movement in Judaism* (1907) recently reprinted with a prolegomenon by Solomon Freehof. Written from the standpoint of a leader in Reform Judaism, the book is extremely detailed for the early years of the movement. Unfortunately, it stops in 1930 and does not have information about subsequent developments. Documents and sources dealing with the theological and historical developments in Europe were compiled by Gunther Plaut in *The Rise of Reform Judaism* (1965). *The Growth of Reform Judaism* (1965) by Plaut contains sources for the understanding of the growth of the movement in America. Jakob J. Petuchowski has written a well-documented study entitled *Prayer Book Reform in Judaism* (1968) in which he recounts the changes in liturgy brought about by the rise of Reform. This aspect is important, since in Judaism reforms in thought and practice are reflected foremost in the official liturgy of the synagogue.

The central figure in early Reform Judaism in Europe and the pioneer figure in modern Jewish scholarship and thought was Rabbi

Abraham Geiger (1810–1874). Selections of his writings together with a detailed bibliography are included in *Abraham Geiger and Liberal Judaism* (1962) by Max Wiener. The book will reward the reader with an insight into the intellectual and scholarly development of Geiger, founder of the *Wissenschaft des Judentums* movement which began the scientific inquiry into Jewish literature, history, and religion.

The central Reform figure in the United States was Rabbi Isaac Mayer Wise (1819–1900). His life and work are treated in Philipson, *op. cit.* Israel Knox's biography *Rabbi in America: The Story of Isaac M. Wise* (1957) and Max Benjamin May, *Isaac Mayer Wise, the Founder of American Judaism: A Biography* (1916) are highly readable and useful.

A basic difference between Reform and traditional Judaism has been its attitude toward Jewish law. Reform abandoned many important traditional Jewish practices and introduced new forms. Solomon Freehof has dedicated himself to the validation and reevaluation of these ritual modifications in the light of the traditional responsa literature. Among his important books in this area are *Reform Jewish Practice and its Rabbinic Background* (1964), *Reform Responsa* (1960), *Recent Reform Responsa* (1963), and *Current Reform Responsa* (1969).

The theological underpinnings of Reform Judaism are discussed by Kaufmann Kohler (1843–1926) in *Jewish Theology, Systematically and Historically Considered* (1918), reprinted in 1968 with an introduction by Joseph Blau. The book presents a liberal approach to Jewish theology highly influenced by Kantian thought. Kohler was president of Hebrew Union College, the Reform rabbinical seminary. More recent developments are reflected in *Contemporary Reform Jewish Thought* (1969), edited by Bernard Martin, in which the movement's central concepts are discussed by its rabbis and scholars. (See also Borowitz and Petuchowski section D.) The last essay by Martin surveys Reform Jewish theology today.

For current thinking, activities, and priorities in the movement, the student should turn to the *Yearbook of the Central Conference of American Rabbis,* the *CCAR Journal,* and *Dimensions,* a magazine produced by the movement's lay organization, the Union of American Hebrew Congregations.

Conservative Judaism:

Conservative Judaism was born in reaction to Reform Judaism. It asserts the possibility of combining tradition with change and seeks to modify traditional Judaism in the spirit of moderation, maintaining its essential character and contours while modifying those aspects which needed modification in the light of differing needs and interpretations. It stresses the freedom of historical research and the importance of *K'lal Yisrael* (Catholic Israel).

The origins of Conservative Judaism were in Germany in the 1840's; today, its intellectual center is at the Jewish Theological Seminary of America in New York. Its two central figures are Zacharias Frankel (1801–1875), who was Chief Rabbi of Dresden, Germany and later head of the Breslau Theological Seminary, and the rabbinic scholar, Solomon Schechter (1850–1915), who served as president of the Jewish Theological Seminary from 1902–1915.

For the early period of Conservative Jewish thought the volume by Blau mentioned above is useful. The best account of Frankel's thought to be found is *Students, Scholars, and Saints* (1928) by Louis Ginzberg (1873–1953), an influential figure in the development of the thought of the Conservative movement and an eminent Jewish scholar. For the early years, see Moshe Davis' *The Emergence of Conservative Judaism: The Historical School in 19th-Century America* (1963), in which he outlines the history and ideology of the forerunners of Conservative Judaism in the United States. *Tradition and Change* (1958), a collection of essays and statements edited by Mordecai Waxman gives a good overview of what has been taught and thought in the Conservative movement.

Studies in Judaism (1896–1919), a three-volume collection of occasional essays on Jewish history and theology by Solomon Schechter, is superbly readable and informative. While it does not deal specifically with the thought of Conservative Judaism (except for the introduction to the first series) it reflects a fine mind, committed to the combination of traditional Judaism and scientific investigation which characterizes Conservative Judaism. Schechter's *Seminary Addresses* (1915), a collection of speeches and essays, is a plea for "traditional Judaism" and for Zionism. Herbert Parzen's *Architects of Conservative Judaism* (1964), written in a popular style, includes biographical sketches of Schechter, Louis Ginzberg, Cyrus Adler, Orientalist and president of the Jewish Theological Seminary (1915–1940), and Louis Finkelstein, its present Chancellor. For later restatements of Conservative Jewish thought the Seminary's Semi-Centennial Volume edited by Cyrus Adler contains some statements about the ideological standpoint of the movement valid today (see especially the essay by Louis Finkelstein, "Tradition in the Making: The Seminary's Interpretation of Judaism"). *Guideposts in Modern Judaism* (1954) by Jacob Agus has essays on central concepts of Judaism interpreted from his point of view. Simon Greenberg, the Seminary's Vice Chancellor has authored a small pamphlet, *The Conservative Movement in Judaism* (1955), as well as a larger volume, *Foundations of a Faith* (1967), in which he discusses God, Torah, and Israel. Robert Gordis' booklet *Conservative Judaism* (1945), is a popular summary of the views dominant in the movement today. The writings of Heschel, Kaplan, and to a certain extent Franz Rosenzweig represent the theological underpinnings of a good deal of Conservative thought today and are discussed separately. *The Condition of Jewish Belief* (1966), edited by Milton Himmelfarb, includes the views of some Conservative rabbis on central concepts of faith and life. The reader should consult the volumes of *The Proceedings of the Rabbinical Assembly*, the organization of Conservative rabbis, as well as its periodical, *Conservative Judaism*, for current issues and opinions.

Marshall Sklare's *Conservative Judaism* (1955) is a sociological analysis which outlines the growth of the movement against the background of the changing sociological character of American Judaism. Sklare's observations and insights are of great value and interest.

Orthodox Judaism:

Modern Orthodox Judaism asserts its essential loyalty to the traditions of Judaism and eschews compromise. Though it seeks to make the Jew part of the modern world, it states that this can be done without sacrificing the authority of Jewish law and life.

It contains within itself many trends and movements, such as Hasidism and the Musar movement,[2] and it is therefore more difficult to outline the literature available to the reader. Of prime importance in the ideology of contemporary Orthodoxy are the writings of Samson Raphael Hirsch (1808–1888), the founder of the "Torah-true" Judaism movement in nineteenth-century Germany. Hirsch is regarded as the progenitor of Neo-Orthodoxy in Western countries which aspired to fuse European culture with unqualified loyalty to rigorously observed traditional Judaism. He was a prolific writer and many of his books are still useful and meaningful. His acknowledged classic is *The Nineteen Letters of Ben Uziel* (1899), written as letters to a questioning student about Judaism. Originally translated by Bernard Drachman, and reissued in 1969, Hirsch attempts, in this book, to prove the viability and necessity of Orthodox Judaism in the modern world. The works of Hirsch have been assiduously translated and published by his disciples. Among the most interesting are *Judaism Eternal: Selected Essays from the Writings of Samson Raphael Hirsch* translated from the German, and annotated with an introduction and a short biography by I. Gruenfeld (1956), in which are included essays on the Jewish calendar, Sabbath, and the concept of freedom in Judaism; and *Horeb* (translation from the German by I. Gruenfeld), which is a handbook of Jewish law and observances. In these works Hirsch presents an Orthodox interpretation of Judaism and Jewish observance. Though the language is somewhat rhetorical, it is a fine introduction to the thought of an important segment of Judaism.

The intellectual center of contemporary American Orthodoxy is Yeshiva University in New York. Samuel Belkin, its president, has published *In His Image* (1960) which is a presentation of Judaism based on *halakhic* literature. There are some questionable generalizations which Belkin makes, but his approach is novel and yet authentic. Belkin has also edited a series entitled Studies in Torah Judaism, which contains essays on aspects of traditional Jewish thought, especially those relating to the observance of Jewish law.

[2] See end of section.

Leo Jung has edited a large number of volumes entitled The Jewish Library. These include essays defending the Orthodox interpretation of Judaism. Outstanding are those on study as a mode of worship, the sexual ethics of Judaism, and the ethics of business according to traditional Judaism. The Jewish Library also contains biographies of important leaders of Orthodox Jewry both in Europe and in America. The essays are of varying quality—but they are important to gain an insight into the character of modern Orthodoxy.

Of special importance in following the developments within this branch of Judaism is the periodical literature produced by the many groups which make up the traditionalist community. Foremost among these periodicals is *Tradition,* published by the Rabbinical Council of America; others include *The Jewish Horizon,* an organ of the Religious Zionists of America; *The Observer,* published by Agudat Yisrael, (an organization inspired by Samson Raphael Hirsch), and *Jewish Life,* published by the Union of Orthodox Jewish Congregations. Many of the journals produced by the Orthodox community are in Hebrew and/or Yiddish and deal with *halakhic* issues (matters of Jewish law).

Hasidism:

Hasidism was a pietistic movement which arose among Eastern European Jews in the middle of the eighteenth century. It was based upon the principles of Jewish mysticism, and emphasized the omnipresence of the Divine in the world. Its method of worship was permeated with joy and enthusiasm, appealing both to the unlearned as well as the learned classes. Its communal structure was built around the *tzadik* (the righteous man) or the *rebbe* to whom many powers were ascribed. Hasidic communities exist until this day. Their spirit and world outlook has been appropriated in modified forms by almost all of the present-day Jewish religious groups. Most responsible for the appreciation of Hasidic spirituality in modern religion is Martin Buber, whose works are discussed elsewhere. Buber's description of Hasidism has been called into question by Gershom Scholem in his essay, "Martin Buber's Hasidism: A Critique," which appeared in *Commentary*

(1961), and is now included in *The Jewish Expression* (ed., Goldin). Scholem asserts that Buber used the legendary material of Hasidism without considering the more theoretical works of the Hasidic masters. Mrs. Rivkah Schatz-Uffenheimer has also criticized Buber's handling of the material in her contribution to *The Philosophy of Martin Buber* (eds. Schilpp and Friedman). Buber replied to both his critics in the Schilpp and Friedman volume in an essay entitled "Interpreting Hasidism" which appeared in *Commentary* (1963). He stated that he was more interested in the actual life of the communities than in their theoretical formulations and that their legends were important in understanding the dimensions of Hasidic spirituality.

The best short introduction to the thought world of Hasidism is to be found in the last chapter of Gershom Scholem's *Major Trends in Jewish Mysticism* (1941). He explicates the relationship between Hasidism and Jewish mysticism and shows how the Hasidic masters converted the mythological foundations of the *kabbala* into a way of life.

The pioneer writer in English was Solomon Schechter who included a chapter on Hasidism in his *Studies on Judaism*. Though not as scholarly as Scholem, Schechter writes with charm and understanding, and his essay is a fine introduction into the meaning of the pietistic movement. More popular accounts can be found in the *Hasidic Anthology* (1934) by Louis I. Newman, and *Maggidim and Hasidim: Their Wisdom* (1962) by Newman, translated in collaboration with Samuel Spitz. In these two volumes we have short sayings of the Hasidic teachers on the various aspects of Judaism and religion arranged alphabetically. One of the first full-length accounts was by Jacob Minkin, *The Romance of Hassidism* (1935). This volume is a popular study and does not include the considerable scholarship that has since been created on the subject. More recently, Harry Rabinowicz has written *A Guide to Hassidism* (1960) which is a scholarly presentation of trends and personalities in Hasidic history. It is one of the few volumes in English giving an account of the development of the different schools and *rebbes*.

As was mentioned previously, most important in understanding the dimensions of spirituality are the tales and legends which were created around the central personalities of Hasidism. Preeminent among the collections of these stories are those of Buber. However, in recent years other collections have appeared in English which are of great interest. Jerome Mintz has collected some of the tales which are circulated among Hasidim living in the United States in his book, *Legends of the Hasidim* (1968). This book, written from a cultural standpoint, is a valuable introduction to the life of the Hasidim in their communities in the New World. Mintz has collaborated with Dan Ben-Amos in publishing a translation of the classic work about the founder of the movement, Rabbi Israel Baal Shem Tov (c. 1700–1760), *Shivhei Ha-Besht: In Praise of the Baal Shem*. This book, which was published after the death of the founder, is a legendary account of his life and works. The translation of this most important text, together with the notes, introduction, and bibliography, are first-rate. Written from a different point of view is Jiri Langer's *Nine Gates to the Chasidic Mysteries* (1961). Langer, living in Prague between the two World Wars, became enchanted with Hasidism, abandoned his westernized way of living and joined the pietistic communities. His account of Hasidic spirituality is permeated with understanding and warmth. Langer's book is a neglected source for understanding the dynamics of the movement and is highly recommended. Another book written from a sociological point of view is Solomon Poll's *The Hasidic Community of Williamsburg* (1967), which describes the way of life in the largest enclave of Hasidism in the United States.

Joseph Weiss was a scholar who lived in England and Israel and who, unfortunately, died at a young age. He was an original and incisive student of the movement. His essays, which have appeared in various journals and collections, are invaluable for the student who wishes to go deeper into the sources and variations in Hasidic religion and life. Most important is his essay "Contemplative Mysticism and Faith in Hasidic Piety" which appeared in the *Journal of Jewish Studies* (1954). Weiss traces two trends in Hasidic thought and life: one more inclined to contemplative mysticism stressing the immanence of God; the other trend, more existentialist, stressing the transcendence of God and the establishing of a relationship with God through faith and decision. Other studies by Weiss include

"Via Passiva in Early Hasidism," in the *Journal of Jewish Studies* (1958); and "The Great Maggid's Theory of Contemplative Magic" in the *Hebrew Union College Annual* (1960).

Since Hasidism is based on earlier Jewish mystical speculation, it becomes necessary, of course, to understand the underpinnings of Jewish mysticism. In this field, Gershom Scholem is preeminent. *Major Trends in Jewish Mysticism* (1941) is his classic presentation of the subject. His collection of essays *On the Kabbala and its Symbolism* (1965), in which he discusses aspects of kabbalistic thought such as the place of the Torah, Commentary, Tradition, and the Golem, is crucial to an understanding of mysticism in Jewish garb. An interesting essay on *Devekuth,* or Communion with God (an important foundation of Hasidic piety) appeared in the *Review of Religion* (1950).

Hasidism stimulated a great deal of opposition on the part of the more established religious circles in Eastern European Jewry. Mordecai Wilensky has devoted a great deal of effort in examining the bases of this opposition. A good introduction to the polemical literature created around the Hasidic movement can be found in Wilensky's article "The Polemic of Rabbi David of Makow Against Hasidism" which appeared in the *Proceedings of the American Academy for Jewish Research* (1956).

The notion of the Hasidic leader is discussed in *The Zaddik* (1960), by Samuel Dresner. He presents some of the early sources and explains the role of the Hasidic teacher as the center of the community and as a model for its adherents in their efforts to establish a concrete relationship with God.

A long-neglected work is that of the Swedish cleric, Torsten Ysander: *Studien zum Bescht'schen Hassidismus in seiner religionsgeschichtlichen Sonderart.* Ysander studied the communities and relates their approach and way of life to the general developments within European religion, especially in the Russian Orthodox Church. This is very important since the Hasidic communities arose and flourished in Russia and Poland. Extremely valuable is *Judaism,* Volume 9, #3 (1960) which devoted an entire issue to Hasidism.

A glimpse into the way of life of the Hasidic conventicle can be found in Heschel's moving account of the life of the Eastern European Jews, *The Earth is the Lord's* (1950), in which he evokes both the beauty and profundity of Hasidic communal life.

Herbert Weiner has written two excellent popular books describing some of the developments within the religious groups in Israel—especially the mystical and Hasidic elements. *The Wild Goats of Ein Gedi* (1961) deals exclusively with the Israeli religious scene. *Nine and One-Half Mystics* (1969) has reference to the Israeli situation, but also discusses various religious communities and personalities in the United States.

In recent years there have appeared more and more translations of original texts. Needless to say these are crucial in understanding and appreciating the meaning of Hasidism. Shneur Zalman of Liadi (1747–1813), founder of Habad Hasidism, attracted more learned followers than was generally true of other Hasidic *rebbes.* His classic work, *The Tanya* analyses the meaning of God's immanence in the world: "There is no vacuum in which God is not present." *The Tanya* is the basis of the Habad (Lubavitcher) community which is extremely active in the United States and Israel. To date five volumes of *The Tanya,* have appeared in translation. Louis Jacobs has translated two important classics of Hasidic mysticism: *The Seeker of Unity: The Life and Works of Aaron of Starosselje* (1966) and *The Tract on Ecstasy* (1963). Jacobs has appended notes and introductions which explain the meaning and significance of the material.

Musar Movement:

In nineteenth-century Lithuania, a movement stressing the ethical dimension of Judaism arose among the students of the academies (*yeshivot*). The Musar movement (*musar* is the Hebrew word meaning morality, ethics) stressed self-examination and the improvement of the personality through study and discussion of the demands made by Judaism for self-perfection. The movement was not popular and was essentially limited to the students of the *yeshivot.* Its founder was Rabbi Israel Salanter (1810–1883), a saintly teacher. There is not too much literature on the subject in English. The best introductions can be found in Louis Ginzberg's essay "Rabbi Israel Salanter" in *The Jewish Expression* edited by Judah Goldin, and the essay of Gedalyahu Alon, "The Lithuanian

Yeshivas" in the same collection. Both writers, themselves students of the *yeshivot,* write movingly and concisely about the aspirations and achievements of Musar. Mendel (Menachem) Glenn has written a full-length study of Rabbi Israel Salanter entitled *Israel Salanter: Religious-Ethical Thinker* (1953). There are, as well, individual essays on the leaders of the Musar movement in the collections *Guardians of Our Heritage* and *Men of the Spirit* edited by Leo Jung. Outstanding is Dr. J. J. Weinberg's "Lithuanian Musar" in *Men of the Spirit.*

Zionism:

Although not a religious movement (there are, however, religious groups within it), Zionism represents the most important development within modern Jewish life. Jewish identity and loyalty has been profoundly affected by the ideologies of Zionism, and more important, through the overwhelming achievements of the founders of the State of Israel. Thus, it is not invalid to include Zionism among the "movements in Judaism."

An excellent collection of the writings of Zionist ideologists compiled by Arthur Hertzberg in *The Zionist Idea: A Historical Analysis and Reader* (1969), includes excerpts from the works of Moses Hess, Theodor Herzl, Ahad Ha-Am, Martin Buber, Chaim Weizmann, David Ben-Gurion, etc. Hertzberg's monograph-size introduction places the selections into perspective. It is the best introduction to Zionist thought available.

The classic Zionist work remains *Der Judenstaat* (*The Jewish State*), written in 1896, in which Theodor Herzl (1860–1904), the founder of political Zionism, described his envisioned Jewish commonwealth. This small book, available in English translation, should be read by everyone who desires an understanding of the rise of Jewish nationalism. One of the most interesting personalities among the early Zionist theorists was Moses Hess (1812–1875), who was an early associate of Karl Marx. He was, in his youth, a fervent disciple of revolution and communism, and broke with Marx and Engels on the issues of the materialistic interpretation of history and the theory of the class struggle. Later he realized the importance of his Jewishness and had a profound insight into the role of the Jewish people as the bearers of the idea of social justice and of the importance of a Jewish commonwealth to put this idea into concrete realization. Hess's work, *Rome and Jerusalem* (1862), is an expression of the kind of idealism that motivated the early pioneers in Palestine. Sir Isaiah Berlin has written a penetrating and highly readable account of the ideology of Moses Hess in a booklet, *The Life and Opinions of Moses Hess.*

The most important ideologue of "cultural Zionism," stressing the role of the Zionist movement in the revival of the Jewish national spirit, was Asher Ginzberg (1856–1927) who assumed the pen name of Ahad Ha-Am, "one of the people." The reader will find his most important writings in the *Selected Essays of Achad Ha-Am* (1912). His essays set the ideological tone of the movement for a long time, and are of decisive importance in understanding its development.

Martin Buber, a lifelong Zionist, has written what is probably the best description of the development of the Zionist idea in his book *Israel and Palestine: The History of an Idea* (1952). This volume contains essays on the main trends in the development of the Zionist concept with emphasis on the religious element.

Of special interest in understanding the role of Israel in Jewish thought and life is Abraham J. Heschel's *Israel: An Echo of Eternity* (1968) in which the philosopher evokes the resonances which the Holy Land produces in the Jewish soul.

One of the most interesting aspects of the Jewish revival in Israel has been the development of the communal settlements—the *kibbutzim.* These settlements were created as experiments in a new type of social life and have attracted worldwide attention. Melford Spiro's *The Kibbutz: Venture in Utopia* (1956) gives a good description of the ideology of the *kibbutzim.*

The student is also directed to the periodical literature. *The Jewish Frontier* and *Midstream* are both excellent Zionist journals. Practically every Jewish periodical deals with some aspect of Israeli life, and every Zionist organization publishes its own magazine. In addition, the Herzl Press specializes in publications on Zionism and Israel, and the Zionist Archives and Library is the major repository in this country.

For an overview of the non-Zionist and even anti-Zionist trends within Judaism, Michael Selzer's *Zionism Reconsidered* (1970) is a convenient anthology of writings.

Jewish Socialism:

Jewish socialism, as was stated previously, is not a religious movement. The founders of this movement were, for the most part, anti-religious. However interpreted, their socialist commitment in terms of Jewish ethical values and concerns and their impact on Jewish life was considerable. We therefore include them in this account.

The best short introduction to the ideology and personalities involved in promoting Jewish socialism is that of Abraham Menes, who contributed the article on the Jewish movement in the collection, *The Jewish People, Past and Present* (1948). For a detailed description of the ideology of the founders of the Bund (the Jewish organization of socialist workers in Poland and Russia), the student may consult Koppel Pinson's article "Arkady Kremer, Vladimir Medem and the Ideology of the Jewish Bund," which describes the development of the thought of the leaders of this movement and details their relationship to Jewish life and leadership. Two full-length books about the growth of the Jewish labor movement in Europe—A. L. Patkin's *Origins of the Russian Jewish Labour Movement,* and Bernard Johnpoll's *The Politics of Futility,* deal with the development of the Bund in Poland between the two wars. Both are interesting accounts of the labor movement, although they deal only tangentially with the relationship of the socialist theory of the Bund and traditional Judaism. The work by Hess referred to in the section on Zionism is of importance in this connection. Another pamphlet of interest in the understanding of the movement is *Bund, Galuth Nationalism, Yiddishism,* by Bezalel Sherman (1958).

The movement for religious socialism was part of Zionist history; the sources for that development will be found in Hertzberg's *The Zionist Idea,* alluded to previously. Another departure in the area of religious socialism was Martin Buber who founded a movement for socialism in Germany during the Weimar Republic. Buber's *Paths in Utopia,* though dealing mainly with the history of socialism, does present, especially in the epilogue, his own thesis for a religious socialism. Most interesting is "Three Theses of a Religious Socialism" in *Pointing the Way*. In this essay, Buber expounds his dialogic philosophy as a basis for a socialism which escapes the traps of both collectivism and individualism: True community leads to socialism.   [s.s.]

V.

JEWISH THINKERS FROM MENDELSSOHN TO THE PRESENT

In the Middle Ages, Jewish philosophy owed its origin to the encounter of Judaism with Greek-Islamic philosophy. A number of thinkers attempted to reconcile their ancestral faith with the truths of regnant philosophical systems or to set forth the substance of Jewish faith in terms of the conceptual tools supplied by Plato, the Neoplatonists, Aristotle and his commentators.

A similar development took place since the eighteenth century, when European (especially German) Jews left the ghetto and encountered the philosophical systems of modern and secular thinkers. Beginning with Mendelssohn, a number of thinkers tried to explicate Judaism in accordance with, and sometimes in opposition to, contemporary philosophies. Thus the rationalism of the German Enlightenment—Kant, Schelling, Hegel, Neo-Kantianism in Europe and pragmatism and naturalism in America—are the backdrop against which the story of modern Jewish philosophy unfolds, whether by thinkers who expound the doctrines of Judaism through the conceptual apparatus of such secular philosophers as, in the case of Mendelssohn, Leibniz-Wolff, in the case of Formstecher, Schelling, of Samuel Hirsch, Hegel, and of Hermann Cohen, Kant; or, in opposition to dominant systems, as Solomon Ludwig Steinheim against Kant and Hegel, or Franz Rosenzweig, who repudiated the philosophy of Hegel. Of course, the relationship between Jewish philosophers of religion and general philosophy has not always been simply a one-way street. Especially since the first World War, some Jewish thinkers have developed their own original approaches which, in turn, have affected general philosophy—most notably, of course, the I-Thou philosophy of Buber, which has influenced philosophical anthropology and existential philosophy.

1. Moses Mendelssohn (1729–1786) was both a philosopher of the European Enlightenment and the inaugurator of modern Jewish religious thought. Although these two strands were united in his personal life, the attempt to reconcile them philosophically proved less than successful. As a son of the Enlightenment he believed that the basic ideas of the religion of reason, the existence of a wise and beneficent God, the immortality of the soul, and the universal moral law are available to all men. To limit these truths to the recipients of a particular revelation, such as Israel, would contradict the goodness of the Creator and the dignity of human reason. The eternal truths necessary for human happiness and blessedness cannot therefore depend on revelation. Thus we see that Mendelssohn, writing as a general philosopher, tried to demonstrate the existence of God in his *Morgenstunden* (1785; *Morning Hours, or about the Existence of God*), and the immortality of the soul in his *Phädon* (1767) as doctrines of rational religion and general metaphysics. Judaism presupposes these truths of natural religion. It reveals no eternal truths of its own, but functions to strengthen and maintain among its adherents the pure beliefs of rational universal religion. Thus Judaism is not revealed *religion* but revealed *legislation*. Mendelssohn developed this concept of Judaism in his *Jerusalem* (1783) and a number of other publications and letters. Most of these (except for some repetitions) are now available in a modern English translation, *Jerusalem and Other Jewish Writings,* translated and edited by Alfred Jospe (1969). His collected works, *Gesammelte Schriften* was published in 7 volumes (Leipzig, 1843–1845); of a critical new edition (Jubiläumsausgabe), only seven volumes appeared (1929–32, 1938) before the rise of Nazism brought this undertaking to a halt. The standard biography of Mendelssohn is by Meyer Kayserling, *Moses Mendelssohn: Sein Leben und seine Werke* (Leipzig, 1862). In addition to the brief introduction to this volume the student should read Jospe's more detailed essay on Mendelssohn in *Great Jewish Personalities in Modern Times* (1960), edited by Simon Noveck, pp. 11–38. A vivid depiction of Mendelssohn against the background of his time

is found in Shalom Spiegel's *Hebrew Reborn* (1930). Excellent expositions of Mendelssohn's thought are presented in Julius Guttmann, *Philosophies of Judaism* (1956) and Nathan Rotenstreich, *Jewish Philosophy in Modern Times.* The reader is also referred to Mordecai M. Kaplan, *The Greater Judaism in the Making*; Arthur A. Cohen, the *Natural and the Supernatural Jew*, and the detailed paper by Isaac Eisenstein Barzilay, "Moses Mendelssohn, A Study in Ideas and Attitudes," in the *Jewish Quarterly Review,* Vol. 52 #1 (July 1961) and #2 (October 1961).

2. Samuel Hirsch (1815–1889) attempted to elucidate Judaism in terms of Hegel's philosophy; at the same time, as a *Jewish* Hegelian, he tried to correct Hegel's image of Judaism. He differs from Hegel by making the true religion the radical alternative to all kinds of paganism and not the comprehensive system which includes all their partial truths. The God of Judaism is asserted to be a present and transcendent God, the Creator and Lord of nature, not dependent on man's action for his reality. Hirsch affirms man's freedom to decide for or against God; yet he also denies the possibility of a divine-human relationship, while at the same time affirming the fact of divine revelations in history which are actual incursions of God. This contradiction is never solved in Hirsch's system.

His book *Die Religionsphilosophie der Juden* (1842) was not translated into English, and the English-speaking reader is referred to the following for expositions of his philosophy: Julius Guttmann, *Philosophies of Judaism;* Jacob B. Agus, *Modern Philosophies of Judaism;* Nathan Rotenstreich, *Jewish Philosophy in Modern Times* and Mordecai M. Kaplan, *The Greater Judaism in the Making.* The most lucid and penetrating study of Hirsch's system is Emil L. Fackenheim, "Samuel Hirsch and Hegel: A Study of Hirsch's *Religionsphilosophie der Juden* (1842)," in *Studies in Nineteenth-Century Jewish Intellectual History,* edited by Alexander Altmann (1964).

3. Solomon Formstecher (1808–1889) was another thinker who tried to depict Judaism in terms of German Idealistic philosophy. His work *Die Religion des Geistes* (*The Religion of the Spirit;* 1841) uses the ideas of Schelling to expound Judaism and manages to express Jewish ethical monotheism by not only subordinating nature to spirit, but by also subordinating the esthetic sphere to

the ethical one, thus diverging from Schelling's pantheistic nature philosophy. Expositions of Formstecher's system can be found in: Julius Guttman, *Philosophies of Judaism*; Jacob B. Agus, *Modern Philosophies of Judaism*; Nathan Rotenstreich, *Jewish Philosophy in Modern Times* and Mordecai M. Kaplan, *The Greater Judaism in the Making*.

4. A thinker who propounded an interpretation of Judaism opposed to the rationalistic systems of his time was Solomon Ludwig Steinheim (1789–1886). By profession a physician, his original and suggestive ideas were largely ignored by his contemporaries and successors, although he anticipated some of the ideas of such twentieth-century thinkers as Franz Rosenzweig and Yehezkel Kaufmann, the historian of Jewish religion. His chief work, *Die Offenbarung nach dem Lehrbegriff der Synagoge. (Revelation according to the Doctrine of the Synagogue;* 1835–1865) appeared in four volumes over a period of thirty years and contains a good deal of repetitious material. It is an attack on speculative reason and tries to validate revelation as the foundation of Judaism. However, he does not oppose rationalism in the name of feeling, subjective faith, or authority. Using the Kantian doctrine that critical reason is able to point to its own limits, he tries to show that speculative reason, although unable to attain a priori knowledge of reality, can admit the truth proclaimed by revelation as the most adequate explanation of reality when confronted with it.

Unaided human reason as expressed in natural religion, paganism, and philosophy is based on the idea of necessity; revelation, on the idea of freedom. Thus the God of speculative reason is subject to the law of causality. The rational principle that *ex nihilo nihil fit* precludes the possibility that material reality should have had an absolute, temporal beginning. The teaching of revelation as it appears in the Bible is based on freedom and proclaims God as the Creator of a world that is good. Steinheim asserts that, far from being irrational, the teachings of revelation are more adequate to empirical reality than the constructions of speculative reason. Thus man's self-consciousness, as a free and responsible moral agent, can only make sense in the light of revelation's doctrine of freedom, while reason's two a priori principles of necessity, namely that (1) every effect has a cause and (2) that nothing comes out of nothing, lead to contradictions.

Steinheim's work is not available in English. For expositions of his thought the reader should consult Guttmann, Agus, Rotenstreich and the informative article by Joshua O. Haberman, "Solomon Ludwig Steinheim's Doctrine of Revelation" in *Judaism,* Vol. 17 (Winter 1968), pp. 22–41. A German volume, issued on the occasion of the hundredth anniversary of his death by Hans-Joachim Schoeps, *Salomon Ludwig Steinheim zum Gedenken* (1966), contains papers on Steinheim, extracts from his published works and some hitherto unprinted pieces and letters.

5. Nachman Krochmal (1785–1840), one of the great pioneers of Jewish scholarship, was the first modern thinker to develop a Jewish philosophy of history. His remarkable system, based on German idealism, especially Hegel, attempts to uncover an inner pattern in the history of Israel. Combining the concepts of medieval Jewish Neo-Platonic ontology with Hegelian notions of Spirit as the process of alienation and reintegration in time, he fashioned a new systematic historiosophy. Each nation represents a distinct "national spirit" which informs all the various aspects of its life and culture. But since each national culture embodies only a limited aspect of Spirit and thus manifests only a special spiritual substance, its duration must come to an end when it has passed through its finite cycle of growth, maturity and decline. Only Israel, being grounded in Absolute Spirit is not subject to this law of decay, but after each cycle of growth, maturity, and decline renews itself and begins a new period of creativity and development.

The Guide for the Perplexed of the Times (*Moreh Nevukhe ha-Zeman),* Krochmal's work on Jewish history and historiosophy in Hebrew was edited and published posthumously by Leopold Zunz. A good essay on its author and his scholarly contributions can be found in Solomon Schechter's *Studies in Judaism.* Shalom Spiegel's *Hebrew Reborn* contains a fascinating chapter on Krochmal's life and background. For expositions of his thought the reader ought to consult Guttmann, Rotenstreich and Mordecai Kaplan, and also the following two articles: Ismar Schorsch, "The Philosophy of History of Nachman Krochmal" in *Judaism,* Vol. 10

(Summer 1961), pp. 237–245 and Jacob Taubes, "Nachman Krochmal and Modern Historicism" in *Judaism*, Vol. 12 (Spring 1963), pp. 150–164. A few central paragraphs of Krochmal's *Guide* with expository comments are published in Louis Jacobs' *Jewish Thought Today*, pp. 131–135.

6. Samuel David Luzzatto (1800–1865), like Nachman Krochmal, is chiefly known for his contributions to the *Wissenschaft des Judentums*, and made his mark as a major philologian and minor poet. Nevertheless his contribution to Jewish theology is noteworthy, although his temperament was basically non-philosophical and anti-rationalistic. As a professor at the Rabbinical College in Padua, Italy he also taught theology, and his writings on this subject (in Hebrew and Italian) are related to this aspect of his career. Luzzatto opposed the attempts of philosophical theologians like Maimonides to reconcile Jewish religion and Greek philosophy and maintained that these two represent incompatible world views. Philosophy aims at truth, Judaism at morality. To "Atticism" the highest value is intellectual understanding, to "Abrahamism," the faith which originated with the patriarchs and was codified and spelled out in the period of Moses, the highest value is compassion. He identifies philosophy with naturalism and religious supernaturalism with the pursuit of ethics. Judaism as a moral discipline embraces all of life, and faith in God and his revealed laws are the basic preconditions for the attainment of ethical living.

An English translation of Luzzatto's work, *The Foundations of the Torah* appeared in 1965 and forms a part of Noah H. Rosenbloom's book *Luzzatto's Ethico-Psychological Interpretation of Judaism*. A good summary of his thought is presented in the second chapter of Agus' *Jewish Philosophy in Modern Times* and very briefly in M. M. Kaplan's *The Greater Judaism in the Making*. An excellent treatment of Luzzatto the man, scholar, and poet is presented in Sh. Spiegel's *Hebrew Reborn*.

7. Hermann Cohen (1842–1918) is the only academic philosopher of the nineteenth century who made a major contribution to Jewish religious thought. Founder of the Marburg school of Neo-Kantianism, he began his career with a series of works expounding

and interpreting Kant from the viewpoint of absolute idealism. He followed this with three works in which he presented his own system, *Logic of Pure Knowledge (Die Logik der reinen Erkenntnis)* (1902), *Ethics of Pure Will (Die Ethik des reinen Willens)* (1904) and *Aesthetics of Pure Feeling (Die Aesthetik des reinen Gefühls)* (1912). The God concept in this system remains that of an idea within the Kantian meaning of that term, needed to link the realms of natural science and ethics and to validate the ethical ideal in reality. "God means that the duration of nature is guaranteed as surely as morality is eternal." After his retirement from the University of Marburg he produced his own original philosophy of Judaism in which the center of his philosophical interest shifted from ethics to religion. In 1915 he published *The Concept of Religion within the System of Philosophy (Der Begriff der Religion im System der Philosophie)*. His mature philosophy of Judaism found its fullest expression in his magnum opus, *Religion of Reason from the Sources of Judaism (Religion der Vernunft aus den Quellen des Judentums)* published posthumously in 1919 (2nd edition, 1929). Cohen's collected essays, articles and addresses on Jewish topics were published in three volumes under the title *Jüdische Schriften* (Jewish Writings) in 1924 with a long introductory essay by Franz Rosenzweig which is probably the most brilliant and illuminating piece written on Cohen's contribution to Jewish thought.

Although Cohen's work had not been translated into English, except for a few short selections (for which the reader should turn to *Contemporary Jewish Thought,* edited by Simon Noveck [pp. 133-173]), now, for the first time, a volume of selections from his Jewish writings has appeared in English under the title *Reason and Hope* (1971) in a translation by Eva Jospe.

From *Religion of Reason*—one chapter (XIII) on "The Day of Atonement" was published in English in *Judaism* magazine Vol. 17 #3 (1968) and Vol. 18 (1969) #1 and #2. A section from his *Ethics of Pure Will* with an interpretive preface by Steven S. Schwarzschild was presented in English in *Judaism* Vol. 14 #4 (Fall 1966).

Mordecai M. Kaplan in his book *The Purpose and Meaning of Jewish Existence* (1964) gives an almost 200-page epitome of

Cohen's *Religion of Reason* with critical comments. This is certainly a valuable contribution in the absence of a full translation, but in no way can it serve as a substitute for the author's original formulations. Jehuda Melber's *Herman Cohen's Philosophy of Judaism* (1968) is another analysis of Cohen's thoughts.

Excellent expositions of Cohen's thought are contained in Guttmann, Agus, and Rotenstreich. A more popular treatment is found in Samuel H. Bergman. The reader is also referred to the relevant sections of Borowitz and Arthur A. Cohen.

Finally, the question whether Cohen's thought in the *Religion of Reason* is still part of his system of speculative idealism or whether it constitutes a decisive breakthrough towards a philosophy of dialogue and existentialism, as claimed by Rosenzweig, is treated with scholarly skill and thoroughness in A. Altmann's paper "Hermann Cohens Begriff der Korrelation" in the Siegfried Moses Jubilee Volume *In zwei Welten* (1962).

8. Leo Baeck (1874–1956), one of the leading liberal rabbis in Germany, is perhaps best known for his fortitude in giving leadership to the threatened Jewish community under the Nazi regime and refusing to abandon his people in their hour of crisis. He was deported to Theresienstadt concentration camp and survived the war, continuing his teaching and writing career in England and America until his death. Baeck, who was a theologian rather than a philosopher, shows the influence of Hermann Cohen. His major work *The Essence of Judaism* (1905; the second greatly expanded edition of 1922 constitutes almost a new book), was stimulated by Harnack's popular book *The Essence of Christianity*. Although agreeing with Cohen on the primacy of ethics in the Jewish religion, Baeck refused to see it as exclusively defined in this way and tried to understand Judaism in terms of its peculiar religious consciousness.

The English-speaking reader is fortunate in having most of Baeck's writings available in very good translations, especially *The Essence of Judaism,* translated by V. Grubenwieser and L. Pearl (1948), and *Judaism and Christianity* (1958), a collection of essays, translated and with a stimulating biographical introduction by Walter Kaufmann. Perhaps the best insight into Baeck's theology can be gained from two essays included in the latter volume: "Mystery and Commandment" and "Romantic Religion." Brief selections from Baeck's writings are also included in *Contemporary Jewish Thought: A Reader,* edited by Simon Noveck (1963). Good treatments of his thought can be found in Eugene Borowitz, *A New Jewish Theology in the Making,* Arthur A. Cohen, *The Natural and the Supernatural Jew,* and in *Great Jewish Thinkers of the Twentieth Century,* edited by Simon Noveck. The most detailed study of Leo Baeck's lifework is Albert H. Friedlander, *Leo Baeck: Teacher of Theresienstadt* (1968), a full-length sympathetic exposition which also contains a detailed bibliography.

9. Franz Rosenzweig (1886–1929) is one of the most important Jewish thinkers of our time. Finding his way back to Judaism from a background of modern secularism and Hegelian philosophy he produced his magnum opus, *Der Stern der Erlösung (The Star of Redemption)* toward the end of the First World War. Until recently, neither this work nor the bulk of his smaller works (collected in his *Kleinere Schriften*) were available in English.

At long last the *Star of Redemption* has been published in English (1971). William W. Hallo's translation of this highly complex work, written in rich and subtle German full of literary allusions, is a major achievement and will, for the first time, enable English-speaking philosophers and theologians to evaluate the author's system.

Rosenzweig, who began as a Hegelian, takes his starting point from the philosophy of German idealism which he submits to a destructive critique, claiming that philosophy, from Thales to Hegel, belies its claim to an understanding of reality without presuppositions, since all the great systems assumed that the three basic elements of prephilosophical experience, God(s), Man and World could be reduced to one common element. This monistic fallacy led to cosmologies in which God and man were understood as parts of nature; theologies where a mystical reduction of man and world into the Godhead was asserted and, in the final development in Hegel, to anthropological idealism, where God and world are reduced to forms of Thought or consciousness understanding itself. Against these reductivisms, he sets ancient Greek pagan consciousness which experienced the three elements in isolation as the plastic cosmos, the Olympian gods, and the tragic human hero of Attic tragedy. The teaching of the Bible sees these three elements neither as isolated nor as identical, but as related: Between God and world there is the relation of creation; between God and man, revelation; and between man and world (and God) there is the relationship of redemption. To Rosenzweig the central category is revelation in which man experiences himself as reached by God's love. Rosenzweig developed (under the influence of his friend, Eugen Rosenstock) a method of "language thinking" *(grammatisches Denken)* in which the abstract, timeless structure of traditional logic is replaced by the living forms of speech which define and constitute the possible modes of human existence. Thus the narrative is the typical expression of the facticity of created things, the I-thou dialogue is the form of revelation, and the common "we" form of the choral praise anticipates the future redemption. Rosenzweig's break with Hegelianism led him to an existentialism which anticipated many insights and ideas of such philosophers as Heidegger, and his linguistic thinking bears a striking similarity to Buber and Ebner who developed their ideas independently around the same time. His *Star of Redemption* is remarkable for its blending of this New Thinking (as its author calls it) with a profound exploration and interpretation of traditional Judaism in the light of Rosenzweig's philosophical approach.

For the English-speaking reader Nahum N. Glatzer's valuable *Franz Rosenzweig: His Life and Thought* (1961) is required reading. After the editor's introduction, the first part of the book presents Rosenzweig's life through well-chosen extracts from letters and diaries, while the second part contains selections from his work. Indispensable as this volume is, it does not contain sufficiently lengthy extracts from the *Star* and other writings to give an adequate understanding of Rosenzweig's system. Glatzer also edited a minor work by Rosenzweig, *Understanding the Sick and Healthy* (1954), in which the author tried to give a popular summary of the main ideas of his *Star* but which he thought inadequate, and whose publication he refused to allow during his lifetime. *On Jewish Learning* (1955) contains three papers by Rosenzweig and some interesting letters (including an exchange with Martin Buber). For an exposition of Rosenzweig's thought the reader is referred to the following books: Agus, *Modern Philosophies of Judaism*, Guttmann,

Philosophies of Judaism, Bergman, *Faith and Reason,* Schwarz-schild's pamphlet, *Franz Rosenzweig: Guide of Reversioners* (1960), Bernard Martin's *Great Twentieth-Century Jewish Philosophers* (1970), Arthur A. Cohen, *The Natural and the Supernatural Jew,* N. Rotenstreich, *Jewish Philosophy in Modern Times* and Nahum Glatzer's essay in *Great Jewish Thinkers of the Twentieth Century* edited by Simon Noveck. Rosenzweig's correspondence with his friend, Eugen Rosenstock, together with essays on its meaning by Alexander Altmann and Dorothy M. Emmett, and additional comments by Rosenstock under the title *Judaism Despite Christianity,* have been edited by Eugen Rosenstock-Huessy (1969). The reader who understands German should go to the sources: *Der Stern der Erlösung* (first edition, 1920; second edition, 1930; third edition, 1954); *Kleinere Schriften* (1937) and *Briefe* (1935), the latter over 700 pages of letters which contain much valuable material on the life and thought of the author. A study on the *Stern* by Else Freund, *Die Existenzphilosophie Franz Rosenzweigs* (second edition, 1959) though technical, is useful, and Bernard Casper, a Catholic philosophy professor, has an excellent and extended chapter on Rosenzweig in his work, *Das dialogische Denken* (1967).

Rosenzweig's "Philosophy of Speech" *(Sprachdenken)* is treated in Harold Stahmer, *"Speak that I May See Thee!": The Religious Significance of Language* (1968), and in Rivka Horwitz, "Franz Rosenzweig on Language," in *Judaism,* Vol. 13, #4 (Fall 1964); his views of history, in Alexander Altmann, "Franz Rosenzweig on History," in *Between East and West,* edited by Alexander Altmann (1958). [F.A.R.]

10. Martin Buber (1878–1965) is the best-known Jewish philosopher and thinker of our time. His work is studied among all groups and he has made his mark not only on religion, but also on psychoanalysis, art, literature, sociology and politics. Though Buber's thought is drawn—according to his own testimony—from Jewish sources and ideas, there is, nonetheless, some question about the Jewishness of some of his writings; but there is no doubt that contemporary Judaism in all its phases bears the mark of Buber's thought and terminology. The literature on Buber and the publica-

tions of Buber are enormous. The Bialik Institute in Jerusalem has published a bibliography of his writings, including various editions and translations up to 1957. The bibliography, which contains 852 items, was compiled by Moché Catane. Additional bibliographies are available in Hans Kohn's *Martin Buber: Sein Werk und seine Zeit* (1930 and now reprinted) and Maurice S. Friedman's *Martin Buber: The Life of Dialogue* (1955). The student is also directed to the annual *Yearbooks* of the Leo Baeck Institute which contain references to articles, books, and other publications dealing with Buber (and with other German-Jewish personalities).

Buber's most influential work is his *I and Thou,* published in German in 1923. The book was first translated into English by Ronald Gregor Smith with a postscript by the author. An excellent new translation with a very interesting introduction by Walter Kaufmann now exists which should supersede previous ones. Kaufmann insists on the use of I-You instead of I-Thou, on the grounds that the latter usage is an archaism in English, and, therefore, removes the immediacy and intimacy of the dialogue.

A paragraph-by-paragraph analysis of *I and Thou* has been published by Robert E. Wood, entitled *Martin Buber's Ontology: An Analysis of I and Thou* (1969). Wood includes references to other works by Buber in which some of the themes in *I and Thou* are discussed and expanded. The work is sometimes quite technical, but it is a useful tool for teachers and students.

First published in 1913, *Daniel* (translated into English by Maurice Friedman in 1964) is a poetical philosophical work which predated *I and Thou.* This book is useful in understanding the transition that Buber made from his early mysticism to his later philosophy of dialogue. The English edition contains a long introductory essay of Maurice S. Friedman setting the work in retrospect and perspective. *Between Man and Man* (1948) contains some of Buber's most famous essays on the general question of dialogue. These include "Dialogue and the Question to the Single One" (which is an answer to Kierkegaard). The final section contains Buber's inaugural lectures at the Hebrew University, "What Is Man?" in which he surveys the history of philosophical anthropology and shows that the reality of man is grasped not by individualism or collectivism but by focusing on the mutual relationships between man and man. Another collection of important essays on the dialogue principle is *The Knowledge of Man* (1965) edited with an introductory essay by Maurice Friedman. The book analyzes the nature of man—Buber's continuous concern—and concludes with a dialogue between Buber and Carl R. Rogers, the psychotherapist.

Buber's specifically Jewish concerns, and his reflections on the meaning of Judaism, have been collected in a volume entitled *On Judaism* (1967) edited by Nahum Glatzer. This book contains addresses delivered by Buber between 1909 and 1918 when he was in his thirties. They have been widely disseminated and discussed. Addresses delivered between 1939 and 1951 (three of them delivered in the United States) represent Buber's more mature thought on the nature of Judaism. They include the powerful "The Dialogue Between Heaven and Earth," a theological reflection on the problem of evil, especially as it impinges on the Holocaust. The last of these addresses has also been published in a separate book, *At The Turning: Three Addresses on Judaism* (1952). Buber describes *Israel and the World* (1948), a highly readable and influential series of essays on the problems of Judaism in the modern world, as a "discussion of the encounter between the historic spirit of Israel and a world which regards it as foreign, incomprehensible, or irrelevant." The essays were written over a period of thirty years and cover Zionism, the meaning of biblical life, and Jewish religiosity.

In *The Eclipse of God: Studies in the Relation Between Religion and Philosophy* (1952), Buber deals with the problems raised by modern philosophy and psychoanalysis for religion and theology. These essays (originally lectures) are important elements in his philosophic system. The title indicates Buber's belief that there are periods when the relationships between man and God are disturbed. This represents a period of eclipse—not of God's absence.

Buber, perhaps more than any other contemporary Jewish writer, has been responsible for bringing the treasures of Hasidic spirituality to the attention of Jews and non-Jews who have not had access to the original sources. His two volumes, *Tales of the Hasidim: The Early Masters* (1947) and *Tales of the Hasidim: The Later Masters* (1947) have attained the status of classics. *The Ten Rungs: Hasidic*

Sayings (1947), a brief book, gives the best of the Hasidic sayings. *The Way of Man According to the Teachings of Hasidism* (1951), another brief book, utilizes Hasidic tales and their lessons to instruct those who wish to learn something about Hasidic spirituality. Buber's novel, *For the Sake of Heaven* (1944), whose setting is Eastern Europe during the Napoleonic wars, is an evocation of the life of the Hasidic masters and their striving for spiritual redemption in the midst of war and political upheaval. Buber has devoted special volumes to individual members, e.g., *Tales of Rabbi Nachman* (1956) which includes an essay on Jewish mysticism, "The Legend of Baal Shem" and "The Legends of the Great Maggid." These books were collected in an earlier German edition, *Die Chassidischen Bücher* (1927).

His views of Hasidism have been collected in two volumes: *Hasidism* (1948), essays on the beginnings of the movement and some of its symbols; and *Hasidism and Modern Man* (1960), edited and translated by Maurice S. Friedman, an exposition of the Hasidic way as well as an autobiographical essay, "My Way to Hasidism." The book includes the collection, *The Way of Man According to the Teachings of Hasidism* (see above) and a translation of some of the writings ascribed to its founder, Israel Baal Shem Tov (1700–1760). It is a valuable introduction to Buber's understanding of Hasidism and of the philosophy of religion. Buber avers that he was introduced to the idea of the I-Thou through his Hasidic reading and experience. Therefore, the study of these texts and their interpretation would seem to be an interesting and profitable beginning for the student wishing to understand him.

Buber has made significant contributions to the understanding and appreciation of the Hebrew Scriptures. Outstanding is his translation of the Hebrew Bible into German. This work (begun with the collaboration of Franz Rosenzweig) is considered a classic in German literature. It is an attempt to capture the beauty and rhythm of the original rather than to paraphrase it into idiomatic German. Some notion of the translation's quality is given by Walter Kaufmann in *The Philosophy of Martin Buber* (1967) (p. 674).

King James: Samaria shall become desolate; for she hath re-
                     belled against her God; they shall fall by the
                     sword; their infants shall be dashed in pieces,
                     and their women with child shall be ripped up.
Revised Standard: Samaria shall bear her guilt, because she has re-
                     belled against her God; they shall fall by the
                     sword, their little ones shall be dashed in pieces,
                     and their pregnant women ripped open.
After Buber: Atone must Samaria the guilt that it was ob-
                     stinate to its God. By the sword they must fall,
                     their toddlers are smashed, their pregnant women
                     slashed.

Buber utilizes his I-Thou philosophy to interpret the stages of Israelite religion and the essence of biblical faith. (For two interesting discussions of his contributions to biblical scholarship see the essays by Nahum Glatzer and James Muilenburg in *The Philosophy of Martin Buber*.) Of great importance is *The Prophetic Faith* (1950). Buber describes the aim of the book thusly: "The task of this book is to describe a teaching which reached its completion in some of the writing prophets from the last decades of the Northern kingdom to the return from the Babylonian exile, and to describe it both as regards its historical process and as regards its antecedents. This is the teaching about the relation between the God of Israel and Israel." Buber's history of biblical faith goes back to the beginnings of Israelite religion and is an imaginative as well as solidly based description of the unfolding of the biblical way of life and thought. *Moses* (1952) is a masterful presentation of the life of the founder of Judaism. The introductory essay, "Saga and History," describes Buber's attitude toward the use of Scripture for history. In *Good and Evil* (1953), Buber presents specific interpretations of some psalms and some themes in the Hebrew Bible. He develops the tool of focusing on the "key words" in any passage; that is, words that are repeated in various sentences. It is these words which can serve as an exegetical tool in getting at the main concern of the author of the passages. Buber's collection, *The Kingship of God* (1932) explains the meaning of Jewish faith in early biblical times, especially its attempt to create a Jewish polity which would dispense with earthly government and live in response to God who was to be the theo-political head of the community.

Buber was one of the historians and the theoreticians of Zionism. His view did not concur with the political orientation of the important Zionist leaders. He saw the resettlement of the Holy Land as an opportunity for the Jewish spirit to find a new home where it could renew and revive its ancient *élan*.

Israel and Palestine: The History of an Idea (1952) is a history of the idea of Zion and the Holy Land in the faith of Israel. It begins with the biblical idea and continues to discuss the concept of Zion in the writings of great Jewish figures as well as in Zionist thinkers. *Israel and Palestine* can serve as an introduction to the idea of national renaissance in Judaism. *Paths in Utopia* (1950), though not concerned only with the Zionist enterprise, gives the reader a philosophical and historical perspective on the development of the *kibbutzim* (communes) in Israel. Buber discusses the underlying assumptions of socialism in its various forms—Marxist, communist, utopian—and concludes with an essay on the *kibbutz*, an experiment which did not fail.

Several collections of Buber's shorter statements on the problems of existence and social philosophy can serve as good introductions. Buber's views of community are explained in "Pointing the Way" in *Collected Essays* (1957) edited by Maurice Friedman. Of special importance is the essay, "Three Theses of a Religious Socialism," in which he attempts to ground his socialism, not in Marxism, but in a dialogical relationship between members of a community. A comprehensive collection also edited by Maurice Friedman is *A Believing Humanism* (1967) which is part of the Credo Perspectives series. Here a wide area of concerns is covered from education to psychoanalysis and will be read with great profit. Another collection of smaller pieces is provided by Nahum Glatzer in *The Way of Response: Martin Buber* (1966).

There has been a voluminous literature on the writings of Buber and analyses of his thought. In America one of the first was Agus in *Modern Philosophies of Judaism* (1941), which is based on the then available writings of Buber. Maurice Friedman's *Martin Buber: The Life of Dialogue* (1955) is a painstaking analysis of all Buber's creativity, and Malcolm Diamond's *Martin Buber: Jewish Existentialist* (1960) is more focused on Buber's religious philosophy. Both are excellent handbooks. Arthur A. Cohen's small volume, *Martin Buber* (1957) is impressionistic but extremely evocative. *The Philosophy of Martin Buber* (1967), part of the Library of Living Philosophers series is an excellent analysis of aspects of Buberian thought by a group of experts and also includes replies by Buber to his critics. Very useful is *Philosophical Interrogations* (1964), edited by Sydney and Beatrice Rome, in which several scholars and writers pose questions to Buber and give him an opportunity to reply.

Finally, Buber's critique and analysis of Christianity, *Two Types of Faith* (1950), in which he explains the differences of faith *in (emuna)* and faith *that (pistis),* is a most important analysis of Christian spirituality from the Jewish point of view.

The definitive edition of Buber's writings in German, arranged by the author himself, is Martin Buber, *Werke,* three volumes, (1962–63) and the additional volume, *Der Jude und sein Judentum: Gesammelte Aufsätze und Reden,* with an introduction by Robert Weltsch (1963).

11. Mordecai M. Kaplan (1881–   ) served for half a century as a teacher of rabbis and religious teachers in his capacity as dean of the Teachers Institute and professor at the Jewish Theological Seminary. He is the founder of the Reconstructionist movement, which calls for a total restructuring of the philosophical, theological, and organizational forms of Judaism. His thought, based on naturalism, pragmatism, and sociology has been analyzed in a series of books by Professor Kaplan and by his disciples.

Judaism as a Civilization, generally considered his magnum opus, was first published in 1934. In it, Kaplan outlines his proposals for the restructuring of Judaism; he criticizes the other versions of Judaism as being inadequate to meet the crisis which modern science, political theory and sociology pose to an ancient faith, and he suggests that Judaism be seen as a civilization; that is to say, that the distinctive quality of Judaism should not be understood in terms of religious dogma and principle. "Judaism is something far more comprehensive than Jewish religion. It includes that nexus of history, literature, language, social organization, folk sanctions, standards of conduct, social and spiritual ideals, esthetic values, which in their totality form a civilization." Kaplan discusses his

views about the way Jewish life should be organized and his view
of God as "the Power that makes for salvation." It is a thorough
program for Jewish life. Kaplan elaborates upon these themes in
The Future of the American Jew (1948), in which he discusses
other problems of Jewish faith such as the problem of evil, the place
of women, the role of Jewish law, etc., and in *The Greater Judaism
in the Making: A Study of the Modern Evolution of Judaism*
(1960). In this volume Kaplan gives a historical survey of the
growth of the important movements of Judaism and concludes the
reinterpretation of Jewish faith in naturalistic terms and the interpretation of Jewish life in civilizational terms. In *The Meaning of
God in Modern Jewish Religion* (1937), Dr. Kaplan reinterprets
traditional terms and concepts in Jewish faith in his distinctive way
—asking how the terms functioned in the past and how they can
function today in a new universe of discourse. As the title indicates,
the main interest of the author is in the idea of God. *Judaism Without Supernaturalism* (1958), is a collection of essays on problems
in Jewish ideology, and *Questions Jews Ask* (1966) are replies Dr.
Kaplan has given to audiences all around the country. His latest
volume is *The Religion of Ethical Nationhood* (1970) in which he
applies Reconstructionist ideology to the problem of nation-states.
Kaplan believes that Judaism can show the way toward the creation
of national entities which will be dedicated not to power but to
ethical values. In addition to these works, Kaplan has written *A
New Zionist* (1955) dealing with the future of the Zionist movement after the establishment of the state of Israel and calling for a
strengthening of ties among Jews around the world.

Mordecai Kaplan's teachings have stimulated a number of disciples to formulate their own versions of Judaism based on the principles of Reconstructionism. Among these volumes are *The Case
for Religious Naturalism* (1958) by Jack J. Cohen which presents
an analysis of religious philosophy and of Judaism in line with the
naturalistic conceptions of some contemporary philosophy. Alan
Miller's *The God of Daniel S.* (1969) is a popular presentation of
Reconstructionist philosophy which takes the form of discussions
with a young Jew, Daniel S., seeking to find his way back to
Judaism. Of special importance is the volume edited by Ira Eisenstein and Eugene Kohn, *Mordecai Kaplan: An Evaluation* (1952),

which contains important essays by Kaplan's disciples analyzing aspects of his thought as well as an important autobiographical essay by Professor Kaplan describing his intellectual metamorphosis. Summaries of Kaplanian thought can be found in volumes previously mentioned especially Agus, *Modern Philosophies of Judaism* and Borowitz, *A New Jewish Theology in the Making.*

A trenchant criticism of Reconstructionist theology is Eliezer Berkovits' "Reconstructionist Theology: A Critical Evaluation," reprinted from *Tradition* (1959). Berkovits, an Orthodox scholar, assails the God-Idea of Kaplan finding it religiously unacceptable. Judaism, says Berkovits, teaches the Living God, and Kaplan's God is a mere abstraction.

A long analytical review of Reconstructionism from the sociological point of view is presented by Charles Liebman in the *American Jewish Yearbook 1970* in which he shows how the principles of Reconstructionism have permeated all aspects of American Jewish life. The periodical *The Reconstructionist* is an important source for the student interested in developments within the circle around Professor Kaplan.   [s.s.]

12. Abraham Joshua Heschel, born in Warsaw in 1907 and descended from a family of Hasidic rabbis, received a traditional Jewish education in Poland, acquired a Western academic education at the University of Berlin, and came to the United States in 1940. His major works appeared in the 1950's and have made him the most widely read living Jewish thinker, not only in America but also in other English-speaking countries and in Europe, where his work is known through translations into French, Italian, and Spanish. His thought, although addressed to the modern reader and his concerns, draws on the total Jewish religious tradition, biblical, rabbinic, medieval, and Hasidic. His lifework consists of two parallel strands—(1) studies and interpretations of classical sources of Judaism which resulted in a number of scholarly publications beginning with *Die Prophetie* (1936; in German), and encompassing rabbinic, medieval, and Hasidic studies; (2) the exposition of his own original philosophy of Judaism and its application to contemporary problems (comprising the bulk of his work written in English). This exposition of his theology is found in his two

major books: *Man Is Not Alone: A Philosophy of Religion* (1951) and *God in Search of Man: A Philosophy of Judaism* (1956).

Religion is defined as the answer to man's ultimate questions. Since modern man is largely alienated from the reality which informs genuine religion, Heschel tries to recover the significant existential questions to which Judaism offers the answer. This leads to a *depth theology* which goes below the surface phenomena of modern doubt and rootlessness and leads to an exposition of the living God of the Bible, who is neither a philosophical abstraction nor a psychological projection, but is a living reality who takes a passionate interest in his creatures. The *divine concern* is the central category of Heschel's philosophy; man's ability to transcend his egocentric interests and to respond with love and devotion to the divine demand is the root of Jewish observance and ethics. This ability to rise to the holy dimension of the divine imperative is the ground of human freedom; the failures and successes of Israel to respond to God's call constitute the drama of Jewish history as seen from the viewpoint of theology. The polarity of law and life, the pattern and the spontaneous, inform all of life and produce the creative tension in which Judaism is a way of prescribed and regular *mitzvot* as well as a spontaneous and always novel reaction of each Jew to the divine reality. Heschel also develops a philosophy of *time* in which the modern tendency to think in spatial categories is contrasted with the Jewish idea of *hallowing time* of which the Sabbath and the holidays are the most outstanding examples.

His thesis that Judaism is a religion of time is developed in *The Sabbath: Its Meaning for Modern Man* (1951). *Man's Quest for God* (1954) contains studies on prayer and symbolism; *The Prophets* (1962) is his major contribution to Biblical theology; his *Theology of Ancient Judaism (Torah min ha-shamayim be-aspaklaryah shel ha-dorot)* in Hebrew (two volumes 1962–65) deals with two major strands in rabbinic thought on the nature of the Torah and revelation. *The Earth Is the Lord's*, originally published in 1950 and now reissued together with *The Sabbath*, deals with the inner life and spirituality of Eastern European Jewry; *The Insecurity of Freedom* (1966) is a collection of essays dealing with contemporary problems; and *Israel: An Echo of Eternity* (1969) deals with the meaning of the land and state of Israel and was

written in the aftermath of the Six Day War. Heschel has planned
to present his philosophical anthropology in a major work and
considers his Stanford University lectures, published under the title
Who Is Man? (1965) as a prolegomenon to such a fully worked
out treatment on the nature of man. Among Heschel's contributions to Jewish-Christian dialogue the reader is referred to the
following two papers: "No Religion Is an Island," in *Union Seminary Quarterly Review,* Vol. 21 #2 (January 1966), and "The
Jewish Notion of God and Christian Renewal," in *Renewal of
Christian Thought,* ed. L. K. Shook, C.S.B. (1967).

For the reader who wants to acquaint himself with Heschel's
thought there are a number of helpful articles and books. *Between
God and Man: An Interpretation of Judaism from the Writings of
Abraham J. Heschel* edited by Fritz A. Rothschild (1959) is a
representative anthology which arranges material from his various
books to display as clearly as possible the underlying systematic
pattern of his thought. It contains an introductory essay by the
editor which tries to present Heschel's basic categories and concepts, to offer the reader a key to his philosophy of religion. It also
has a full bibliography.

A more popular sketch of Heschel's thought is to be found in
Rothschild's chapter on Heschel in *Modern Theologians, Christians
and Jews,* edited by Thomas E. Bird (1967). The Fall 1968 issue
of *Conservative Judaism* contains two papers presented on the occasion of Heschel's sixtieth birthday by Fritz A. Rothschild and Edmond La B. Cherbonnier; a third one dealing with his contributions
to Jewish scholarship by Seymour Siegel was published in Volume
32 of the *Proceedings of the Rabbinical Assembly for 1968.* A perceptive and insightful volume, *The Promise of Heschel* by Franklin
Sherman (1970) is the work of a Lutheran theologian who devotes
his last chapter to Heschel's contribution to the Jewish-Christian
dialogue. Brief expositions of Heschel's theology are also found in
Eugene Borowitz, *A New Jewish Theology in the Making* and
Arthur A. Cohen, *The Natural and the Supernatural Jew.* [F.A.R.]

13. *Contemporary Jewish Thought:* The thinkers and writers
here discussed are mainly Americans and are, for the most part,
writing in English.

a. A writer of particular power and lucidity is Will Herberg.

Herberg, influenced by Niebuhr as well as by Buber and Rosenzweig, is the author of several important volumes which have had
a profound impact on the thought of contemporary Jews. His
Judaism and Modern Man, a superb statement on the main problems of theology and ethics, is written from the standpoint of one
who had previously been committed to a secular ideology and had
found his way back. The spiritual autobiography of Herberg is
contained in his article "From Marxism to Judaism," which appeared first in *Commentary* and was reprinted in *Arguments and
Doctrines* edited by Arthur A. Cohen and is included in the Cohen
anthology alluded to above. His volume, *Protestant, Catholic, Jew,*
which has reached the status of a classic in religious sociology, is
particularly important for contemporary Judaism in that it analyzes
the change in the status of American Jews as a participant in one
of the three "great religions of democracy"—Protestantism, Catholicism, and Judaism. Other articles of Herberg which should be
read to gain an understanding of his view of the role of Judaism
in contemporary life are "Jewish Existence and Survival" and
"Prophetic Faith in an Age of Crisis"—both of them in the first
volume of the periodical, *Judaism,* "The 'Chosenness' of Israel
and the Jew of Today" in *Doctrines and Arguments,* edited by
Arthur A. Cohen, "Religious Trends in American Jewry" in *Judaism,* Vol. 3 (1954), and "Judaism as Personal Decision," in
Conservative Judaism, Vol. 22, #4 (Summer 1968).

b. Louis Jacobs, a British rabbi and scholar, has attempted in
several of his volumes to restate the case for traditional Judaism
in the light of modern philosophy and research. His first important
book, *We Have Reason to Believe* (1957), is especially useful in
regard to the problem of revelation. The *Principles of the Jewish
Faith* has already been mentioned as a survey of Judaism based on
the thirteen articles of faith of Maimonides. A small volume, *Jewish
Values* (1960), is made up of discussions of some of the values of
Jewish spirituality. His volume *Faith* is a useful introduction to the
problem of the meaning and validation of faith in the light of
modern philosophy and thought. Jacobs is one of the few Jewish
writers who deals with the problems posed by the school of British
Linguistic Analysis. Jacobs has also edited collections of sources in
Jewish Law and in *Jewish Ethics, Philosophy* and *Mysticism.*

The excerpts are short but good for introductory courses and discussions.

c. Milton Steinberg was one of the most influential writers on Judaism in his time. His lucid and charming style captivated his readers. Though written a quarter of a century ago, *Basic Judaism* (1947) is still considered by many the best introduction to Jewish religion. *Anatomy of a Faith* (1960), edited posthumously by Arthur A. Cohen, contains some of his most important essays. Most important is a "Guide to Contemporary Trends in Religious Thought." Among his previous volumes, particularly useful is *A Partisan Guide to the Jewish Problem* (1945), which traces the history of modern Judaism.

d. Jacob Bernard Agus is the author of *Modern Philosophies of Judaism,* to which reference has already been made. While uneven in quality, his collection of essays, *Guideposts in Modern Judaism* (1954), contains interesting material about contemporary Jewish thought. His compilation, *The Vision and the Way* (1966), is a statement of Jewish ethics. While it is not entirely satisfactory, it is one of the few existing volumes in this field. His two-volume work, *The Meaning of Jewish History* (1963), a discussion of the meaning and élan of Jewish history, is highly regarded by scholars and, again, is one of the few volumes dealing with the problem of the philosophy of Jewish history.

e. Robert Gordis, a biblical scholar, has written several books on Jewish religion. *Faith for Moderns* (1960) is a statement of his religious faith cast in a modern idiom. In *Judaism for the Modern Age* (1955), he deals with the problems of Conservative Judaism, the meaning of Jewish law, the problem of revelation, and other subjects with clarity. *The Root and the Branch* (1962) is a book of essays concerned with problems of the relationship between ethics and international relations and other social issues. Another compilation of essays, *Judaism in a Christian World* (1966), treats the relationships between Judaism and Christianity calling for fairness and rectification of historic inaccuracies.

f. Arthur Allen Cohen is a lay theologian whose works have attracted attention. His prose, though elegant, is sometimes difficult for readers to follow. *The Natural and the Supernatural Jew* (1962), is both a review of contemporary Jewish thought and a statement of Cohen's own faith, based on existentialism. Cohen has also edited a useful anthology of articles written on problems in contemporary Judaism, entitled *Arguments and Doctrines* (1970). The collection is good—although for some inexplicable reason he has omitted the writings of the leading Jewish thinkers of our time, such as Heschel, Buber, and Rosenzweig. Cohen's *The Myth of the Judeo-Christian Tradition* (1969) attempts to prove that the phrase Judeo-Christian is not accurate either historically or theologically.

g. Richard L. Rubenstein is one of the few articulate voices in American Judaism espousing a version of radical theology. His collection of essays *After Auschwitz* (1966) is a statement of Jewish life and thought which dispenses with the belief in the traditional God of history. This volume was followed by *The Religious Imagination* (1968), a study of the rabbinic mind in the light of psychoanalysis. *Eros and Morality* (1970) is a discussion of some of the problems of morals.

h. Max Kadushin, although primarily interested in expounding the theological method of the Talmudic sages, asserts that contemporary Judaism should follow the lead of the rabbis in pursuing what he calls organic thinking. This mode of thinking consists of a series of "value concepts" which are not definable in abstract definition, but are concretized in stories, parables, and prescribed actions. Kadushin's main works which developed this thesis are *Organic Thinking* (1938), *The Rabbinic Mind* (1952), and *Worship and Ethics* (1964).

i. Louis Finkelstein's essay, "Judaism as a System of Symbols," which originally appeared in the fifth volume of the journal *The Thomist* (the Maritain volume) is an exposition of Judaism as a system of action symbols.

j. Gershom G. Scholem (b.1897) has made the study of Jewish mysticism his life's work and is the acknowledged scholarly authority in this field. But although the classical works of Kabbalah are part of pre-modern thought, his book, *Major Trends in Jewish Mysticism* (1941, 2nd ed. 1946), is indispensable for all who want to understand the development of Jewish thought in the last three centuries, since it includes chapters on "Sabbatianism and Mystical Heresy" and on Hasidism. His latest volume in English, *The Messianic Idea in Judaism and Other Essays on Jewish Spirituality*

(1971), contains essays written between 1930 and 1970, a number of which will be of interest to the student of modern Jewish thought. Thus, one paper deals with the relationship between Messianism and early Hasidism, another with Martin Buber's interpretation of Hasidism which Scholem subjects to a searching critique. The volume also includes the famous paper on Sabbatian nihilism, "Redemption through Sin," an essay on the motivations and methodologies of nineteenth-century Jewish scholarship (*Wissenschaft vom Judentum*) and a shorter piece written on the occasion of the second edition of Rosenzweig's *Star of Redemption* in 1930.

k. The late Chief Rabbi of Palestine, Abraham Isaac Kook (1865–1935), has been very important in contemporary Jewish thought. All his writings stress the centrality of the land of Israel in Judaism. Very few of his works are available in English. His thought was permeated by the thought-world of Kabbala and resembles in many ways the writings of Teilhard de Chardin. His book, *Orot Hateshuva,* on the aspects of holiness in the newborn nationalism was translated by A. B. Z. Metzger, and excerpts from his writings are included in the collection, *Contemporary Jewish Thought,* edited by Noveck. Jacob Agus' *Banner of Jerusalem* (1946), is the only full-length study in English of the thought of Rabbi Kook.

l. Among orthodox Jewish leaders, Rabbi Joseph B. Soloveitchik, (b. 1903) Talmudist and professor of Philosophy of Religion at Yeshiva University, is considered to be a mentor and guide. Unfortunately, Rabbi Soloveitchik has resisted attempts to have his works fully published. However, two essays, "The Lonely Man of Faith" and "Confrontation," both appearing in the journal *Tradition,* have attracted wide attention.* An article by Aharon Lichtenstein on the thought of J. B. Soloveitchik is included in *Great Jewish Thinkers of the Twentieth Century* and Eugene Borowitz deals with the theological aspects of Soloveitchik's writings including *"Ish Ha-Halakhah"* in *New Jewish Theology in the Making* (pp. 160–173).

m. Eliezer Berkovits has been influential among Orthodox writers

---

* A lengthy Hebrew essay, *"Ish HaHalakhah"* ("Halakhic Man"), which is considered the most important exposition of his thought has not as yet been translated into English. It appeared in *Talpiot* Vol. 1. (1945).

and thinkers. *God, Man, and History* (1959) is an Orthodox statement of Judaism in the light of Rosenzweigian and Buberian thought. Berkovits has been particularly critical of some of the trends in contemporary studies and has written trenchant criticism of Reconstructionism in *Reconstructionist Theology: A Critical Evaluation* (1959), and the *Philosophy of Martin Buber: A Jewish Critique* (1962; both are part of Yeshiva University's Studies in Torah Judaism). He has also written a long essay on *Prayer* (1962) published by Yeshiva University.

n. A group of younger Jewish theologians are engaged in restating the premises of Reform Judaism. Their outlook is more traditional than their predecessors' and makes use of the insights and stresses of existentialism. Eugene Borowitz's two books, *A New Jewish Theology in the Making* (1968) and *How Can a Jew Speak of Faith Today* (1969) restate some of the issues in Jewish belief with vigor and freshness without sacrificing the traditional base. His book *Choosing a Sex Ethic* is an urbane discussion of the issues in sex ethics from the Jewish traditional point of view.

o. One of the most competent Jewish theologians today from the point of view of philosophic rigor and experience is Emil Fackenheim. Trained in the discipline of philosophy, Fackenheim has been an outstanding voice in contemporary Jewish thought. His collection of essays, *Quest of Present and Future* (1968) and his small volume, *God's Presence in History* (1970), are a powerful argument for traditional Judaism. He is particularly influenced by the events in Europe under Hitler and has made the religious demand upon the Jew to survive his touchstone.

p. *Eternal Dissent* (1961) by David Polish and *The Face of God After Auschwitz* (1965) by Ignaz Maybaum, a British liberal rabbi, are expositions of Jewish religion in the light of the events in the twentieth century. The character of Jewish destiny is to stand firm in the face of the new barbarians who are threatening western civilization as well as all of humankind.

q. Jakob J. Petuchowski is a professor at the Hebrew Union College and is an important factor in the revival of traditional thought amongst Reform rabbis and leaders. *Ever Since Sinai* (1961) is a restatement of the doctrine of revelation in the line of Rosenzweig and Buber. *Heirs to the Pharisees* (1970), a collection of essays, restates traditional Jewish values in the light of the developments within the modern world. Arnold Jacob Wolf has edited a volume entitled *Rediscovering Judaism* (1965), which contains essays by the newer personalities in liberal Judaism who see their faith in the light of existentialist philosophy.   [s.s.]

VI.

BIBLIOGRAPHY IN ALPHABETICAL ORDER

Adler, Cyrus, ed., *The Jewish Theological Seminary of America: Semi-Centennial Volume* (New York: Jewish Theological Seminary, 1939).

Agus, Jacob B., *Banner of Jerusalem* (New York: Bloch, 1946).

————, *The Evolution of Jewish Thought: From Biblical Times to the Opening of the Modern Era* (New York: Abelard-Schuman, 1959).

————, *Guideposts in Modern Judaism: An Analysis of Current Trends in Jewish Thought* (New York: Bloch, 1954).

————, *The Meaning of Jewish History* (New York: Abelard-Schuman, 1963).

————, *Modern Philosophies of Judaism: A Study of Recent Jewish Philosophies of Religion* (New York: Behrman House, 1941; paperback, 1970).

————, *The Vision and the Way* (New York: Ungar, 1966).

Ahad Ha-Am (Asher Ginsberg), *Selected Essays of Achad Ha-Am* (Philadelphia: Jewish Publication Society, 1912).

Alon, Gedalyahu, "The Lithuanian Yeshivas," in Judah Goldin, *The Jewish Expression* (New York: Bantam Books, 1970).

Altmann, Alexander, "Franz Rosenzweig and Eugen Rosenstock-Huessy: An Introduction to Their Letters on Judaism and Christianity," *The Journal of Religion,* Vol. 24, #4 (October 1944).

————, "Franz Rosenzweig on History," in Alexander Altmann, ed., *Between East and West* (London: East and West Library, 1958), pp. 194–214.

————, "Hermann Cohens Begriff der Korrelation," in Hans Tramer, ed., *In zwei Welten: Siegfried Moses zum 75. Geburtstag* (Tel Aviv: Verlag Bitaon, 1962), pp. 377–399.

————, "Theology in Twentieth-Century German Jewry," *Year Book I, The Leo Baeck Institute* (London: East and West Library, 1956), pp. 193–216.

American Jewish Year Book (New York: American Jewish Committee, Philadelphia: Jewish Publication Society, 1970).

Baeck, Leo, *The Essence of Judaism,* translated by V. Grubenwieser and L. Pearl (revised edition, New York: Schocken, 1948; paperback edition, 1961).

————, *Judaism and Christianity,* translated with an introduction by

Walter Kaufmann (Philadelphia: Jewish Publication Society, 1964).

————, "Theology and History," *Judaism,* 13 (1964), pp. 274–284.

————, *Wege im Judentum: Aufsätze und Reden* (Berlin: Schocken, 1933).

————, *Das Wesen des Judentums* (first edition, Berlin: Nathansohn und Lamm, 1905; second revised edition, Frankfurt am Main: J. Kauffmann, 1922).

————, "Why Jews in the World? A Reaffirmation of Faith in Israel's Destiny," *Commentary,* Vol. 3, June 1947, pp. 501–507.

Bamberger, Bernard J., *The Story of Judaism* (New York: Union of American Hebrew Congregations, 1957).

Baron, Salo W., "The Modern Age," in *Great Ages and Ideas of the Jewish People,* Leo W. Schwarz, ed. (New York: Random House, 1956).

Barzilay, Isaac Eisenstein, "Moses Mendelssohn: A Study in Ideas and Attitudes," *Jewish Quarterly Review,* Vol. 52, #1 (July 1961), pp. 69–93; and #2 (October 1961), pp. 175–186.

Belkin, Samuel, *In His Image: The Jewish Philosophy of Man as Expressed in Rabbinic Tradition* (London and New York: Abelard-Schuman, 1960).

————, *The Philosophy of Purpose,* Studies in Torah Judaism series, #1 (third edition, New York: Yeshiva University, 1958).

Ben-Amos, Dan, and Jerome Mintz, *In Praise of the Baal Shem (Shivhei ha-Besht)* (Bloomington: Indiana University Press, 1970).

Bergman, Samuel H., *Faith and Reason: An Introduction to Modern Jewish Thought,* translated and edited by Alfred Jospe (Washington: B'nai B'rith Hillel Foundations, 1961; New York: Schocken, paperback edition, 1963).

Berkovits, Eliezer, "Faith and Law," *Judaism,* 13 (1964), pp. 422–430.

————, *God, Man, and History* (New York: Jonathan David, 1959).

————, *A Jewish Critique of the Philosophy of Martin Buber* (New York: Yeshiva University, 1962).

————, *Prayer* (New York: Yeshiva University, 1962).

————, *Reconstructionist Theology: A Critical Evaluation* (New York: Jonathan David, 1959; reprinted from *Tradition,* Vol. 2, Fall 1959).

Berlin, Sir Isaiah, *The Life and Opinions of Moses Hess* (Cambridge: Published for the Jewish Historical Society of England, 1959).

Bird, Thomas E., ed., *Modern Theologians: Christians and Jews* (University of Notre Dame Press, 1967; New York: Association Press, 1968).

Blau, Joseph L., *Modern Varieties of Judaism* (New York: Columbia University Press, 1966).

————, *The Story of Jewish Philosophy* (New York: Random House, 1962).

Bokser, Ben Zion, "Jewish Universalism: An Aspect of the Thought of HaRav Kook," *Judaism* 8 (1959), pp. 214–219.

————, *Judaism: A Profile of a Faith* (New York: Knopf, 1963).

Borowitz, Eugene, "Hope Jewish and Hope Secular," *Judaism,* 17 (1968), pp. 131–147.

————, *A New Jewish Theology in the Making* (Philadelphia: Westminster, Press, 1968).

————, *How Can a Jew Speak of Faith Today?* (Philadelphia: Westminster Press, 1968).

————, "The Problem of the Form of a Jewish Theology," *Hebrew Union College Annual,* Vols. 40/41, Cincinnati, 1969–1970, pp. 391–408.

Buber, Martin, *At The Turning: Three Addresses on Judaism* (New York: Farrar, Straus & Young, 1952).

————, *Begegnung: Autobiographische Fragmente* (Stuttgart: Kohlhammer, 1960).

————, *A Believing Humanism: My Testament, 1902–1965,* translation, introduction, and explanatory comments by Maurice Friedman (New York: Simon and Schuster, 1967).

————, *Between Man and Man,* translated by Ronald Gregor Smith (New York: Macmillan, 1948; paperback edition, 1965).

————, *Daniel,* translated by Maurice Friedman (New York: McGraw-Hill, 1965, paperback edition).

————, *Die Chassidischen Bücher* (Berlin: Schocken, 1927).

————, *Eclipse of God: Studies in the Relation between Religion and Philosophy* (New York: Harper & Row, 1952; paperback edition, Harper Torchbook, 1957).

————, *Die Erzählungen der Chassidim* (Zurich: Manesse, 1949); 1928 edition titled, *Die Chassidischen Bücher.*

————, *For the Sake of Heaven,* translated by Ludwig Lewisohn, second edition, (Philadelphia: Jewish Publication Society, 1953).

————, *Good and Evil,* translated by Ronald Gregor Smith and Michael Bullock (New York: Scribners, 1953).

————, *Hasidism,* translated by Greta Hort and others (New York: Philosophical Library, 1948).

————, *Hasidism and Modern Man,* translated and edited by Maurice

Friedman (New York: Horizon Press, 1958); second volume of set is *Origin and Meaning of Hasidism.*

————, *I and Thou,* translated by Walter Kaufmann (New York: Scribners, 1970).

————, *I and Thou,* translated by Ronald Gregor Smith (second edition, New York: Scribners, 1958).

————, *Ich und du* (Leipzig: Insel, 1923).

————, "Interpreting Hasidism," *Commentary,* XXXVI (1963), pp. 218–225.

————, *Israel and Palestine: The History of an Idea,* translated by Stanley Godman (London: East and West Library, 1952).

————, *Israel and the World: Essays in a Time of Crisis* (New York: Schocken, 1948; paperback, 1963; second edition, 1965).

————, *Der Jude und sein Judentum: Gesammelte Aufsätze und Reden,* with an introduction by Robert Weltsch (Cologne: Joseph Melzer Verlag, 1963); complements the three-volume edition of Buber's *Werke.*

————, *Kingship of God* (New York: Harper & Row, 1967).

————, *The Knowledge of Man,* edited by Maurice Friedman and translated by Maurice Friedman and Ronald Gregor Smith (New York: Harper & Row, 1965).

————, *The Legend of the Baal-Shem,* translated by Maurice Friedman (New York: Schocken, 1969, also paperback).

————, *Moses: The Revelation and the Covenant* (New York: Harper & Row, 1958; paperback edition).

————, *Nachlese* (Heidelberg: Lambert Schneider, 1965).

————, *On Judaism,* edited by Nahum N. Glatzer (New York: Schocken 1967).

————, *The Origin and Meaning of Hasidism,* edited and translated by Maurice Friedman (New York: Horizon Press, 1960); the first volume is *Hasidism and Modern Man.*

————, *Paths in Utopia* (Heidelberg: Schneider, 1950; Boston: Beacon, 1958).

————, *Pointing the Way,* edited and translated by Maurice S. Friedman (New York: Harper & Row, 1963; paperback edition).

————, *The Prophetic Faith,* translated by Carlyle Witton-Davis (New York: Harper & Row, 1960; paperback edition).

————, *Tales of the Hasidim: The Early Masters,* translated by Olga Marx (New York: Schocken Books, 1947–1948; paperback edition, 1961).

————, *Tales of the Hasidim: The Early Masters,* translated by Olga Marx (New York: Schocken, 1947–1948; paperback edition, 1961).

————, *The Tales of Rabbi Nachman,* translated by Maurice Friedman (New York: Horizon Press, 1956).

————, *Ten Rungs: Hasidic Sayings,* translated by Olga Marx (New York: Schocken, 1947; paperback edition, 1965).

————, *Two Types of Faith* (New York: Harper & Row, 1961; paperback edition).

————, *The Way of Man According to the Teachings of Hasidism* (Chicago: Wilcox Follett, 1951; New York: Citadel Press, 1966).

————, *The Way of Response; Martin Buber,* edited by Nahum N. Glatzer (New York: Schocken, 1966).

————, *Werke,* three vols. (Munich: Kösel and Heidelberg: Lambert Schneider, 1962–1963), Vol. 1: *Schriften zur Philosophie;* Vol. 2: *Schriften zur Bibel;* Vol. 3: *Schriften zum Chassidismus.*

————, *The Writings of Martin Buber,* selected, edited, and introduced by Will Herberg (New York: Meridian-World, 1956; paperback edition).

————, mit Franz Rosenzweig, *Die Schrift und ihre Verdeutschung* (Berlin: Schocken, 1936).

————, mit Franz Rosenweig, *Die Schrift: zu verdeutschen unternommen von Martin Buber gemeinsam mit Franz Rosenzweig* (Berlin: L. Schneider, 1926–1937).

Casper, Bernhard, *Das dialogische Denken: Eine Untersuchung der religionsphilosophischen Bedeutung Franz Rosenzweigs, Ferdinand Ebners und Martin Bubers* (Freiburg-Basel-Wien: Herder, 1967).

Catane, Moché, *Bibliography of Martin Buber's Works* (*1895–1957*) (Jerusalem: Bialik Institute, 1958).

Cherbonnier, Edmond La B., "Heschel as a Religious Thinker," *Conservative Judaism,* Vol. 23 # 1 (Fall 1968), pp. 25–39.

Clawson, Dan, "Rosenzweig on Judaism and Christianity: A Critique," *Judaism,* Vol. 19 #1 (Winter 1970), pp. 91–98.

Cohen, Arthur A., ed., *Arguments and Doctrines: A Reader of Jewish Thinking in the Aftermath of the Holocaust* (Philadelphia: Jewish Publication Society and New York: Harper & Row, 1970).

————, *Martin Buber* (New York: Hillary House, 1957).

————, *The Myth of the Judeo-Christian Tradition* (New York: Harper & Row, 1969).

————, *The Natural and the Supernatural Jew: An Historical and*

Theological Introduction (New York: Pantheon Books, 1962; paperback edition, New York: McGraw-Hill, 1964).

Cohen, Carl, "Franz Rosenzweig," *Conservative Judaism,* Vol. 8, #1 (November 1951), pp. 1–13.

Cohen, Hermann, *Der Begriff der Religion im System der Philosophie* (Giessen: Alfred Töpelmann, 1915).

———, "The Day of Atonement," *Judaism,* 17 (1968), pp. 352–357; 18 (1969), pp. 84–90, 216–222. (English translation from *Religion der Vernunft.*)

———, *Jüdische Schriften,* edited by Bruno Strauss with an introduction by Franz Rosenzweig, three volumes (Berlin: C. A. Schwetschke, 1924).

———, *Reason and Hope: Selections From the Jewish Writings of Hermann Cohen,* transl. and edited by Eva Jospe (New York: W. W. Norton & Co., 1971).

———, *(Die) Religion der Vernunft aus den Quellen der Judentums,* (first edition, Leipzig: Gustav Fock, 1919; second revised edition, Frankfurt am Main: J. Kauffmann, 1929; third edition reprint of second edition Cologne: Josef Melzer, 1959).

Cohen, Jack, *The Case for Religious Naturalism* (New York: Reconstructionist Press, 1958).

Commentary, "Symposium on the State of Jewish Belief" (New York: August 1966).

Davis, Moshe, *The Emergence of Conservative Judaism: The Historical School in 19th-Century America* (Philadelphia: Jewish Publication Society, 1963.)

Dawidowicz, Lucy, ed., *The Golden Tradition: Jewish Life and Thought in Eastern Europe* (New York: Holt, Rinehart & Winston, 1967; paperback edition, Beacon).

Diamond, Malcolm M., "Faith and its Tensions," *Judaism,* 13 (1964), pp. 317–327.

———, *Martin Buber: Jewish Existentialist* (New York: Oxford, 1960; Harper Torchbooks, paperback edition).

Dresner, Samuel H., *The Zaddik: The Doctrine of the Zaddik According to the Writings of Yaakov Yosef of Polnoy* (London-New York-Toronto: Abelard-Schuman, 1960).

Eckstein, Felix, "Judaism—The Traditional, Existentialist and Humanist Approach," *Judaism* 2 (1953), pp. 148–159.

Eisenstein, Ira and Eugene Kohn, eds., *Mordecai M. Kaplan: An Evaluation* (New York: Reconstructionist Foundation, 1952).

Elbogen, Ismar, *A Century of Jewish Life* (Philadelphia: Jewish Publication Society, 1944).

Epstein, Isadore, *The Faith of Judaism* (London: Soncino, 1954).

———, *Judaism: A Historical Presentation* (Baltimore: Penguin, 1959).

Fackenheim, Emil L., *God's Presence in History: Jewish Affirmations and Philosophical Reflections* (New York: New York University Press, 1970).

———, *Quest for Past and Future: Essays in Jewish Theology* (Bloomington: Indiana University Press, 1968).

———, "Samuel Hirsch and Hegel: A Study of Hirsch's *Religionsphilosophie der Juden* (1842)," in A. Altmann, ed., *Studies in Nineteenth-Century Jewish Intellectual History* (Cambridge, Mass.: Harvard University Press, 1964), pp. 171–201.

Finkelstein, Louis, *The Beliefs and Practices of Judaism* (New York: Devin-Adair, 1952).

———, *The Jews*, two volumes (third edition, New York: Harper & Row; Philadelphia: Jewish Publication Society, 1960; New York: Schocken, 1970; three-volume paperback edition).

———, *Judaism as a System of Symbols* (New York: Jewish Theological Seminary, n.d.).

Fleischman, Yaakov, "Franz Rosenzweig as a Critic of Zionism," *Conservative Judaism*, Vol. 22 #1 (Fall 1967), pp. 54 ff.

Formstecher, Salomon, *Die Religion des Geistes* (Frankfurt am Main, 1841).

Freehof, Solomon Bennett, *Current Reform Responsa* (Cincinnati: Hebrew Union College Press, 1969).

———, *Recent Reform Responsa* (Cincinnati: Hebrew Union College Press, 1963).

———, *Reform Jewish Practice and its Rabbinic Background* (New York: Union of American Hebrew Congregations, 1964).

———, *Reform Responsa* (Cincinnati: Hebrew Union College Press, 1960).

Freund, Else, *Die Existenzphilosophie Franz Rosenzweigs: Ein Beitrag zur Analyse seines Werkes* "Der Stern der Erlösung," second revised edition (Hamburg: Felix Meiner, 1959).

Friedlander, Albert H., *Leo Baeck: Teacher of Theresienstadt* (New York: Holt, Rinehart & Winston, 1968).

Friedländer, Michael, *The Jewish Religion* (London: 1891; Shapiro-Vallentine, 1922; New York: Pardes, 1946; American edition revised and enlarged with a biography of the author).

Friedman, Maurice S., "Hasidism and the Contemporary Jew," *Judaism,* 9 (1960), pp. 197–206.

————, *Martin Buber: The Life of Dialogue* (Chicago: University of Chicago Press, 1955; New York: Harper Torchbook, 1960).

Ginzberg, Louis, "Rabbi Israel Salanter," in *The Jewish Expression,* edited by Judah Goldin (New York: Bantam, 1970), pp. 415–488; paperback edition.

————, *Students, Scholars, and Saints* (Philadelphia: Jewish Publication Society of America, 1928; paperback edition, 1958).

Gittelsohn, Roland, *The Meaning of Judaism* (New York: World, 1970).

Glatzer, Nahum N., "Franz Rosenzweig," *Yivo Annual of Jewish Social Science* I (New York: 1946).

————, *Franz Rosenzweig: His Life and Thought* (New York: Schocken, 1961; paperback edition).

————, "Franz Rosenzweig, the Story of a Conversion," *Judaism* I (New York: 1952), pp. 69–79.

————, *The Judaic Tradition; Texts edited and introduced* (Boston: Beacon Press, 1970; paperback edition).

————, *The Way of Response: Martin Buber* (New York: Schocken, 1966).

Glenn, Mendel Gershon, *Israel Salanter: Religious-Ethical Thinker* (New York: Dropsie College Press, 1953).

Goldin, Judah, ed., *The Jewish Expression* (New York: Bantam, 1970; paperback edition).

Gordis, Robert, *A Faith for Moderns* (New York: Bloch, 1960).

————, *Judaism for the Modern Age* (New York: Farrar, Straus & Cudahy, 1955).

————, *Judaism in a Christian World* (New York: McGraw-Hill, 1966).

————, "Reform and Conservative Judaism," *Judaism* 1 (1952), pp. 110–120.

————, *The Root and the Branch: Judaism and the Free Society* (Chicago: University of Chicago Press, 1962).

Graetz, Heinrich, *History of the Jews,* six volumes (Philadelphia: Jewish Publication Society, 1891–1898).

Greenberg, Hayim, *The Inner Eye* (New York: Jewish Frontier, 1953).

Greenberg, Irving, "The New Encounter of Judaism and Christianity," *The Barat Review,* Lake Forest, Ill., Vol. 3, #2, (June–September 1968) pp. 113–125.

Greenberg, Simon, *The Conservative Movement in Judaism* (New York: United Synagogue of America, 1955).

————, *Foundations of a Faith* (New York: Burning Bush Press, 1967).

Gruenewald, Max, "Leo Baeck: Witness and Judge," *Judaism,* (Autumn 1957).

Guttmann, Julius, *Philosophies of Judaism: The History of Jewish Philosophy from Biblical Times to Franz Rosenzweig,* translated by David W. Silverman (New York: Holt, Rinehart & Winston, 1964; paperback edition, Garden City: Doubleday Anchor Books, 1966).

————, "The Principles of Judaism," in *Conservative Judaism,* Vol. 14 #1 (Fall 1959), pp. 1–24.

Haberman, Joshua O., "Franz Rosenzweig's Doctrine of Revelation," *Judaism,* 18 (1969), pp. 320–336.

————, "Solomon Ludwig Steinheim's Doctrine of Revelation," *Judaism,* 17 (1968), pp. 22–41.

Harris, Monford, "Theology and Jewish Scholarship," *Judaism,* 9 (1960), pp. 331–338.

Herberg, Will, "Jewish Existence and Survival: A Theological View," *Judaism,* 1 (1952), pp. 19–26.

————, *Judaism and Modern Man: An Interpretation of Jewish Religion* (New York: Farrar, Straus & Cudahy, 1951; paperback edition, New York: Atheneum, 1970).

————, "Judaism as Personal Decision," in Alfred Jospe, ed., *Tradition and Contemporary Experience* (New York: Schocken-Hillel Books, 1970), pp. 77–90; also in *Conservative Judaism,* Vol. 22, #4 (Summer) 1968.

————, "Prophetic Faith in an Age of Crisis," *Judaism* 1 (1952), pp. 195–202.

————, *Protestant, Catholic, Jew,* second edition (Garden City: Doubleday Anchor Books, 1960, paperback edition).

————, "Religious Trends in American Jewry," *Judaism* 3 (1954), pp. 229–240.

————, "Rosenzweig's Judaism of Personal Existence," *Commentary,* Vol. X, #6 (December 1950), pp. 541–550.

Hertzberg, Arthur, ed., *Judaism* (New York: George Braziller, 1962; also New York: Washington Square Press, 1963, paperback edition).

————, *The Zionist Idea: A Historical Analysis and Reader* (Garden City, N.Y.: Doubleday and Herzl Press, 1959; Atheneum paperback edition, 1970).

Herzl, Theodor, *The Jewish State,* translated by Sylvia D. Avigdor (New York: Federation of American Zionists, 1917; American Zionist Emergency Council, 1946).

Heschel, Abraham J., *Between God and Man: An Interpretation of Judaism from the Writings of Abraham J. Heschel,* selected, edited, and introduced by Fritz A. Rothschild (New York: Harper & Bros., 1959; New York: The Free Press–Macmillan, 1965, paperback edition).

————, "The Concept of Man in Jewish Thought," in *The Concept of Man,* edited by S. Radhakrishnan and P. T. Raju (London: Allen and Unwin, 1960), pp. 108–157.

————, *The Earth is the Lord's: The Inner Life of the Jew in East Europe* (New York: Henry Schuman, 1950). *The Earth is the Lord's and The Sabbath* (New York: Harper Torchbook, paperback edition).

————, *God in Search of Man: A Philosophy of Judaism* (New York: Farrar, Straus & Cudahy, 1956; Philadelphia: Jewish Publication Society, 1956; New York: Harper Torchbook, paperback edition).

————, "A Hebrew Evaluation of Reinhold Niebuhr," in *Reinhold Niebuhr: His Religious, Social, and Political Thought,* Vol. 2 of the Library of Living Theology, edited by Ch. W. Kegley and R. W. Bretall (New York: Macmillan, 1956), pp. 391–410.

————, *The Insecurity of Freedom: Essays in Applied Religion* (New York: Farrar, Straus & Giroux, 1965; Farrar, Straus, paperback edition).

————, *Israel: An Echo of Eternity* (New York: Farrar, Straus & Giroux, 1969; paperback edition).

————, "The Jewish Notion of God and Christian Renewal," in *Renewal of Religious Thought: Proceedings on the Congress of the Theology of the Renewal of the Church, Centenary of Canada, 1867–1967* (Dorval, Quebec: Palm Publishers, n.d.).

————, *Man Is Not Alone: A Philosophy of Religion* (New York: Farrar, Straus, and Young, 1951; and Philadelphia: Jewish Publication Society, 1951; New York: Harper Torchbook, paperback edition).

————, *Man's Quest for God: Studies in Prayer and Symbolism* (New York: Scribners Sons, 1954; paperback edition).

————, "The Mystical Element in Judaism," in *The Jews: Their History, Culture and Religion,* edited by Louis Finkelstein (New York: Harper & Row; Philadelphia: Jewish Publication Society, 1949), pp. 602–623 (in Vol. 1 of the 2-volume edition, and in Vol. 2 of the 3-volume paper edition).

————, "No Religion Is an Island," in *Union Seminary Quarterly Review,* Vol. XXI, No. 2, Part I (January 1966), pp. 117–134.

————, *Die Prophetie* (German), Cracow: The Polish Academy of Sciences (Mémoires de la Commission Orientalist No. 22), 1936.

————, *The Prophets* (New York and Evanston: Harper & Row, 1962; Philadelphia: Jewish Publication Society, 1962; New York: Harper Torchbook in 2 vols., paperback edition).

————, "Protestant Renewal: A Jewish View," in *The Christian Century,* Vol. 80, No. 49 (December 4, 1963), pp. 1501–1504.

————, "The Religious Message," in *Religion in America: Original Essays on Religion in a Free Society,* edited by John Cogley (New York: Meridian, 1958, paperback edition), pp. 244–271.

————, *The Sabbath: Its Meaning for Modern Man* (New York: Farrar, Straus, and Young, 1951).

————, *Theology of Ancient Judaism (Torah Min Ha-Shamayim Be-Aspaklaryah Shel Ha-Dorot)* in Hebrew (London and New York: Soncino, Vol. I, 1962; Vol. II, 1965)

————, "What We Might Do Together," in *Religious Education,* Vol. LXII, No. 2 (March–April, 1967), pp. 133–140.

————, *Who is Man?* (Stanford, Calif.: Stanford University Press, 1965; also paperback edition).

Hess, Moses, *Rome and Jerusalem,* translated by Meyer Waxman (New York: Bloch, 1918); translated by Maurice J. Bloom (New York: Philosophical Library, 1958).

Himmelfarb, Milton, ed., *The Condition of Jewish Belief* (New York: Macmillan, 1966).

Hirsch, Samson Raphael, *Fundamentals of Judaism. Selections from the Works of S. R. Hirsch and Outstanding Torah-true Thinkers* (New York: Feldheim, 1949).

————, *Horeb: A Philosophy of Jewish Laws and Observances,* translated by Isidor Gruenfeld (London: Soncino, 1962).

————, *Judaism Eternal: Selected Essays from the Writings of Samson Raphael Hirsch,* translated by Isidor Gruenfeld (London: Soncino, 1956).

————, *The Nineteen Letters of Ben Uziel: Being a Spiritual Presentation of the Principles of Judaism,* translated by Bernard Drachman (New York: Funk and Wagnalls, 1899; reissued New York: Feldheim, 1969).

————, *Timeless Torah: An Anthology of the Writings of Samson Raphael Hirsch,* edited by J. Breuer (New York: Feldheim, 1957).

Hirsch, Samuel, *Das System der religiösen Anschauung der Juden und sein Verhältnis zum Heidentum, Christentum und zur absoluten Philosophie;* Vol. I (only one to appear): *Die Religionsphilosophie der Juden* (Leipzig, 1842).

Horwitz, Rivka G., "Franz Rosenzweig on Language," *Judaism,* Vol. 13, #4 (Fall 1964), pp. 393–406.

Jacob, Walter, "Leo Baeck and Christianity," *Jewish Quarterly Review* (October 1965).

Jacobs, Louis, *Faith* (London: Vallentine, Mitchell, 1968).

———, *Jewish Ethics, Philosophy, and Mysticism* (New York: Behrman House, 1969).

———, *Jewish Law* (New York: Behrman House, 1968).

———, *Jewish Thought Today,* The Chain of Tradition series, Vol. 3 (New York: Behrman House, 1970).

———, *Jewish Values* (London: Vallentine, Mitchell, 1960).

———, *Principles of the Jewish Faith* (New York: Basic Books, 1964).

———, *The Seeker of Unity: The Life and Works of Aaron of Starosselje* (New York: Basic Books, 1966).

———, *The Tract on Ecstasy,* translated with introduction and notes (London: Vallentine, Mitchell, 1963).

———, *We Have Reason to Believe,* third edition (London: Vallentine, Mitchell, 1965).

Johnpoll, Bernard K., *The Politics of Futility: The General Jewish Workers' Bund of Poland, 1917–1943* (Ithaca, N.Y.: Cornell University Press, 1967).

Jospe, Alfred, ed., *Tradition and Contemporary Experience: Essays on Jewish Thought and Life* (New York: Schocken and B'nai B'rith Hillel Foundations, 1970, paperback edition).

Judaism, Vol. 3, #4 (1954), pp. 302–361, Tercentenary Issue: articles on "Philosophies of Judaism in America," by E. Rackman, Th. Friedman, H. M. Schulweis, S. S. Cohon, and C. B. Sherman.

———, Vol. 9, #3 (Summer 1960), pp. 197–284, Hasidism Issue: articles by M. Friedman, Z. S. Schachter, J. Orent, et al.

———, Vol. 10, #4 (Fall 1961), pp. 291–352, Symposium: "My Jewish Affirmation."

———, Vol. 15, #2 (Spring 1966), pp. 133–163, "Toward Jewish Religious Unity: A Symposium": Articles by Irving Greenberg, Jacob J. Petuchowski, Seymour Siegel, and Mordecai M. Kaplan, and discussion.

————, Vol. 16, #3 (Summer 1967), pp. 269–299, "Jewish Values in the Post-Holocaust Future: A Symposium," papers by Emil L. Fackenheim, Richard H. Popkin, George Steiner, Elie Wiesel, and discussion.

Jung, Leo, *Guardians of our Heritage* (New York: Macmillan).

————, ed., The Jewish Library (London: Soncino 1968), 23 volumes, including *Jewish Faith and Life*.

Kadushin, Max, *Organic Thinking: A Study in Rabbinic Thought* (New York: Jewish Theological Seminary, 1938).

————, *The Rabbinic Mind,* second edition (New York: Blaisdell, 1965).

————, *Worship and Ethics* (Evanston, Ill.: Northwestern University Press, 1964).

Kaplan, Mordecai M., *The Future of the American Jew* (New York: Macmillan, 1948).

————, *The Greater Judaism in the Making: A Study of the Modern Evolution of Judaism* (New York: Reconstructionist Press, 1960).

————, *Judaism as a Civilization: Toward a Reconstruction of American-Jewish Life* (New York: Schocken, [1934], 1967).

————, *Judaism without Supernaturalism* (New York: Reconstructionist Press, 1958).

————, *The Meaning of God in Modern Jewish Religion* (New York: Behrman House, 1937).

————, *A New Zionism* (New York: Theodor Herzl Foundation, 1955).

————, *Questions Jews Ask* (New York: Reconstructionist Press, 1966).

————, *The Religion of Ethical Nationhood* (New York: Macmillan, 1970).

Kaplan, Simon, "Hermann Cohen's Philosophy of Judaism," *Judaism* 1 (1952), pp. 140–149.

Katz, Jacob, "Judaism and Christianity against the Background of Modern Secularism," *Judaism* 17 (1968), pp. 299–315.

Kayserling, Meyer, *Moses Mendelssohn: Sein Leben und seine Werke* (Leipzig: Hermann Mendelssohn, 1862; second edition, 1888).

Kertzer, Morris, *What Is a Jew?* (Cleveland: World, revised edition, 1960; paperback edition, Collier, Macmillan).

Knox, Israel, *Rabbi in America: The Story of Isaac M. Wise* (Boston: Little, Brown, 1957).

Kohler, Kaufmann, *Jewish Theology, Systematically and Historically Considered* (New York: Macmillan, 1918; Ktav, 1968).

Kohn, Hans, *Martin Buber, Sein Werk und seine Zeit* (Hellerau: J. Hegner, 1930).

————, *Martin Buber: Sein Werk und seine Zeit—Ein Beitrag zur Geistesgeschichte Mitteleuropas 1880–1930*. Nachwort: 1930–60 by Robert Weltsch (Cologne: Joseph Melzer, 1961).

Kook, Abraham, *Orot Hateshuva,* translated by E. B. Z. Metzger (Jerusalem: Or Etzion, 1966).

Krochmal, Nachman, *The Writings of Nachman Krochmal,* in Hebrew, edited and with an introduction by Simon Rawidowicz, second enlarged edition (London and Waltham, Mass.: Ararat Publishing Society, 1961).

Kurzweil, Zvi E., "Three Views on Revelation and Law," *Judaism 9* (1960), pp. 291–298.

Langer, Jiri, *Nine Gates to the Chasidic Mysteries* (New York: David McKay, 1961).

Levinthal, Israel H., *Judaism, An Analysis and an Interpretation* (New York: Funk & Wagnall, 1935).

Lewisohn, Ludwig, *What is This Jewish Heritage?* (Washington, D.C.: Hillel Little Books, 1954; revised edition with additional material plus an introduction by Milton Hindus, New York: Schocken, 1964, paperback edition).

Liebeschütz, Hans, "Jewish Thought and Its German Background," *Year Book I,* Leo Baeck Institute (London: East and West Library, 1956), pp. 217–236.

————, *Von Georg Simmel zu Franz Rosenzweig: Studien zům Jüdischen Denken im Deutschen Kulturbereich,* (Tubingen: J. C. B. Mohr, 1970).

Löwith, Karl, "M. Heidegger and Franz Rosenzweig or Temporality and Eternity," *Philosophy and Phenomenological Research,* Vol. 3 (September 1942), pp. 53–77; revised version in: Karl Löwith, *Nature History and Existentialism,* edited by A. Levison (Evanston, Ill.: Northwestern University Press, 1966, pp. 51–78).

Martin, Bernard, ed., *Contemporary Reform Jewish Thought* (Chicago: Quadrangle, 1968).

————, *Great Twentieth Century Jewish Philosophers: Shestov, Rosenzweig, Buber, with Selections from their Writings,* edited and with an introduction (New York: Macmillan, 1970; paperback edition).

May, Max Benjamin, *Isaac Mayer Wise, the Founder of American Judaism: A Biography* (New York: G. P. Putnam's Sons, 1916).

Maybaum, Ignaz, *The Face of God After Auschwitz* (Amsterdam: Polak and Van Gennep, 1965).

Melber, Jehuda, *Hermann Cohen's Philosophy of Judaism* (New York: Jonathan David, 1968).

Mendelssohn, Moses, *Gesammelte Schriften,* edited by G. B. Mendelssohn, 7 volumes [really 8—vols. 4(I) and 4(II) are separate] (Leipzig: F. A. Brockhaus, 1843–1845).

———, *Gesammelte Schriften (Jubiläumsausgabe),* edited by I. Elbogen, J. Guttmann, E. Mittwoch, et al., Vols. 1, 2, 3, 7, 11, 16 (Breslau: Akademie-Verlag, 1929–1932; Vol. 4, Breslau: Marcus, 1938).

———, *Jerusalem and Other Jewish Writings,* translated and edited by Alfred Jospe (New York: Schocken, 1969).

Menes, Abraham, "The Jewish Socialist Movement in Russia and Poland (1870's–1897)" *The Jewish People Past and Present* Vol. II (New York: Jewish Encyclopedic Handbooks, 1948).

———, "Religious and Secular Trends in Jewish Socialism," *Judaism* 1 (1952), pp. 218–226.

Meyer, Herrmann M. Z., *Moses Mendelssohn Bibliographie,* mit einer Einführung von Hans Herzfeld, *Veröffentlichungen der Historischen Kommission zu Berlin,* Band 26; *Bibliographien,* Band 2 (Berlin: Walter de Gruyter, 1965).

Meyer, Michael A., *The Origins of the Modern Jew: Jewish Identity and European Culture in Germany 1789–1824* (Detroit: Wayne State University Press, 1967).

Miller, Alan W., *The God of Daniel S.* (New York: Macmillan, 1969).

Minkin, Jacob S., *The Romance of Hassidism* (New York: The Macmillan Co., 1935; second edition, Thomas Yoseloff paperback edition; No. Hollywood, California: Wilshire, 1971).

Mintz, Jerome, *Legends of the Hasidim: An Introduction to Their Culture and Oral Tradition in the New World* (Chicago: University of Chicago Press, 1968).

Neusner, Jacob, *History and Torah: Essays on Jewish Learning* (New York: Schocken, 1965).

———, *Judaism in the Secular Age* (New York: Ktav, 1970).

———, *The Way of Torah: An Introduction to Judaism,* from The Life of Man series (Belmont, California: Dickenson, 1970, paperback edition).

Newman, Louis, *The Hasidic Anthology;* contains an Introduction on "The Hasidim; their History, Literature, and Doctrines" (New York: Scribners, 1934; paperback edition, Schocken, 1963).

————, *Maggidim and Hasidim: Their Wisdom* (New York: Bloch, 1962).

Noveck, Simon, ed., *Contemporary Jewish Thought: A Reader* (Washington: B'nai B'rith Department of Adult Jewish Education, 1963).

————, ed., *Great Jewish Personalities in Modern Times* (Washington: B'nai B'rith Dept. of Adult Jewish Education, 1963).

————, ed., *Great Jewish Thinkers of the Twentieth Century* (Washington: B'nai B'rith Department of Adult Jewish Education, 1963; also in paperback edition).

Parzen, Herbert, *Architects of Conservative Judaism* (New York: Jonathan David, 1964).

Patkin, A. L., *The Origins of the Russian-Jewish Labour Movement* (Melbourne: 1947).

Petuchowski, Jakob J., "The Concept of Revelation in Reform Judaism," *Yearbook* LXXIX, Central Conference of American Rabbis (Cincinnati: 1959).

————, *Ever Since Sinai: A Modern View of Torah* (New York: Scribe Publications, 1961).

————, *Heirs to the Pharisees* (New York: Basic Books, 1970).

————, "The Limits of Liberal Judaism," *Judaism* 14 (1965), pp. 146–158.

————, *Prayerbook Reform in Europe: The Liturgy of European Liberal and Reform Judaism* (New York: World Union for Progressive Judaism, 1968).

Philipson, David, *The Reform Movement in Judaism* (New York: 1907; Ktav, 1967; reprint).

Pinson, Koppel, "Arkady Kremer, Vladimir Medem, and the Ideology of the Jewish Bund," *Jewish Social Studies* (July 1945).

Plaut, W. Gunther, *The Growth of Reform Judaism* (New York: World Union for Progressive Judaism, 1965).

————, *The Rise of Reform Judaism* (New York: World Union for Progressive Judaism, 1965).

Polish, David, *Eternal Dissent,* London-New York: Abelard-Schuman, 1961.

———— and Frederic Doppelt, *A Guide for Reform Jews* (New York: Bloch, 1967).

Poll, Solomon, *The Hasidic Community of Williamsburg: A Study in the Sociology of Religion* (New York: Free Press, 1962; paperback edition, Schocken, 1969).

Rabinowicz, Harry M., *A Guide to Hassidism* (New York: T. Yoseloff, 1960).

Reichmann, Eva H., ed., *Worte des Gedenkens für Leo Baeck* (London: 1959).

Rome, Sydney and Beatrice, eds., *Philosophical Interrogations* (New York: Holt, Rinehart & Winston, 1964).

Rosen, Kopul, *Rabbi Israel Salanter and the Mussar Movement* (London: Narod Press, 1945).

Rosenbloom, Noah H., *Luzzatto's Ethico-Psychological Interpretation of Judaism* (New York: Yeshiva University, 1965; paperback edition). Contains a translation of S. D. Luzzatto's *The Foundations of the Torah.*

Rosenstock-Huessy, Eugen, ed., *Judaism Despite Christianity: The "Letters on Christianity and Judaism" between Eugen Rosenstock-Huessy and Franz Rosenzweig* (University, Alabama: University of Alabama Press, 1969).

Rosenzweig, Franz, *Briefe,* edited and selected by Edith Rosenzweig with the cooperation of Ernst Simon (Berlin: Schocken, 1935).

———, *Das Büchlein vom gesunden und kranken Menschenverstand,* edited by Nahum N. Glatzer (Düsseldorf: Joseph Melzer, 1964).

———, *Kleinere Schriften* (Berlin: Schocken, 1937).

———, *On Jewish Learning;* English translation of the three epistles: "Zeit ists," "Bildung und kein Ende," "Die Bauleute," and additional material, edited by Nahum N. Glatzer (New York: 1955; Schocken paperback edition, 1965).

———, *The Star of Redemption,* translated from the second edition of 1930 by William W. Hallo (New York: Holt, Rinehart & Winston, 1971).

———, *Der Stern der Erlösung,* first edition (Frankfurt am Main: J. Kauffmann, 1921; second edition, 1930; third edition, Heidelberg: Lambert Schneider, 1954).

———, *Understanding the Sick and the Healthy: A View of World, Man and God* (English translation from the manuscript of *Das Büchlein vom gesunden und kranken Menschenverstand),* edited and with an introduction by Nahum N. Glatzer (New York: Noonday Press, 1953).

Rotenstreich, Nathan, "Common Sense and Theological Experience on the Basis of Franz Rosenzweig's Philosophy," in *Journal of the History of Ideas,* 5 (1967), pp. 353–360.

————, *Jewish Philosophy in Modern Times: From Mendelssohn to Rosenzweig* (New York: Holt, Rinehart & Winston, 1968; translated from the Hebrew original which appeared in Tel Aviv: Am Oved, 1950).

————, "Solomon Ludwig Steinheim—Philosopher of Revelation," *Judaism,* 2 (1953), pp. 326–338.

Roth, Leon, *Judaism: A Portrait* (New York: Viking, 1961).

Rothschild, Fritz A., "Abraham Joshua Heschel," in Thomas E. Bird, ed., *Modern Theologians: Christians and Jews* (Notre Dame, Ind.: University of Notre Dame Press, and New York: Association Press, 1967), pp. 169–182.

————, ed., *Between God and Man: An Interpretation of Judaism from the Writings of Abraham J. Heschel* (New York: Harper & Bros., 1959; New York, The Free Press–Macmillan, 1965, paperback edition).

————, "The Concept of God in Jewish Education," *Conservative Judaism,* Vol. 24, #2 (Winter 1970), pp. 2–20.

————, "The Religious Thought of Abraham Heschel," *Conservative Judaism,* Vol. 23, #1 (Fall 1968), pp. 12–24.

————, "Truth and Metaphor in the Bible: An Essay on Interpretation," *Conservative Judaism,* Vol. 25, #3 (Spring 1971), pp. 3–23.

Rubenstein, Richard L., *After Auschwitz* (Indianapolis: Bobbs-Merrill, 1966; also paperback edition).

————, *Eros and Morality* (New York: McGraw-Hill, 1970).

————, *The Religious Imagination* (Indianapolis: Bobbs-Merrill, 1968).

Rudavsky, David, *Emancipation and Adjustment: Contemporary Jewish Religious Movements, their History and Thought* (New York: Diplomatic Press, 1967).

Sachar, Howard Morley, *The Course of Modern Jewish History* (New York: Dell, 1963).

Schatz-Uffenheimer, Rivka, "Contemplative Prayer in Ḥasidism," in *Studies in Religion Presented to Gershom G. Scholem on His Seventieth Birthday* (Jerusalem: Magnes, 1967), pp. 209–226.

Schechter, Solomon, *Seminary Addresses* (New York: Burning Bush Press, 1959). .

————, *Studies in Judaism,* three volumes (Philadelphia: Jewish Publication Society, 1896–1919).

————, *Studies in Judaism: A Selection* (New York: paperback edition, 1958, pp. 150–189; new paperback edition, Atheneum, 1970).

Schilpp, Paul Arthur and Maurice Friedman, eds., *The Philosophy of Martin Buber,* The Library of Living Philosophies, Vol. 12 (La Salle, Illinois: Open Court Publishing Co., 1967). Contains contributions by thirty authors and Buber's replies.

Schneider, Herbert W., "On Reading Heschel's *God in Search of Man:* A Review Article," in *The Review of Religion,* Vol. 21, Nos. 1–2 (November 1956), pp. 31–38.

Schneur, Zalman, of Liadi, *Tanya.* Vol. 1, *Liqqutei Amarim,* Vol. 2, *Shaar Hayichud VeHaemunah,* Vol. 3, *Iggeret Hateshuvah,* Vol. 4, *Iggeret Hakodesh,* Vol. 5, *Kuntres Acharon* (Brooklyn: Kehot, 1962).

Schoeps, Hans-Joachim, ed., *Salomon Ludwig Steinheim zum Gedenken: Ein Sammelband* (Leiden: E. J. Brill, 1966).

Scholem, Gershom G., "Devekuth or Communion with God," *The Review of Religion,* Vol. XIV, (1950), pp. 115–139.

————, *Major Trends in Jewish Mysticism* (Jerusalem: Schocken, 1941, second revised edition 1946; paperback edition, N.Y.: Schocken,1961)

————, "Martin Buber's Hassidism: A Critique," *Commentary,* Vol. 32, #4 (October 1961), pp. 305–316; reprinted in *The Jewish Expression,* edited by Judah Goldin (New York: Bantam, pp. 397–414).

————, *The Messianic Idea in Judaism and Other Essays on Jewish Spirituality* (New York: Schocken, 1971).

————, *On the Kabbalah and its Symbolism* (New York: Schocken, 1965).

Schorsch, Ismar, "The Philosophy of History of Nachman Krochmal," *Judaism,* 10 (1961), pp. 237–245.

Schwarzschild, Steven S., "The Democratic Socialism of Hermann Cohen," in *Hebrew Union College Annual,* Vol. 27 (1956), pp. 417–438.

————, "Franz Rosenzweig and Existentialism," *Yearbook LXII The Central Conference of American Rabbis* (Cincinnati: 1952).

————, *Franz Rosenzweig (1886–1929), Guide of Reversioners.* Makers of Modern Jewish History series, No. 3 (London: Hillel Foundation, 1960).

————, "Franz Rosenzweig on Judaism and Christianity," *Conservative Judaism,* Vol. 10, #2 (Winter 1956), pp. 41–48.

————, "The Lure of Immanence—the Crisis in Contemporary Religious Thought," *Tradition,* Vol. 9, #1–2 (Spring–Summer 1967), pp. 70–99.

Selden, Ruth, *Image of the Jew: Teachers' Guide to Jews and their Religion* (New York: Ktav, 1970).

Selzer, Michael, *Zionism Reconsidered* (New York: Macmillan, 1970).

Sherman, C. Bezalel, *Bund, Galuth, Nationalism, Yiddishism* (New York: Herzl Press, 1918); 28-page pamphlet.

Sherman, Franklin, *The Promise of Heschel* (Philadelphia: J. B. Lippincott, 1970; paperback edition).

Siegel, Seymour, "Contributions of A. J. Heschel to Jewish Scholarship," *Proceedings of the Rabbinical Assembly,* Vol. XXXII, (1968), pp. 72–85.

Silver, Abba Hillel, *Where Judaism Differed* (Philadelphia: Jewish Publication Society, 1957).

Sklare, Marshall, *Conservative Judaism* (New York: Free Press, 1955).

Soloveitchik, Joseph B., "The Lonely Man of Faith," *Tradition,* Vol. 7, #2 (Summer 1965), pp. 5–67.

———, "Confrontation," *Tradition,* Vol. 6, #2 (Spring–Summer 1964), pp. 5–29.

Spero, Shubert, "Is There an Indigenous Jewish Theology?" *Tradition,* Vol. 9, #1–2 (Spring–Summer 1967), pp. 52–69.

Spiegel, Shalom, *Hebrew Reborn* (New York: Macmillan, 1930; paperback edition, Meridian, 1962).

Spiro, Melford, *Kibbutz: Venture in Utopia* (Cambridge, Mass.: Harvard University Press, 1956; New York: Schocken, 1965; paperback edition).

Stahmer, Harold, *"Speak that I May See Thee!": The Religious Significance of Language* (New York: Macmillan, 1968).

Steinberg, Milton, *Anatomy of a Faith,* edited by Arthur Cohen (New York: Harcourt Brace, 1960).

———, *Basic Judaism* (New York: Harcourt Brace, 1947).

———, *A Partisan Guide to the Jewish Problem* (Indianapolis: Bobbs-Merrill, 1945).

Steinheim, Salomon Ludwig, *Die Offenbarung nach dem Lehrbegriff der Synagoge,* 4 volumes (Frankfurt am Main, Leipzig, Altona: 1835–1865).

Stitskin, Leon D., ed., *Studies in Torah Judaism* (New York: Yeshiva University Press–Ktav, 1969).

Streiker, Lowell D., "Martin Buber," in *Modern Theologians: Christians and Jews,* edited by Thomas E. Bird (New York: University of Notre Dame Press and Association Press, 1967), pp. 1–17.

Taubes, Jacob, "The Issue Between Judaism and Christianity," *Commentary,* Vol. XVI (New York: 1953).

———, "Nachman Krochmal and Modern Historicism," *Judaism* 12 (1963), pp. 150–164.

Tillich, Paul, "An Evaluation of Martin Buber: Protestant and Jewish Thought" in *Theology of Culture* (New York: Oxford University Press, 1959), pp. 188–199.

Trepp, Leo, *Eternal Faith, Eternal People* (Englewood Cliffs: Prentice-Hall, 1962).

Waxman, Meyer, *Judaism: Religion and Ethics* (New York: T. Yoseloff, 1958).

Waxman, Mordecai, ed., *Tradition and Change* (New York: Burning Bush Press, 1958, 1964).

Weinberg, J. J., "Lithuanian Mussar," in *Men of the Spirit,* edited by Leo Jung (New York: KYM Son, 1963).

Weiner, Herbert, *Nine and One-Half Mystics* (New York: Holt, Rinehart & Winston, 1969).

———, *The Wild Goats of Ein Gedi* (Garden City: Doubleday Co., 1961; paperback edition, Atheneum, 1970).

Weiss, Joseph, "Contemplative Mysticism and 'Faith' in Hasidic Piety," *Journal of Jewish Studies,* IV (1953), pp. 19–29.

———, "Via Passiva in Early Hasidism," *The Journal of Jewish Studies,* XI (1960), pp. 137–55.

———, "The Kavanoth of Prayer in Early Hasidism," *The Journal of Jewish Studies,* IX (1958), pp. 163–92.

———, "The Great Maggid's Theory of Contemplative Magic," *Hebrew Union College Annual,* XXXI (1960), pp. 137–48.

Wiener, Max, *Abraham Geiger and Liberal Judaism* (Philadelphia: Jewish Publication Society, 1962).

———, *Jüdische Religion im Zeitalter der Emanzipation* (Berlin: Philo, 1933).

Wiener, Theodore, *The Writings of Leo Baeck: A Bibliography,* Studies in Bibliography and Booklore, Vol. 1, #3 (Cincinnati: Hebrew Union College Press, 1954).

Wilensky, Mordecai L., "The Polemic of Rabbi David of Makow Against Hasidism," *Proceedings of the American Academy for Jewish Research,* XXV (1956), pp. 137–156.

Wolf, Arnold J., ed., *Rediscovering Judaism: Reflections on a New Theology* (Chicago: Quadrangle, 1965).

Wood, Robert E., *Martin Buber's Ontology: An Analysis of I and Thou* (Evanston: Northwestern University Press, 1969).

Wouk, Herman, *This Is My God* (Garden City, N.Y.: Doubleday, 1959).

Ysander, Torsten, *Studien zum Bescht'schen Hasidismus in seiner religionsgeschichtlichen Sonderart* (Uppsala: 1933).

THE CONTEMPORARY
JEWISH COMMUNITY

by LLOYD GARTNER

Lloyd T. Gartner, Associate Professor of History of the City College of the City University of New York, is currently on the faculty of the Institute of Contemporary Jewry at the Hebrew University in Jerusalem. Among his publications are *The Jewish Immigrant in England* and *The History of the Jews of Milwaukee,* co-authored with L. J. Swichkow.

To grasp what has happened to the Jewish people in the contemporary world it may be best to begin with numbers.

At the opening of the twentieth century there were about 11,500,000 Jews in the world, of whom 7,000,000 lived in Central and Eastern Europe; 1,000,000 lived in the United States, most of them recent arrivals from the same area. In 1939 there were some 16,700,000 Jews in the world, of whom 7,500,000 lived in Central and Eastern Europe; the number of Jews in the United States stood at around 5,000,000, and the new Jewish community of Palestine could count 500,000. Nearly 6,000,000 European Jews perished during World War II, the vast majority of them systematically murdered by the Nazis during their short-lived conquest of Europe. Three years after the war's conclusion, the State of Israel was founded in 1948 with a population of 650,000. In 1971 there are about 13,000,000 Jews in the world; the State of Israel is the home of 2,500,000, the United States has almost 6,000,000, and Soviet Russia about 3,000,000.

These abruptly changing numbers reflect the revolutionary changes which the Jewish people has undergone in the twentieth century. Mass migration and mass murder; settlement in new countries and the founding of a Jewish state in the ancient homeland; religious diversity and secular ideologies; notable participation in Western culture and a brilliant flowering of Hebrew and Yiddish letters; extensive assimilation to majority cultures and intense communal life—such a list of contrasts could be much longer yet barely suggest the drama and tragedy in contemporary Jewish life and history. And the Jews, as a people who read and write voluminously, already possess a huge literature on all these subjects. The value of this literature, however, is very uneven. Some areas have hardly been explored in a careful, serious manner—Latin America, to cite one instance—while Israel and American Jewry have become, in recent years, the subjects of reliable scholarly study. Jewish migration and anti-Semitism, perhaps surprisingly, still call for basic study. Our list inevitably reflects these strengths and weaknesses.

The following bibliography contains, with few exceptions, books and articles in the English language, providing full citation and critical comments on each work. A few works in French, German, Spanish, and Italian have been cited where necessary. It should be noted that a separate bibliography is being issued on the European Holocaust, so that subject is accordingly omitted here.

I.

GENERAL WORKS

There is no good general survey of contemporary Jewish life or history on a worldwide scale. The works cited here are broad essays and studies.

Salo W. Baron, "The Modern Age" in *Great Ages and Ideas of the Jewish People,* edited by Leo W. Schwarz (New York: Random House, 1956), pp. 315–484.
    A learned and stimulating essay by a foremost Jewish historian.

Ben Zion Dinur, *Israel and the Diaspora* (Philadelphia: Jewish Publication Society of America, 1969).
    A leading Israeli historian's strongly Palestinocentric interpretation of Jewish history, especially in modern times. Stimulating and controversial.

Louis Finkelstein, ed., *The Jews: Their History, Culture and Religion,* third edition, 2 volumes (Philadelphia and New York: Jewish Publication Society of America, Harper & Row, 1960); fourth edition, 3 volumes, paperback (New York: Schocken, 1970).
    Contains substantial sections on modern Jewish history and contributions to civilization, also on the demography and economics of the Jews, by generally expert authors. Chapters of interest include: "East European Jewry" (B. D. Weinryb); "The Decline of European Jewry" (A. Tartakower); "Jewish Religious Life and Institutions in America" (M. Davis); "The Rise of the State of Israel" (O. I.

Janowsky); "Jewish Migration" (J. Lestschinsky); "Economic Structure and Life of the Jews" (S. Kuznets); "The Jews Outside of Israel, the United States, and the Soviet Union" (M. Himmelfarb); "Social Characteristics of American Jews" (N. Glazer).

Solomon Grayzel, *A History of the Contemporary Jews from 1900 to the Present* (Philadelphia: Jewish Publication Society of America, 1960), paperback: Atheneum.
   A sketchy short history.

Koppel S. Pinson, ed., *Essays on Anti-Semitism*, second edition, (New York: Conference on Jewish Relations, 1946).
   An excellent collection of historical and analytic studies, with emphasis on modern Europe. There are chapters on France (H. Arendt), Germany (W. Gurian), Russia (M. Vishniak), Poland (R. Mahler), and on psychological aspects (I. S. Wechsler, Z. Diesendruck).

Arthur Ruppin, *The Jewish Fate and Future* (London: The Macmillan Co., 1940).

————, *The Jews in the Modern World* (London: The Macmillan Co., 1935).

————, *The Jews of To-Day* (London: G. Bell and Sons, 1913).
   Three cross-sectional, thoroughly informed surveys of the Jewish people—demographic and ideological—at three different periods during the recent past.

Jacob L. Talmon, *The Unique and the Universal* (New York: George Braziller, 1965).
   On the interrelation between modern European and Jewish history, especially in ideas of nationalism, socialism, and totalitarianism. Highly provocative.

Mark Wischnitzer, *To Dwell in Safety: The Story of Jewish Migration since 1800* (Philadelphia: Jewish Publication of America, 1949).
   A fair history of the vast migration of Jews from East to West.

II.

UNITED STATES

Jews have lived as a community in what is now the United States since approximately 1654, at New Amsterdam, but the great numerical growth occurred between 1880 and 1925, when American Jewry multiplied, thanks to East European immigration, from 280,000 to 4,500,000. The major phase of American Jewish history therefore lies in this century. As mentioned above, there is already a substantial literature of merit. In order to deal adequately with American Jewry, however, it is necessary to view it in the dual perspective of American and of Jewish history. Comparative studies with other American religious and ethnic groups, and with the worldwide Jewish past, greatly deepen our understanding.

The literature on American Jewry has been divided into three parts: A. Periodicals; B. History and Sociology; C. Cultural and Religious Life (an area of study still rather weak). It should be noted that most works cited in Section I above treat American Jewry in some detail.

A. PERIODICALS

Numerous fine periodicals appear which furnish the best view of current affairs and outlooks.

American Jewish Year Book (Philadelphia: Jewish Publication Society of America and American Jewish Committee).

Annual, since 1899. Basic population and communal data, and a review of yearly events throughout the world. Since the 1950's important articles have appeared each year. Invaluable is Elfrida C. Solis-Cohen, *American Jewish Year Book: Index to Volumes 1–50, 1889–1949 (5660–5709)*, New York: 1967. The length and careful detail of the *American Jewish Year Book* make it a source of rare value for contemporary Jewish history.

Commentary (New York: American Jewish Committee).

Monthly since 1946. An influential journal of general opinion and of Jewish affairs, somewhat to the left of center.

Judaism (New York: American Jewish Congress).

Quarterly published since 1952 by the American Jewish Congress, specializing in religious thought.

Midstream (New York: Herzl Institute).

A monthly since 1955 mostly of Jewish affairs, Zionist in orientation, published by the Theodor Herzl Foundation.

Leo W. Schwarz, *The Menorah Treasury: Harvest of Half a Century* (Philadelphia: Jewish Publication Society of America, 1964).

A splendid selection of essays, poems, and studies from the leading American Jewish magazine, ca. 1913–1950. Reflective of the cultural, literary, and intellectual trends of its time.

B. History and Sociology

General histories and studies of major communities are included, besides studies of the status of the Jew in American society.

Stephen Birmingham, *"Our Crowd": The Great Jewish Families of New York* (New York: Harper & Row, 1966); also paperback.

Notwithstanding its inaccuracies and superficiality, this work sheds much light on the Jewish upper bourgeoisie during its important years, ca. 1870–1920.

Rudolf Glanz, *Studies in Judaica Americana* (New York: Ktav, 1970).

Studies of immigration culture and social life during the nineteenth century. Unusual materials are quarried, and the results are very suggestive for the relations among American ethnic groups.

Nathan Glazer, *American Judaism* (Chicago: University of Chicago Press, 1957); also paperback.

A good short account. Its emphasis on the "religious revival" marks it as a book of the 1950's. In the Chicago History of American Civilization series.

Charles Y. Glock and Rodney Stark, *Christian Beliefs and Anti-Semitism* (New York: Harper & Row, 1965); also paperback.

Based on a study conducted by the Survey Research Center of the University of California, Berkeley. Shows that certain patterns of Christian belief play a major role in developing and maintaining anti-Jewish prejudice in this country. Part of the Patterns of American Prejudice series.

Arthur Goren, *New York Jews in Quest of Community: The Kehillah Experiment 1908–1922* (New York: Columbia University Press, 1970).

A fine study of Jewish communal and cultural efforts during the climax of the immigrant period. Supplemented by Rischin, below.

Ben Halpern, *The American Jew: A Zionist Analysis* (New York: Herzl Press, 1956).

An able statement of the position that America is a Christian society, and that Jewish status within it will always be limited.

Will Herberg, "The Jewish Labor Movement in the United States," *American Jewish Year Book,* LIII (1952), pp. 3–74.

A well-informed survey, emphasizing the Jewish labor movement's acculturation to the English language, and its transition to liberal instead of radical politics.

John Higham, *Strangers in the Land: Patterns of American Nativism, 1860–1925* (New Brunswick, New Jersey: Rutgers University Press, 1954); paperback: Atheneum, 1963.

An outstanding treatment of nativist anti-immigration sentiment, and of the rise of intellectualized racist doctrines including anti-Semitism.

Robert Morris and Michael Freund, eds., *Trends and Issues in Jewish Social Work in the United States, 1899–1952* (Philadelphia: Jewish Publication Society of America, 1962).

A good selection from contemporary sources illustrating the most typical activity of Jews in America. Changing programs and objectives are emphasized over administrative and financial matters.

Moses Rischin, *The Promised City: New York's Jews, 1870–1914* (Cambridge, Mass.: Harvard University Press, 1962); paperback: Corinth Books, 1964.

A basic study of Jewish immigrants in New York City, dealing principally with economic and social life as well as Yiddish cultures and trade unionism, against the general American background. Supplemented by Goren, above.

Stuart E. Rosenberg, *The Jewish Community in Rochester, 1843–1925.* (New York: American Jewish Historical Society, 1954).

A comprehensive study of a prosperous upstate New York city, especially its religious and cultural phases. About 21,000 Jews live there.

Gertrude J. Selznick and Stephen Steinberg, *The Tenacity of Prejudice* (New York: Harper & Row, 1969).

First intensive nationwide analysis of the degree and sources of anti-Semitism. Part of Patterns of American Prejudice series. Shows extent to which Americans are committed in their attitudes to a democratic and pluralistic society.

C. Bezalel Sherman, *The Jew within American Society: A Study in Ethnic Individuality* (Detroit: Wayne State University Press, 1960); also paperback.

A well-informed study of the place of Jews within American life, utilizing much comparative data with other ethnic groups. Last revised during the 1950's, its conclusions are now somewhat dated.

Marshall Sklare, ed., *The Jews: Social Patterns of an American Group* (New York and London: The Free Press, 1958).

An extremely well-selected group of sociological studies by various authors illuminating the principal phases of American Jewish life.

————, director, *The Lakeville Studies.* Volume I: Marshall Sklare and Joseph Greenblum, *Jewish Identity on the Suburban Frontier: A Study of Group Survival in the Open Society;* Volume II: Benjamin B. Ringer, *The Edge of Friendliness: A Study of Jewish-Gentile Relations* (New York: Basic Books, 1967).

A comprehensive, penetrating study of Jewish life, status, and group dynamics in an affluent Midwestern suburb. This is the deepest analysis of contemporary American Jewish thought and group life.

Charles Herbert Stember and others, *Jews in the Mind of America* (New York: Basic Books, 1966).

A survey of the depth and extent of anti-Semitism in America by means of public-opinion polling, together with astute evaluations by various experts. The general evaluation is optimistic.

Louis J. Swichkow and Lloyd P. Gartner, *The History of the Jews of Milwaukee* (Philadelphia: Jewish Publication Society of America, 1963).

This city and its Jewish community of 24,000 are noteworthy for their Germanic and socialist past, which this detailed work stresses.

Judd L. Teller, *Strangers and Natives: The Evolution of the American Jew from 1921 to the Present* (New York: Delacorte, 1968).

Well informed and interesting, but tends to emphasize the curious over the basic, and New York's lower East Side. It is very good for New York City during the 1920's and 1930's.

Max Vorspan and Lloyd P. Gartner, *A History of the Jews of Los Angeles* (San Marino, California and Philadelphia: Huntington Library and Jewish Publication Society of America, 1970).

This metropolis is America's boom city par excellence, and its Jewish community has developed in similar fashion. A comprehensive study.

C. CULTURAL AND RELIGIOUS LIFE

Robert Alter, *After the Tradition: Essays on Modern Jewish Writing* (New York: E. P. Dutton, 1969).

Probably the best critical analysis of the American Jewish writers of the 1950's and 1960's.

Lloyd P. Gartner, *Jewish Education in America: A Documentary History* (New York: Teachers' College Press, 1970); also paperback.

Introduction and documents, emphasizing the relations between public and Jewish education, cultural pluralism, and the place of education in Jewish communal life.

Hutchins Hapgood, *The Spirit of the Ghetto,* edited by Moses Rischin (Cambridge, Mass.: Harvard University Press, 1967). Illustrations by Jacob Epstein.

Excellent edition of a minor classic, first published in 1902. Another edition by Harry L. Golden, New York: Schocken Books, 1965, in a paperback edition. Scenes from the social and cultural life of immigrants on New York's Lower East Side, absorbingly written.

Oscar I. Janowsky, ed., *The American Jew: A Reappraisal* (Philadelphia: Jewish Publication Society of America, 1967).

A good although unimaginative collection of studies on contemporary American Jewry. Strongest on Jewish education.

Mordecai M. Kaplan, *Judaism as a Civilization: Toward a Reconstruction of American Jewish Life* (New York: The Macmillan Co., 1934; Schocken, 1967); also paperback.

A major work of theology, deriving in part from a social analysis of American Jewry of the 1920's and 1930's; a classic of Jewish thought. The author is the founder of the Reconstructionist religious movement.

Charles S. Liebman, "Orthodoxy in American Jewish Life," *American Jewish Year Book,* LXVI (1965), pp. 21–97.

A well-informed, thoughtful account of the least-studied sector of

American Judaism, demonstrating that Orthodox Judaism has passed the stage of an immigrant religion and found its place in American Judaism.

W. Gunther Plaut, *The Growth of Reform Judaism: American and European Sources until 1948* (New York: World Union for Progressive Judaism, 1965).

A serviceable collection of sources, thematically arranged, covering 1870–1948. Like Reform Judaism itself, the focus is on America.

Marshall Sklare, *Conservative Judaism: An American Religious Movement* (Glencove, Ill.: The Free Press, 1955).

A discerning history and analysis of Conservative Judaism, emphasizing its social background more than its religious thought. Supplemented by Waxman, below.

Carl Hermann Voss, ed., *Stephen S. Wise: Servant of the People* (Philadelphia: Jewish Publication Society of America, 1969).

Selected letters of the foremost public rabbinic figure and Zionist of his time.

Mordecai Waxman, *Tradition and Change: The Development of Conservative Judaism* (New York: Burning Bush Press, 1958).

A good collection of sources for its subject, emphasizing theology and Jewish law. An important supplement to Sklare, above.

III.

THE WESTERN HEMISPHERE

Literature on Jews in Canada and Latin America is rather scanty. The following is perforce a small selection.

Jacob Beller, *Jews in Latin America* (New York: Jonathan David, 1969).

An interesting but uncritical survey and history.

Mauricio J. Dulfano, "Anti-Semitism in Argentina: Patterns of Jewish Adaptation," *Jewish Social Studies* XXXI, 2 (April 1969), pp. 122–144.

A description of Jewish reactions to Argentine anti-Semitism.

Irving Louis Horowitz, "The Jewish Community of Buenos Aires," *Jewish Social Studies,* XXIV, 4 (October 1962), pp. 195–222.

A well-conceived sociological analysis of Jewish outlooks and communal structure in Buenos Aires, where about 350,000 Jews dwell.

Robert M. Levine, "Brazil's Jews During the Vargas Era and After," *Luso-Brazilian Review,* Vol. V, No. 1 (June 1968), pp. 45–58.

Concentrates on legal status and anti-Semitism, 1930–1950.

Abraham Monk and Jose Isaacson, eds., *Comunidades judias de Latinoamerica 1968* (Buenos Aires: Editorial Candelabro, 1968).

A useful survey by country, including directories of institutions, with some brief special articles.

Louis Rosenberg, *Canada's Jews* (Montreal: Canadian Jewish Congress, 1939).

The standard social and demographic study, now somewhat antiquated. The same author's supplementary, briefer studies published subsequently round out the picture.

IV.

WESTERN EUROPE

In 1900, Western Europe—specifically Germany, France, and England—was the center of emancipated Jewry, the model of aspiration for the East European Jewish masses. The high political and social status of the Jews of Western Europe, and the distinguished contributions they made to their respective national cultures, corresponded to the world dominance exercised by that region. That picture has changed altogether. The tragedy of German Jewry in the twentieth century is well known; as to the Jews of France, they underwent serious native anti-Semitism, Nazi rule, and a revival, thanks to the large-scale immigration of North African Jews during recent years. Only English Jewry remained comparatively unscathed, but its influence in Jewish life declined with that of England itself.

Not much is available on the Jews of Western Europe, aside from England, in the English language. An exception is Nazism and its impact, not covered in this bibliography.

H. G. Adler, *The Jews in Germany: From the Enlightenment to National Socialism* (Notre Dame: University of Notre Dame Press, 1969).

A capable, brief account emphasizing the tensions and ambiguities of German-Jewish relations.

Georges Benguigui, Josiane Bijaoui-Rosenfeld, Georges Levitte, *Aspects of French Jewry*. Introductory essay by Otto Kleinberg (London: Vallentine, Mitchell, 1969).

After the introduction, a sketch of recent French Jewry, and sociological studies of Jewish students at the University of Paris and the integration in France of North African Jews. A worthwhile addition to the very limited knowledge of French Jewry.

Pierre Aubéry, *Milieux juifs de la France contemporaine* (Paris: Plon, 1957).

Based on Jewish memoirs and novels with Jewish characters, the author skillfully describes the various circles and outlooks of French Jews.

Centre national des études juives-Bruxelles [and] Institute of Contemporary Jewry at the Hebrew University, Jerusalem, *La vie juive dans l'Europe contemporaine: Jewish Life in Contemporary Europe* (Brussels: Editions de l'Institut de Sociologie de l'Université Libre de Bruxelles, 1965).

Demographic and cultural topics are treated in a series of papers and discussions on continental Western Europe since 1945. The papers are in French and English.

Rezo De Felice, *Storia degli ebrei italiani sotto il fascimo* (Turin: Einaudi, 1962).

The standard work, which should be translated into English.

Ismar Elbogen, *Geschichte der Juden in Deutschland* (Berlin: Jüdische Buch Vereinigung, 1935).

Although antiquated, this short history by one of the great German Jewish scholars has not been superseded.

Maurice Freedman, ed., *A Minority in Britain: Social Studies of the Anglo-Jewish Community* (London: Vallentine, Mitchell, 1955).

A brief history followed by demographic, psychological, and sociological studies of British Jewry. A valuable work.

Lloyd P. Gartner, *The Jewish Immigrant in England, 1870–1914*
(London and Detroit: George Allen and Unwin, Wayne State University Press, 1960).
 The formative period of contemporary Anglo-Jewry, dealing with
the era of the great immigration from Eastern Europe.

Julius Gould and Shaul Esh, eds., *Jewish Life in Modern Britain:*
Papers and Proceedings of a Conference . . . 1st and 2nd April,
1962 . . . (London: Routledge Kegan Paul, 1964).
 Valuable papers and stimulating discussion on Jews in contemporary England, especially inner Jewish life.

Leo Baeck Institute of Jews from Germany, *Yearbook* (1956—) 13
vols. to date.
 Concerned with all phases of modern German Jewish life, its greatness, problems, and tragedy, these volumes are a real treasury. They
are quite readable, and all but a few articles are in English. Although
topics of cultural and intellectual history predominate, there are extensive studies of political and economic life.

Paul Massing, *Rehearsal for Destruction: A Study of Political Anti-*
Semitism in Imperial Germany (New York: Harper & Row, 1949).
 An able study of pre-1914 anti-Semitism, with emphasis on the
political structure and parties. It exposes the roots of later disasters.

Rabi [pseud. of Vladimir Rabinowitz], *Anatomie du judaisme français*
(Paris: Editions de Minuit, 1962).
 A stimulating history, discussion and essay on French Jewry's history and mentality.

Society for the History of Czechoslovak Jews, *The Jews of Czecho-*
slovakia: Historical Studies and Surveys (Philadelphia: Jewish Publication Society of America, 1968).
 A substantial collection, mostly on the nineteenth and twentieth
centuries. The value of the studies varies a good deal.

V.

EASTERN EUROPE

 East European Jewry was for three centuries the numerical and
intellectual center of the Jewish people. Notwithstanding oppression and poverty it retained this focal position until World War I

and its aftermath. After 1918, Russian Communism was strongly hostile to Jewish religion and culture with a brief exception made for Yiddish "proletarian culture," while the new Poland was generally ruled by anti-Semitic regimes, although Polish Jews continued in their cultural eminence. The Jewish situation between the wars was little better in the smaller states of East Central Europe. The culminating disaster was the Holocaust during World War II in which almost the entire Jewish population of these countries (except for the unconquered sections of Russia and a less thorough slaughter in Hungary and Rumania) was killed by the Nazis according to plan. Since then East European Jewry has been a shadow of its former greatness. In Russia there live as many as 3,000,000 Jews, but the Communist regime is all but openly anti-Semitic.

Literature in English is unfortunately sparse, with the partial exception of works on the Jews under Communist rule. Books cited in Section I, above, deal extensively with Eastern Europe.

Salo W. Baron, *The Russian Jew under Tsars and Soviets* (New York and London: The Macmillan Co., 1964).
A thorough, dispassionate survey, especially useful for the Soviet period.

Lucy S. Dawidowicz, *The Golden Tradition: Jewish Life and Thought in Eastern Europe* (New York: Holt, Rinehart & Winston, 1967); paperback, Beacon Press.
A comprehensive view of Jewish life, beliefs, and ideologies in Eastern Europe as told from autobiographical sources. There is a fine historical introduction.

Oscar I. Janowsky, *People at Bay: The Jewish Problem in East-Central Europe* (New York: Oxford University Press, 1938).
Brief but comprehensive, this work surveys the desperate condition of the Jews in Poland, Rumania, and the neighboring small states on the eve of World War II.

Lionel Kochan, ed., *The Jews in Soviet Russia Since 1917* (Oxford: University Press, 1970).
A collection of authoritative articles on Soviet Jewry including economics, anti-Semitism, Yiddish, the Birobidzhan project and other subjects. Emphasis is placed on the post World War II period.

Peter Meyer, Bernard D. Weinryb, Eugene Duschinsky, Nicholas Sylvain, *The Jews in the Soviet Satellites* (Syracuse: Syracuse University Press, 1953).

The countries covered are Czechoslovakia, Poland, Hungary, Rumania, and Bulgaria. After a short survey of the condition of the Jews on the eve of World War II and their fate during that conflict, there is a detailed study of the situation until 1953, when this thorough, authoritative book was published.

Perspectives on Soviet Jewry (New York: Academic Committee for Soviet Jewry and the Anti-Defamation League of B'nai B'rith, 1971); paperback.

A compilation of papers by Nathan Glazer, Moshe Decter, William Korey, John A. Armstrong, Alex Inkeles, Hans J. Morgenthau, Maurice Friedberg and Paul Lendvai.

Maurice Samuel, *Blood Accusation: The Strange History of the Beilis Case* (New York: Knopf, 1966).

Authoritative, brilliantly written account of a notorious blood-libel case, 1911–1913, which casts light on Czarist anti-Semitic machinations.

Solomon M. Schwarz, *The Jews in the Soviet Union* (Syracuse: Syracuse University Press, 1951).

The most comprehensive, authoritative work on Communist ideology bearing on the Jews; social and political status of Russian Jews; anti-Semitism in Russia; the Birobidzhan venture. It has not been antiquated or superseded.

Simon Segal, *The New Poland and the Jews* (New York: L. Furman, 1938).

The best general study of the legal, political, and economic position of Polish Jewry between the World Wars. Sharply critical of the Polish government.

VI.

THE ORIENT

The serious study of Jews in Muslim and other Oriental lands during modern times has barely begun. These are two significant works:

Itzhak Ben-Zvi, *The Exiled and the Redeemed,* second edition (Philadelphia: Jewish Publication Society of America, 1963).

Studies of remote and almost forgotten Jewish communities, mainly in the Orient, by the second President of Israel who devoted years to basic research on their life and history.

André N. Chouraqui, *Between East and West: A History of the Jews of North Africa* (Philadelphia: Jewish Publication Society of America, 1968).

One of the few modern studies of Oriental Jewish communities in a Western language. A satisfactory survey.

VII.

ISRAEL

The State of Israel is the Jewish miracle of the twentieth century. An eroded, nearly abandoned land transformed into a fertile, populous one; religious faith in messianic restoration changed into a national movement of revival and resettlement; a surge of Hebrew language and culture; social experiments in new forms of industry and agriculture; a mass of refugees and immigrants from backward countries made into confident, productive citizens; an innovative, functioning system of health, social welfare, and education at all levels; worldwide Jewish support and enthusiasm; military skill and bravery against heavy odds—it is no wonder that the Jewish state has fascinated the world.

A huge literature already exists, and is growing rapidly. Much of it is excellent in quality. In addition to the works listed in this section, most of those in General Works (I) devote considerable attention to Israel.

A. The Zionist Movement and Rebirth of Palestine

Alex Bein, *Theodore Herzl* (Philadelphia: Jewish Publication Society of America, 1940); paperback: Atheneum, 1970.

Standard, well-written biography of the founder of political Zionism. A revised edition would be welcome, in view of recent research.

David Ben-Gurion, *Rebirth and Destiny of Israel* (New York: Philosophical Library, 1954).

Essays and addresses, 1915–1952, by the Israeli leader. Highly expressive of his personal vision and character so influential in his country's development.

ESCO Foundation for Palestine, *Palestine: A Study of Jewish, Arab and British Policies.* 2 volumes (New Haven: Yale University Press, 1947).
Thorough and basic for the period of the British mandate. I. B. Berkson is the principal author.

Ben Halpern, *The Idea of the Jewish State,* Second edition (Cambridge, Mass.: Harvard University Press, 1969).
A sociologically oriented, somewhat abstract history of the conception of a modern Jewish state. Expertly informed.

Arthur Hertzberg, ed. and trans., *The Zionist Idea: A Historical Analysis and Reader* (Garden City and New York: Doubleday & Co. and Herzl Press, 1959); also paperback, Atheneum, 1970.
A substantial anthology of Zionist writings with a fine introduction. The best approach to Zionist thought, which underlies the creation of the State of Israel.

J. C. Hurewitz, *The Struggle for Palestine* (New York: W. W. Norton, 1950).
Thorough but pedestrian diplomatic history of the 1930's and 1940's.

Abraham Revusky, *Jews in Palestine* (New York: Vanguard, 1945).
Very good survey of Palestinian Jewry in the pre-State of Israel period.

Leonard Stein, *The Balfour Declaration* (New York: Simon and Schuster, 1961).
The standard study of the most important event in Zionist diplomatic history, Great Britain's declaration in 1917 of support for a "Jewish National Home."

Chaim Weizmann, *Trial and Error* (New York: Harper & Row, 1949).
Highly personal reminiscences of the Zionist leader and first President of Israel. See Oscar K. Rabinowicz, *Fifty Years of Zionism: A Historical Analysis of Dr. Chaim Weizmann's Trial and Error* (London: R. Anscombe, 1950) for a well-informed critique.

B. POLITICAL AND DIPLOMATIC AFFAIRS

Yehuda Bauer, *From Diplomacy to Resistance* (Philadelphia: Jewish Publication Society of America, 1970).

A study of Palestinian Jewish diplomacy during World War II, showing how military experience was acquired and techniques of armed resistance developed in preparation for the post-war struggle to found the Jewish Commonwealth.

————, *Flight and Rescue: Brichah* (New York: Random House, 1970).

A fascinating masterful account of the organized escape of the Jewish survivors of Eastern Europe, 1944–1948. Based on archival sources and extensive oral documentation.

Marver H. Bernstein, *The Politics of Israel: The First Decade of Statehood* (Princeton: Princeton University Press, 1957).

An authoritative analysis of government in its day-by-day operation which has value well beyond the date of publication. See also L. J. Fein, below, for a different view of government.

Theodore Draper, *Israel and World Politics: Roots of the Third Arab-Israeli War* (New York: Viking Press, 1968).

Able, well-written summary of the background of the Six Day War with a documentary appendix. Emphasizes American activity and Arab backgrounds. Supplements Laqueur, below.

Leonard J. Fein, *Israel: Politics and People* (Boston and Toronto: Little, Brown, 1968); also paperback.

An excellent, well-written study which deals more with "political culture" and attitudes within Israel than with the state's formal political structure and activity. Compare with M. H. Bernstein, above.

Oscar I. Janowsky, *Foundations of Israel: Emergence of a Welfare State* (Princeton: Van Nostrand, 1959); paperback.

An adequate, brief account of the historic background and actual workings of the State of Israel. Useful brief documents are appended.

Jacob M. Landau, *The Arabs in Israel: A Political Study* (London, New York, Toronto: Oxford University Press, 1969).

Well-documented, dispassionate study by an Israeli authority.

Walter Laqueur, *The Road to War 1967: The Origins of the Arab-Israel Conflict* (London: Weidenfeld and Nicholson, 1968).

A thoroughly informed account with a documentary appendix, which focuses on Israeli actions during the diplomatic crisis. Supplements Draper, above.

Netanel Lorch, *The Edge of the Sword: Israel's War of Independence, 1947–1949* (New York: G. P. Putnam, 1961).

A substantial history of the war against the Arab invasion of 1948 to establish the state. Semi-official and authoritative.

Nadav Safran, *From War to War: The Arab-Israeli Confrontation, 1948–1967* (New York: Pegasus, 1969); paperback edition.

A comprehensive, judicious analysis of the relations between Israel and its Arab neighbors taking all principal factors into account.

————, *The United States and Israel* (Cambridge, Mass.: Harvard University Press, 1963).

A volume in the American Foreign Policy Library. Valuable on the Israeli political background; good discussion of diplomatic relations.

Ernest Stock, *Israel on the Road to Sinai 1949–1956* (Ithaca, N.Y.: Cornell University Press, 1967).

"With a sequel on the Six-Day War, 1967." An analysis of Israeli's international situation and foreign policy leading to the Sinai campaign of 1956.

C. THE PEOPLE OF ISRAEL—THEIR BACKGROUNDS, SOCIAL INSTITUTIONS, CULTURAL LIFE

Joseph S. Bentwich, *Education in Israel* (Philadelphia: Jewish Publication Society of America, 1965).

A useful exposition of the varieties of Israeli school systems with a glimpse of some of their characteristic problems.

Shneour Z. Cheshin, *Tears and Laughter in an Israel Courtroom* (Philadelphia: Jewish Publication Society of America, 1959).

Instructive and entertaining work by a Justice of the Supreme Court of Israel. Valuable for judicial procedures and for the types of cases which come to court.

S. N. Eisenstadt, *Israeli Society* (New York: Basic Books, 1967).

A major, full-scale analysis by the leading Israeli sociologist. All significant social movements and institutions are analyzed in this important work.

Georges Friedmann, *The End of the Jewish Peope?* (Garden City, N.Y.: Doubleday, 1967).

A French sociologist's scrutiny of Israel and its transformation into an industrial society; highly stimulating. Some personal speculations are also included.

Judah Matras, *Social Change in Israel* (Chicago: Aldine Press, 1965).

A concise, concentrated sociological study of changes within Israeli social structure and in social roles since the 1940's. A valuable work.

Raphael Patai, *Israel Between East and West: A Study in Human Relations,* Second revised edition (Westport, Conn.: Greenwood, 1970).

An anthropologically oriented study of social and cultural life, problems, and changes among Oriental Jews settling in westernized Israeli society.

Howard Morley Sachar, *Aliyah: The Peoples of Israel* (Cleveland and New York: World Publishing, 1961); from the *Ends of the Earth: The Peoples of Israel* (Cleveland and New York: World Publishing, 1964).

Biographical "case studies" of characteristic members of Israel's diverse population. Instructive and diverting.

Ronald Sanders, *Israel: The View from Masada* (New York: Harper & Row, 1966).

Interesting and competent survey, especially useful for its awareness of the deep links of Israeli reality with Jewish history and Zionist thought.

Judith T. Shuval, *Immigrants on the Threshold* (New York: Atherton Press, 1963).

A very instructive sociological study of 2000 immigrants' first year in Israel, with close attention to their backgrounds and adaptive abilities.

Melford E. Spiro, *Kibbutz: Venture in Utopia* (Cambridge, Mass.: Harvard University Press, 1956); paperback edition.

An anthropologist's penetrating, lucid view of the Israeli collective; the work examines a secular, Marxist-oriented settlement.

Alex Weingrod, *Israel: Group Relations in A New Society* (New York: Praeger, 1965).

Brief, expert account of relations among the various social, economic, and cultural strata of Israel.

————, *Reluctant Pioneers: Village Development in Israel* (Ithaca, N.Y.: Cornell University Press, 1966).

The trials, failures, and achievements of Moroccan Jewish immigrants settled in a new village in the Negev, by an anthropologist.

Ferdynand Zweig, *The Israeli Worker: Achievements, Attitudes and Aspirations* (New York: Herzl Press, 1959).

A lively study of the articulate, variegated working class of Israel.

THE HOLOCAUST:
ANTI-SEMITISM
AND THE JEWISH
CATASTROPHE

---

by HENRY FRIEDLANDER

Henry Friedlander was born in Germany, in 1930. In 1941 he was deported to the Lodz ghetto and from there to Auschwitz. He emigrated to the United States in 1947.

Dr. Friedlander is presently on the faculty of the City University of New York. He served as staff member of the Committee for the Study of War Documents and is the author of *Guides to German Records, Nos. 5, 8, 11, and 13*. In addition, he has written numerous papers and articles on German Socialism, the German Revolution of 1918-19, and the Nazi regime. Currently, he is writing a history of the Holocaust.

The Holocaust forms a separate chapter in Jewish history. For Jews the Catastrophe has become a haunting trauma, punctuating the history that began at Sinai. The destruction of European Jewry, the historical and intellectual center of the Jewish people, has fundamentally transformed Jewish existence in the dispersion, ending the 2000-year-old Christian-Jewish symbiosis. The victory of racial anti-Semitism leading to planned and organized mass murder has cast doubt upon the value of Emancipation and thus conferred legitimacy upon the founding of Israel. Even for non-Jews the murder of millions in the center of Christian Europe in our times has revealed the barbarism that continues to exist under the veneer of civilization.

However, the history of the Holocaust, central to any understanding of 20th-century totalitarianism as well as modern Jewish history, has so far been excluded from most historical accounts—general as well as Jewish, popular as well as academic. Even in the card catalogues of major libraries the Holocaust is a very recent entry; most works on it are still classified under many diverse headings as, for example, "Europe—World War II—German Occupation—Jews." Still, the literature of the Holocaust is already large and is constantly growing. Although much is only accessible to those who read Yiddish, a great deal is now available in English, more if we add French and German.

I.

REFERENCE MATERIALS

A. BIBLIOGRAPHIES

For the serious student interested in pursuing the study of the

Holocaust in greater detail a number of guides and bibliographies
are now available.

Guide to Jewish history under nazi impact. Edited by Jacob Robinson
and Philip Friedman. Yad Vashem and Yivo Joint Documentary
Project, Bibliographical Series No. 1. New York, 1960.

Indispensable. This massive guide contains over 3,500 entries,
explanatory notes, and exemplary indices covering all aspects of the
Holocaust, including interpretations, bibliographies, libraries, and
documents.

Ten further volumes in this series, published by the two leading
research institutes, include bibliographies of Hebrew and Yiddish
books and articles and Randolph L. Braham's *The Hungarian Jewish
Catastrophe: A Selected and Annotated Bibliography* (New York,
1962).

Books on persecution, terror and resistance in nazi Germany. Edited
by Ilse R. Wolff. The Wiener Library Catalogue Series No. 1. 2nd
rev. ed. London, 1960.

From Weimar to Hitler: Germany, 1918–1933. Edited by Ilse R.
Wolff. The Wiener Library Catalogue Series No. 2. 2nd rev. ed.
London, 1964.

German Jewry: its history, life and culture. Edited by Ilse R. Wolff.
The Wiener Library Catalogue Series No. 3. London, 1958.

Three valuable catalogues from the holdings of the Wiener Library
in London.

La France: de l'affaire Dreyfus à nos jours. Centre de Documentation
Juive Contemporaine, Catalogue No. 1. Paris, 1964.

La France, le troisième reich, Israël. Centre de Documentation Juive
Contemporaine, Catalogue No. 2. Paris, 1968.

The two bibliographies from the holdings of the Paris Centre.

B. JOURNALS

A number of scholarly journals cover, exclusively or in part, the
history of the Holocaust. Containing important articles, they are
also essential for the information they bring about the continuing
research into the Jewish Catastrophe.

Le monde juive. Paris, 1946 ff.

The journal of the Parisian Centre de Documentation Juive Contemporaine, perhaps the most impressive of the research institutes dedicated to the study of the Holocaust. The Centre, concentrating on events in France, has also published, in French, a large number of scholarly monographs.

Revue d'histoire de la deuxième guerre mondiale. Paris, 1950 ff.

The most important journal dealing with Nazi domination and anti-Nazi Resistance in occupied Europe. Several times the journal dedicated an entire issue to a problem surrounding the Holocaust: "Le système concentrationaire allemand," IV, 15–16 (1954); "La condition des Juifs," VI, 24 (1956); "Camps de concentration," XII, 45 (1962).

The Wiener library bulletin. London, 1946 ff.

The extremely valuable publication of the Wiener Library, the impressive London institute dedicated to the study of Fascism, racism, and anti-Semitism. Contains excellent bibliographies, short research articles, and a survey of the press. Since 1965 published in conjunction with the ADL, with a changed and less valuable format.

Yad Vashem studies on the European Jewish catastrophe and resistance. Annual, irregular. Jerusalem, 1957 ff.

An annual publication dedicated exclusively to an investigation of the Holocaust, the *studies* are published by the Yad Vashem Martyrs' and Heroes' Memorial Authority, the official institute established in Jerusalem by the Government of Israel. Haphazardly edited and translated, the value of its articles varies a great deal; a few are good, some are fair, and many are poor. Yad Vashem also publishes a *Bulletin* in English (Jerusalem, 1957 ff.).

Yearbook of the Leo Baeck Society. London: East and West Library, 1956 ff.

Annual publication of the Leo Baeck Society (Jerusalem, London, and New York) founded by the Council of Jews from Germany. Expertly edited, the volumes contain valuable articles, many of them scholarly. Concentrating on German Jewish history before 1933, they have recently also included studies of anti-Semitism and of German Jewry in the Nazi era. Most important, each volume includes an annual bibliography compiled by the Wiener Library. The Society also publishes scholarly monographs in English and in German and a *Bulletin* in German (Tel Aviv: Bitaon, 1957 ff.).

Yivo Bleter. Vilna and New York, 1931 ff.

The leading scholarly Yiddish journal, published since 1940 by the Yivo Institute for Jewish Research, the New York successor to the Yiddish Scientific Institute of Vilna. Concentrating on the history and culture of East European Jewry, it also includes articles on the Holocaust; its first and second issue of Vol. 30 (1947) was dedicated to a study of the Catastrophe.

Every year an English translation of the most important articles appears in the *Yivo Annual of Jewish Social Science* (New York, 1946 ff.). The contributions, varying in scholarship, usually contain valuable information not otherwise available. Of special interest is Vol. VIII: "Studies on the epoch of the Jewish catastrophe, 1933–1945."

II.

ANTI-SEMITISM AND THE THIRD REICH

To understand, if possible, the causes of the Catastrophe, it is essential to probe the minds of those who planned and executed the murder of Europe's Jews. Of course, we still cannot truly understand how a supposedly civilized people in the heart of modern Europe could develop murder into an industry, in the process killing millions of men, women, and children with machinelike precision. The following works attempt to explain the mystery posed by the Nazi phenomenon.

The first group includes histories and analyses of anti-Semitism and of Nazi ideology (without, however, listing works by anti-Semites). Some experts see the hatred of Jews in our times as unrelated to that of earlier ages, almost as *sui generis,* because anti-Semitism based on race differed substantially from that based on religion. Others, however, see it only as the last, and most ferocious, expression of an old, traditional hostility. But all agree that anti-Semitism was central to the Nazi phenomenon.

The second group lists studies of the Nazi regime. Because the literature on the Third Reich is already massive, only the most important and relevant works, excluding the writings of the Nazi leaders, have been included here.

A. ANTI-SEMITISM AND THE NAZI IDEOLOGY

Arendt, Hannah. *The origins of totalitarianism.* 2nd rev. ed. Cleveland and New York: The World Publ. Co. (Meridian Books), 1958.

Brilliant, erudite, and influential analysis of the genesis and the nature of Nazi and Stalinist totalitarianism. Miss Arendt, an eminent political theorist, here shows the central importance of anti-Semitism to the ideology and of concentration camps to the organization of the totalitarian system.

Cohn, Norman. *Warrant for genocide: the myth of the Jewish world-conspiracy and the protocols of the elders of Zion.* New York: Harper & Row (Torchbooks), 1969.

Brilliant and intuitive investigation of the roots of Nazi anti-Semitism. Tracing the fabrication and dissemination of the forgery known as *The Protocols of the Elders of Zion,* this scholarly study presents the argument that the Nazi racialist doctrine is a secularized version of medieval demonological anti-Semitism.

Friedrich, Carl J., ed. *Totalitarianism.* New York: Grosset & Dunlap (Universal Library), 1964.

Proceedings of a 1953 conference on modern totalitarianism. Papers and discussion by the leading specialists are of a uniformly high quality.

Hay, Malcolm. *The foot of pride: the pressure of Christendom on the people of Israel for 1900 years.* Boston: Beacon, 1950. Paperback ed. 1960 as *Europe and the Jews.*

Interesting survey of anti-Semitism, strong on the Christian roots, by a Catholic historian.

Klemperer, Victor. *L.T.I. Notizbuch eines Philologen.* Berlin: Aufbau Verlag, 1946.

Illuminating essay dissecting the language of the Third Reich (*Lingua Tertii Imperii*). Klemperer, a German Jewish philologist who escaped deportation, based his study on notebooks compiled during the Nazi years. His perceptive analysis reveals the hidden techniques of Nazi mythology.

Massing, Paul R. *Rehearsal for destruction: a study of political anti-semitism in imperial Germany.* New York: Harper, 1949.

Scholarly history of German anti-Semitism between 1870 and 1914. Thorough discussion of Stöcker's Christian Social movement as well as the rise of the early racial anti-Semites. Also valuable for its treatment of the reactions of the political parties, including the Socialists.

Mosse, George L. *The Crisis of German Ideology: Intellectual Origins of the Third Reich.* New York: Grosset & Dunlap (Universal Library), 1964.

A comprehensive survey of the ideological roots of Nazism, tracing its growth from the early nineteenth century, with special emphasis on education and the youth movement.

Pinson, Koppel S., ed. *Essays on anti-Semitism.* 2nd rev. ed. New York: Conference on Jewish Relations, 1946.

A collection of authoritative articles treating the economic, social, and psychological dimensions of anti-Semitism as well as its appearance in various periods and countries. Includes H. Arendt on France and W. Gurian on Germany.

Poliakov, Leon. *Histoire de l'antisémitisme.* 3 vols. Paris: Calmann-Lévy. Vol. I: *Du Christ aux Juifs de cour* (1958); Vol. II: *De Mahomet aux Marranes* (1961); Vol. III: *De Voltaire à Wagner* (1968).

These massive volumes, scholarly and perceptive, are the best history of anti-Semitism now available. The first volume, which traces the genesis of anti-Semitism from early Christian-Jewish rivalries, is also available in English translation (New York: Vanguard, 1964).

Poliakov has also published a brilliant essay showing how after Hitler anti-Semitism survived as anti-Zionism in the Soviet world, exported from there to the West after the 1967 Arab-Israeli war: *De l'antisionisme à l'antisémitisme* (Paris: Calmann-Lévy, 1969).

Pulzer, Peter G. J. *The rise of political anti-Semitism in Germany and Austria.* New York: John Wiley (paperback ed.), 1964.

A valuable history of anti-Semitism in the German lands. Although more selective than Massing (No. 17 above) on German anti-Semitism, it includes the more virulent Austrian variety. Especially important for its discussion of Schönerer and Lueger.

Reichman, Eva G. *Hostages of civilization: the social sources of national socialist anti-Semitism.* Boston: Beacon ,1951.

An interesting sociological investigation, erudite but not always convincing, which concludes that the Catastrophe does not prove the failure of Emancipation. It argues that hatred of Jews in modern Germany did not reflect actual group conflicts but, based on old stereotypes, represented a projection of German fears and insecurities.

Stern, Fritz. *The politics of cultural despair: a study in the rise of the Germanic ideology.* Garden City, N.Y.: Doubleday (Anchor Books), 1965.

A scholarly study of Paul de Lagarde, Julius Langbehn, and Moeller van den Bruck as intellectual precursors of the Third Reich.

Viereck, Peter. *Metapolitics: the roots of the nazi mind.* New York: Capricorn Books, 1961.

An early and still valuable study first published in 1941 with the subtitle *From the Romantics to Hitler.* Traces the Germanic ideology from Fichte and Father Jahn through Wagner to Rosenberg and Hitler.

Weinrcich, Max. *Hitler's professors.* New York: Yivo, 1946.

Text and documents show how Germany's intellectual community supported the Nazi anti-Jewish program.

B. THE NAZI REGIME

Bracher, Karl Dietrich. *The German dictatorship: the origins, structure, and effects of national socialism.* Transl. from the German by Jean Steinberg. New York: Praeger, 1970.

A detailed, comprehensive, and penetrating analysis of the Third Reich by a leading German political scientist. His earlier German studies—*Die Auflösung der Weimarer Republik* (1955) and *Die nationalsozialistische Machtergreifung* (1962 with W. Sauer and G. Schulz)—have become the standard works.

Bullock, Alan. *Hitler: a study in tyranny.* London: Odhams Press, 1952 (also Harper & Row Torchbook ed.).

The standard scholarly biography.

Commandant of Auschwitz: the autobiography of Rudolf Hoess. Transl. from the German. New York: Popular Library, 1961.

The revealing memoirs of the S.S. commander of the Auschwitz extermination camp, written in a Polish jail before his execution.

Dallin, Alexander. *German rule in Russia, 1941–1945: a study of occupation policies.* New York: St. Martin's Press, 1957.

Extremely valuable. A scholarly study based on captured German documents, it provides the details on how the Nazis planned and implemented their ruthless domination in occupied Russia. Shows how different ministries pushed competing policies; delineates the jurisdictional conflicts between the military, civil, and S.S. authorities.

Heiden, Konrad. *Der Fuehrer: Hitler's rise to power.* Transl. by Ralph Manheim. Boston: Houghton Mifflin, 1944 (also Beacon paperback).
An older but still important work by the earliest student of the Hitler movement. A perceptive, biographical study of Nazism from its inception to 1934.

Höhne, Heinz. *The order of the death's head: the story of Hitler's S.S.* Transl. from the German by Richard Barry. New York: Coward-McCann, 1970.
A thorough study by a German journalist who, trying to revise earlier interpretations, sees the S.S. as split into diverse groups struggling for power, not as a monolithic criminal organization.

Neumann, Franz. *Behemoth: the structure and practice of national socialism.* New York: Harper & Row (Torchbooks), 1966.
An older work by an eminent political scientist originally published in 1942 but still important. The best of the Marxist interpretations, it is especially valuable for its probing analysis of the interrelationship between politics and economics.

Reitlinger, Gerald. *The S.S.: alibi of a nation, 1922–1945.* New York: Viking (Compass Books), 1957.
The best available history of the S.S. Provides a valuable account of the origins, development, and functions of Himmler's empire. Essential for an understanding of the various S.S. Offices like the RSHA, which included the Gestapo, and the WVHA, which included the Inspectorate of the Concentration Camps.

Taylor, Telford. *Sword and swastika: generals and nazis in the third reich.* New York: Simon & Schuster, Inc., 1952 (also Quadrangle paperback ed.).
Valuable history of the German army in the Third Reich by the U.S. prosecutor at the Nuremberg Trials.

Baumont, Maurice, John H. E. Fried, Edmond Vermeil, et al. *The third reich.* New York: Praeger, 1955.
An older, now slightly dated, collection of essays by eminent

specialists written under the auspices of UNESCO. Includes an essay on anti-Semitism by Leon Poliakov.

Trevor-Roper, Hugh R. *The last days of Hitler.* New York: Macmillan, 1947 (also Collier paperback ed.).

Perceptive biographical essay on the final days of the Third Reich. This study by an eminent English historian, ordered by British intelligence at the end of the war to discover the circumstances of Hitler's death, brilliantly dissects the nature of the Nazi regime.

Wheeler-Bennett, John W. *The nemesis of power: the German army in politics, 1918–1945.* New York: Viking (Compass Books), 1967.

Solid and important history of the German army in the Weimar Republic and the Third Reich.

III.

THE CATASTROPHE: HISTORIES AND INTERPRETATIONS

Today, twenty-five years after the end of the Second World War, we still do not possess an adequate history of the Catastrophe. This applies particularly to the Jewish response. Here the sources are still too fragmentary—covering too many countries, buried in too many archives—to permit a synthesis. Only a few brief attempts have so far appeared. Meanwhile, hoping that further research will soon produce the monographic literature essential for any synthesis, we must continue to rely on diaries and memoirs.

The Nazi crime, however, has already found its historians. Although the perpetrators wished to hide their deeds, they left behind massive collections of documents, a tribute to modern bureaucracy and Teutonic thoroughness. From these papers, captured by the Allies and thus opened for research, scholars have been able to reconstruct history's most documented crime.

But the documents alone cannot fully convey to us the experience of the Holocaust. We tend to disbelieve them. We also need stories and pictures, which are listed at the end of this section. Eyewitness accounts, equally important, are listed in Section V.

Arendt, Hannah. *Eichman in Jerusalem: a report on the banality of evil.* New York: Viking (Compass Books), 1964.

A brilliant critical essay on the Jerusalem trial by the foremost analyst of totalitarianism. The leading interpretation of the Catastrophe until now, it includes a penetrating analysis of Eichmann as the technician of mass murder, and a perceptive, but controversial, analysis of the Jewish Councils as unwilling instruments of the Nazi extermination program. Originally published as articles in the *New Yorker*.

Bettelheim, Bruno. *The informed heart: autonomy in a mass age.*
An interesting, but not always convincing, psychological interpretation of the Jewish response by an eminent psychiatrist who spent a short time in Buchenwald before the war.

Braham, Randolph L., ed. *The destruction of Hungarian Jewry: a documentary account.* 2 vols. New York: Pro Arte Publ. for the World Federation of Hungarian Jews, 1963.
This documentary history includes photostatic reproductions of the original documents.

Dawidowicz, Lucy S. "Towards a history of the holocaust," *Commentary,* XLVII, 4 (Apr. 1969), 51–56.
A valuable historiographical essay, including a critical survey of research enterprises and a perceptive analysis of historical problems.

Esh, Shaul. "The dignity of the destroyed: towards a definition of the period of the holocaust," *Judaism,* XI, 2 (Spring 1962), 99–111.
A brief essay attempting a definition of the Holocaust as a subject.

Hausner, Gideon. *Justice in Jerusalem.* New York: Schocken Books (paperback ed.), 1968.
Survey of the Catastrophe and account of the Eichmann trial by the Israeli prosecutor.

Hilberg, Raul. *The destruction of the European Jews.* Chicago: Quadrangle, 1961 (also paperback ed.).
Indispensable. The definitive scholarly history. Based on an exhaustive study of the documentary evidence, this massive work—769 pages of double-column text and numerous charts—describes in minute detail the conception and execution of the Nazi program of extermination, adding a convincing and perceptive analysis.

Levai, Eugene. *Black book on the martyrdom of Hungarian Jewry.* Zurich: The Central European Times Publ. Co. Ltd., 1948.
Detailed account. Documents and illustrations.

Levin, Nora. *The holocaust: the destruction of European Jewry, 1933–1945.* New York: T. Y. Crowell, 1968.

Popular history, conscientious and well-written. Attempts to write "from the inside," emphasizing the "failures" of German Jewry, the "dilemmas" of the Jewish Councils, and resistance.

Pawel, Ernst. "Fiction of the holocaust," *Midstream,* XVI, 6 (June–July 1970), 14–26.

Slick survey of novels and memoirs.

Poliakov, Leon. *Harvest of hate: the nazi program for the destruction of the Jews of Europe.* Translated from the French. Syracuse, N.Y.: Syracuse Univ. Press, 1954.

The best available survey of the Catastrophe. Brief, concise, yet still comprehensive, with extensive quotes from the original sources.

———, and Sabille, Jacques. *Jews under the Italian occupation.* Paris: Éditions du Centre, 1955.

Text and documents (translated) on the interesting problem of Italian policy in the occupied territories. Reveals the paradox that Fascist Italy refused to collaborate with the Nazis in killing the Jews. Poliakov treats occupied France, Sabille occupied Croatia and Greece. The only English publication of the Centre de Documentation Juive Contemporaine.

Presser, Jacob. *The destruction of the Dutch Jews.* Translated from the Dutch by Arnold Pomerans. New York: E. P. Dutton, 1969.

Scholarly account of the Nazi murder of the Jews in Holland. The first comprehensive history of the Jewish fate in one European country. Treats Jewish Councils, transit camps, deportations, extermination as well as the German policies.

Reitlinger, Gerald. *The final solution: the attempt to exterminate the Jews of Europe, 1939–1945.* New York: A. S. Barnes (Perpetua Books), 1961.

The first comprehensive history, first published in 1953. Provides a scholarly description of the Nazi plan and a detailed account of its country-by-country implementation.

Robinson, Jacob. *And the crooked shall be made straight: the Eichmann trial, the Jewish catastrophe, and Hannah Arendt's narrative.* New York: Macmillan, 1965.

A vitriolic attack on Hannah Arendt and her *Eichmann in Jeru-*

salem. Attempts to refute her, page-by-page. Disjointed and apologetic, but unusually valuable for the details and bibliography provided in the text and in the massive end-notes.

————. *Psychoanalysis in a vacuum: Bruno Bettelheim and the holocaust*. New York: Yivo, 1970.
A similar, but much shorter and more readable, attack and refutation of Bettelheim's work.

Sosnowski, Kiryl. *The tragedy of children under nazi rule*. Warsaw and Poznan: Zachodnia Agencja Prasowa (Western Press Agency), 1962.
English edition of a Polish work. Discusses the fate of children, including Jews, in the occupied countries, and concentrating on Poland. Sections treat birth and death rates, education and health, ghettos and camps. Illustrations, charts, documents.

Syrkin, Marie. "The literature of the holocaust," *Midstream, XII*, 5 (May, 1966), 3–20,
A sensitive and discriminating essay on diaries and memoirs.

Tenenbaum, Joseph. *In search of a lost people: the old and the new Poland*. New York: Beechhurst Press, 1948.
A Jewish historian's account of his visit to Poland in 1946, recording his experiences and discoveries about the Jewish fate. Includes valuable information on ghettos and camps.

————. *Race and reich: the story of an epoch*. New York: Twayne, 1956.
An early, not very successful, attempt to analyze Nazism in thought and action. Treats racism, economic spoilation, and extermination.

ART AND LITERATURE

Borowski, Tadeusz. *This way for the gas, ladies and gentlemen and other stories*. Translated from the Polish. London: Jonathan Cape, 1967.
A Polish poet's short stories, terrible in their simplicity, based on his experiences in Auschwitz. The best "literature" of the Holocaust.

Eschwege, Helmut, ed. *Kennzeichen J: Bilder, Dokumente, Berichte zur Geschichte der Verbrechen des Hitlerfaschismus an den deutschen Juden 1933–1945*. Berlin: VEB Deutscher Verlag der Wissenschaften, 1966.

A pictorial record and accompanying documents. Particularly strong on the pre-war years and on the deportations of the German Jews.

Frank, Anne. *The diary of Anne Frank.* New York: Pocket Books.

The touching and optimistic diary of a young German Jewish girl, who later perished in Belsen, while hiding from the Nazis in Amsterdam. Now world famous.

. . . I never saw another butterfly . . . Children's drawings and poems from Terezin concentration camp 1942–1944. New York: McGraw-Hill, 1962.

Captivating and haunting poems and drawings by Jewish children incarcerated in the Ghetto of Theresienstadt.

Salomon, Charlotte. *Charlotte: a diary in pictures.* New York: 1963.

A young German Jewish girl's surviving record in the form of colored drawings and brief text. Drawn in southern France before her deportation to Auschwitz, it provides a visual and somewhat gloomy counterpart to the more hopeful diary of the younger Anne Frank.

Schoenberner, Gerhard. *The yellow star: the persecution of the Jews in Europe 1933–1945.* London: Transworld Publ., Corgi Books, 1969.

A comprehensive pictorial record. The photographs in the original German edition (*Der gelbe Stern: die Judenverfolgung in Europa,* Hamburg: Rütten and Loening, 1960) are reproduced with far more clarity.

Schwarz-Bart, André. *The last of the just.* Translated from the French. New York: Atheneum, 1961.

Novel emphasizing the demonic nature of the Holocaust and treating the Catastrophe as only the last, though more destructive and more modern, of a long line of persecutions.

Wiesel, Elie. *The gates of the forest.* Translated from the French. New York: Avon Books, 1967.

———. *A beggar in Jerusalem.* Translated from the French. New York: Random House, 1970.

Two of Wiesel's novels probing the demonological dimensions of the Holocaust and blending its experiences—a link and an explanation—with stories of past and present Jewish travail.

IV.

GHETTOS AND CAMPS

The ghettos and camps erected by the Nazis formed the actual arena of the Catastrophe. To understand the Jewish response—and to solve the problems posed by Jewish resistance and the Jewish Councils (*Judenräte*)—we must therefore study these institutions as well as the round-ups and deportations that preceded them. No history of the Holocaust can be complete without insight into the world of the concentration camps. However, only a few monographs cover this important topic; they are listed in this section. For understanding we must still turn to the valuable and indispensable eyewitness accounts. Only a portion have been published, and of those only a few are available in English. Still, the list is already so long that only the most important can be included here. They will be listed in the next section.

Adler, H. G. "Ideas toward a sociology of the concentration camp," *American journal of sociology,* LXIII, 5 (March 1958), 513–22.

————. *Theresienstadt 1941–1945: das antlitz einer zwangsgemein-schaft.* Tübingen: J. C. B. Mohr (Paul Siebeck), 1955.

Definitive work on Theresienstadt. This massive scholarly study provides an historical account, a sociological analysis, and a psychological interpretation of this camp society, including its *Judenrat.* Model study of a ghetto as a "society under compulsion."

————. *Die verheimlichte Wahrheit: Theresienstädter Dokumente.* Tübingen: J. C. B. Mohr (Paul Siebeck), 1958.

A volume of annotated documents to accompany his history.

Arendt, Hannah. "Social science techniques and the study of concentration camps," *Jewish Social Studies,* XII, 1 (Jan. 1950), 49–64.

Two eminent specialists explore methodological problems of research on the camp world.

Bloom, Solomon F. "Dictator of the Lodz ghetto: the strange history of Mordechai Chaim Rumkowski," *Commentary,* VII, 2 (Feb. 1949), 111–22.

Brief history of the "Getto Litzmannstadt" in Lodz, including an analysis of its *Judenrat* chief, the "Elder" Rumkowski.

Central Commission for Investigation of German Crimes in Poland. *German crimes in Poland.* Vol. I. Warsaw, 1946.

An early comprehensive account. Includes chapters on extermination and concentration camps. Of special interest is the coverage of Auschwitz-Birkenau, Treblinka, and Chelmno (Kulmhof).

Cohan, Elie A. *Human behavior in the concentration camp.* Transl. from the Dutch. New York: Grosset & Dunlap, Inc. (Universal Library), n.d.

A valuable study of the camp society by a survivor of Auschwitz and Mauthausen. Originally a thesis in psychiatry at the University of Utrecht, this analysis emphasizes psychological motivations and reactions.

Fisher, Julius S. "How many Jews died in Transnistria?" *Jewish social studies,* XX, 2 (Apr. 1958), 95–101.

Brief documented paper on Rumanian massacres.

Friedman, Philip. "Problems of research in Jewish 'self-government' (Judenrat) in the nazi period," *Yad Vashem Studies,* II (1958), 95–113.

Important analysis of the Jewish Councils. Valuable for its bibliographical notes.

———. "Jewish resistance," *Yad VashemStudies,* II (1958), 113–31.

A significant essay on Jewish resistance, one of the few available. Valuable for its bibliographical notes.

———. *This was Oswiecim: the story of a murder camp.* Transl. from the Yiddish by Joseph Leftwich. London: United Jewish Relief Appeal, 1946.

A brief history of Auschwitz.

Gringanz, Samuel. "The ghetto as an experiment of Jewish social organization," *Jewish Social Studies,* XI, 1 (Jan. 1949), 3–20.

———. "Some methodological problems in the study of the ghetto," *Jewish Social Studies,* XII, 1 (Jan. 1950), 65–72.

Two attempts to probe ghetto life.

Katz, Robert. *Black sabbath: a journey through a crime against humanity.* New York: Macmillan, 1969.

Detailed popular account of the round-up and deportation of the Jews in Rome on 16 October 1943.

Kogon, Eugen. *Der SS-Staat: das System der deutschen Konzentrationslager*. Frankfurt on the Main: Verlag der Frankfurter Heft, 1946. English paperback edition as *The Theory and Practice of Hell* (Berkley Publ. Corp., 1950).
    Early survey and analysis, originally composed for the U.S. Army, describing the camp world's organization, structure, and function. Concentrates on Buchenwald, where Kogon spent the war years as an Austrian anti-Nazi, but also applicable to other camps.

Kolb, Eberhard. *Bergen-Belsen: geschichte des 'Aufenthaltslagers' 1943–1945*. Hanover: Verlag fuür Literatur und Zeitgeschehen, 1962.
    Scholarly, perhaps a little pedantic, history of the Belsen camp by a young German historian, the most detailed account of a camp available. Text, documents, notes, and charts.

Lévy, Claud and Paul Tillard. *Betrayal at the Vel d'Hiv*. Transl. from the French. New York: Hill and Wang, 1969.
    Detailed account of the round-up of Parisian Jews on 16 July 1942, their confinement in the Vélodrome d'Hiver, and their deportation.

Poliakov, Leon. *Auschwitz*. Paris: Julliard Collection Archives, 1964.
    A valuable short history of the Auschwitz-Birkenau extermination camp. Text and documents. French paperback.

Roth, Cecil. "The last days of Jewish Salonica," *Commentary*, X, 1 (July 1910), 49–55.
    An essay on the deportations of the Greek Jews from Salonica, the oldest Sephardic community.

Steiner, Jean-François. *Treblinka*. Translated from the French. New York: Simon & Schuster, 1967 (also Signet paperback).
    A documentary novel about the Treblinka extermination camp. Factual and powerful story, including a revolt by the prisoners.

Tenenbaum, Joseph. "The Einsatzgruppen," *Jewish Social Studies*, XVII. 1 (Jan. 1955), 43–64.
    A documented survey of the activities of the S.S. execution squads in occupied Russia.

Trunk, Isaiah. *Lodzer geto*. New York: Yivo, 1962.
    A Yiddish history of the ghetto in Lodz. The best study of an eastern ghetto. Text and documents treat the foundation, organization, and destruction of the ghetto. Includes chapters on forced

labor, health, and the *Judenrat*. Important information on deportations, including those of the German Jews sent to Lodz in 1941.

————. "Religious, educational and cultural problems in the eastern European ghettos under German occupation," *Yivo Annual of Jewish Social Science,* XIV (1969), 159–95.
   A valuable essay on life in the ghettos.

Wellers, Georges. *De Drancy à Auschwitz.* Paris: Éditions du Centre, 1946.
   Important history of the French transit camp Drancy, from which Jews were deported to Auschwitz. Text and documents.

Wulf, Josef. *Lodz: das letzte Ghetto auf polnischem Boden.* Schriftenreihe der Bundeszentrale für Heimatdienst No. 59. Bonn, 1962.
   Brief history of the Lodz ghetto. Text and documents.

Yivo colloquium on the German-imposed representations before and during World War Two. New York: Yivo, 1967.
   Worthwhile collection of papers on the *Judenräte,* covering Germany, France, and Holland as well as East Europe.

V.

EYEWITNESS ACCOUNTS

Donat, Alexander. *The holocaust kingdom: a memoir.* New York: Holt, Rinehart and Winston, 1963.
   Valuable report by a journalist and his wife about their experiences in the Warsaw ghetto, including the revolt, the extermination camp of Maydanek, and various other concentration camps.

Goldstein, Bernard. *The stars bear witness.* Transl. from the Yiddish. New York: Viking, 1949. Dolphin paperback, ed. 1961 as *Five years in the Warsaw ghetto.*
   Important report on the life and death of the Warsaw ghetto by the leader of the Jewish Socialist Bund.

Kaplan, Chaim Aron. *Scroll of agony: the Warsaw diary of Chaim A. Kaplan.* Ed. and transl. by Abraham I. Katsh. New York: Macmillan, 1965.
   Important Hebrew diary of the Warsaw ghetto by a Russian-born Jewish educator.

Levi, Primo. *If this is a man*. Transl. from the Italian. New York: Orion Press, 1959. Collier paperback ed. 1961 as *Survival in Auschwitz: the nazi assault on humanity*.

A dispassionate report about his experiences in Auschwitz by an Italian Jewish chemist. The best available eyewitness account of the camp world.

Nyiszli, Miklos. *Auschwitz: a doctor's eyewitness account*. Translated from the Hungarian. Greenwich, Conn.: Crest Books, 1960.

Revealing account by a Hungarian Jewish physician who served in the crematoria of Auschwitz.

Ringelblum, Emmanuel. *Notes from the Warsaw ghetto: the journal of Emmanuel Ringelblum*. Ed. and transl. by Jacob Sloan. New York: McGraw-Hill, 1958.

Important Yiddish diary of the Warsaw ghetto by a Jewish historian.

Wells, Leon Weliczker. *The Janowska road*. New York: Macmillan, 1963.

Valuable and impressive report by a young Jewish boy about the murder of Jewry in Eastern Galicia, including an account of the Janowska camp in Lvov (Lemberg) and of its "death brigade."

Wiesel, Elie. *Night*. Transl. from the French. New York: Avon Books, 1969.

Powerful account of the experiences of a young Jewish boy deported from Transylvania to Auschwitz and Buchenwald.

VI.

WORLD REACTIONS

The Nazi program of destruction was a true national effort, demanding for its success the cooperation of the entire German people and requiring as well the complicity—tacit if not open—of the conquered nations, the satellite governments, the churches, the neutrals, even the Allies. In the pervasive atmosphere of world-wide acquiescence, the few instances of rescue stand out as unique acts of humanity. The works in this section probe and record this world reaction.

Bernadotte, Count Folke. *The fall of the curtain: last days of the third reich.* Translated from the Swedish by Count Eric Lewenhaupt. London and Toronto: Cassell, 1945.

Significant account of the Swedish relief mission during the final hours of the war.

Bertelsen, Aage. *October '43.* Translated from the Danish by Milly Lindholm and Willy Agtby. New York: Putnam, 1954.

Story of the rescue of Danish Jewry in 1943 by a man and his wife active in the Danish student Christian movement to save Jews.

Brand, Joel and Alex Weissberg. *Desperate mission: Joel Brand's story.* Translated from the German. New York: Criterion Books, 1958.

Meaningful report about the failure to ransom Hungarian Jewry. Brand, the messenger sent to Palestine, was arrested by the British, who refused to receive his proposals.

Conway, John S. *The nazi persecution of the churches, 1933–45.* New York: Basic Books, 1968.

Comprehensive and scholarly treatment of Nazi policy vis-à-vis the German Protestant and Catholic churches and of their reaction. Covers both persecution and compliance.

Conzemius, Victor. "Églises chrétiennes et totalitarisme national-socialiste," *Revue d'histoire ecclésiastique,* LXIII (1968), No. 2, 437–503 and Nos. 3–4, 868–948.

A scholarly and extremely valuable history of the relationship between the European churches and the Nazi regime.

Feingold, Henry L. *The politics of rescue: the Roosevelt administration and the holocaust, 1938–1945.* New Brunswick, N.J.: Rutgers University Press, 1970.

The scholarly history of the failure of the United States to rescue European Jewry. It treats the evasions of the government, showing how it refused to admit the Jews before or to rescue them during the slaughter. Also probes the futility of the intervention by the official American Jewish agencies. Valuable.

Flender, Harold. *Rescue in Denmark.* New York: Simon and Schuster, 1963.

Popular, moving account by an American journalist.

Friedländer, Saul. *Pius XII and the third reich: a documentation.*

Translated from the French and German by Charles Fullman. New York: Knopf, 1966.

Interweaving text and documents, this book tells the story of Vatican silence during the Second World War.

————. *Kurt Gerstein: the ambiguity of good.* Transl. from the French and German by Charles Fullman. New York: Knopf, 1969.

A documentary biography of the tragic figure of Gerstein, the believing Christian who served in the S.S. and delivered the gas to the camps while trying to alert the world. Gerstein was the protagonist in Hochhut's play *The Deputy.*

Friedman, Philip. *Their brothers' keepers.* New York: Crown, 1957.

Country by country survey of the rescue of Jews by their neighbors.

Häsler, Alfred. *The lifeboat is full: Switzerland and the refugees, 1933–1945.* Transl. from the German by Charles Lane Markmann. New York: Funk and Wagnalls, 1969.

A valuable, critical history about the Swiss policy toward Jewish refugees, showing how that nation reversed its traditional policy of granting asylum to the persecuted.

Horbach, Michael. *Out of the night.* Transl. from the German. London: Vallentine, Mitchell, 1967.

Rescue of Jews by Germans based on interviews by a German journalist.

Kastner, Rudolf. *Der Kastner-Bericht über Eichmanns Menschenhandel in Ungarn.* Munich: Kindler, 1961.

Report about the negotiations with the Nazis concerning the ransoming of Hungarian Jewry by the Jewish negotiator for the Hungarian Jewish Rescue Committee.

Lewy, Guenter. *The catholic church and nazi Germany.* New York: McGraw-Hill (paperback edition), 1964.

The valuable, scholarly history of the relationship between the Nazi regime and German Catholicism, showing how the Church supported the national effort.

————. "Pius XII, the Jews, and the German catholic church," *Commentary,* XXXVII, 2 (Feb. 1964), 23–25.

A documented essay dissecting the attitudes towards the Jews in the German church, this book probes the anti-Semitism of the clergy in the Weimar Republic and the acquiescence of the episcopate in the Third Reich.

Littell, Franklin Hamlin. *The German phoenix: men and movements in the church in Germany.* Garden City, N.Y.: Doubleday, 1960.
    History of the resistance of the Protestant Church against Nazism.

Morse, Arthur D. *While six million died: a chronicle of American apathy.* New York: Random House, 1967.
    A valuable documented popular history of the American failure to rescue Jews.

Oppen, Beate Ruhm von. "Nazis and Christians," *World politics,* XXI, 3 (April 1969), 392–424.
    Scholarly essay stressing the resistance of the German Protestant Churches.

Sharf, Andrew. *The British press and Jews under nazi rule.* London: Oxford University Press, 1964.
    An interesting, scholarly study on the reports and reaction of the British press to the Catastrophe.

Wyman, David S. *Paper walls: America and the refugee crisis 1938–1941.* Amherst, Mass.: The University of Massachusetts Press, 1968.
    A valuable, documented history of the failure of the United States to admit Jewish refugees before the war.

Yahil, Leni. *The rescue of Danish Jewry: test of a democracy.* Transl. from the Hebrew by Morris Gradel. Philadelphia: The Jewish Publication Society, 1969.
    Scholarly history of the rescue of the Jews of Denmark in October 1943.

Zahn, Gordon C. *German catholics and Hitler's wars: a study in social control.* New York: Sheed and Ward, 1962 (also paperback).
    A sociological attempt to analyze the reasons for Catholic acquiescence.